Lipstick Brigade

THE UNTOLD TRUE STORY OF
WASHINGTON'S WORLD WAR II
GOVERNMENT GIRLS

Cindy Gueli

Tahoga History Press
Washington, D.C.

ANNE,
CAN'T WAIT TO TALK
ABOUT THESE GIRLS
GOVERNMENT WITH YOU!
INDY

Tahoga History Press
Washington, D.C.

Lipstick Brigade/ Cindy Gueli. —1st ed.
ISBN 978-0-692-37410-8
ISBN 978-0-692-37411-5 (ebook)
LCCN 2015931705

Contents

For the women of the Lipstick Brigade,
whose courage and dedication remade Washington

Phyllis Grothjan shows her winning design for the Government Girl warplane.

Introduction

The women who are here now are a problem. A major problem in wartime; a potentially tragic problem after the war. Numerically, at least, the problem is becoming worse... These women—girls mostly, and pretty young girls at that—come from everywhere... What will happen then to the girls of the lipstick brigade?
  ~NEW YORK TIMES, DECEMBER 1942[1]

Mother's Day 1943 broke with a surprising burst of sunshine. The cool rain that showered Washington the previous night left the grassy expanse of the Ellipse damp but the air fresh with early summer. The wheels of the P-51 Mustang and F4U Corsair sunk into the soft earth as the Army and Navy towed their respective warplanes behind the White House in preparation for the 3 p.m. dedication ceremony. Government Girls dressed in their Sunday best followed the booming sounds of the Army Air Force and the Navy Bluejacket Bands brought in to entertain the gathering crowd. More than fifteen thousand people showed up to witness the culmination of what the *Washington Post* dubbed "the greatest demonstration of mass patriotism ever witnessed in the nation's capital."[2]

A glance at the nose art of each newly painted aircraft revealed the reason for the day's highly anticipated event. The insignia showed an attractive young woman, hand boldly raised in a "V" for Victory gesture, surfing the back of an American eagle clutching bombs in its talons. The words curving around the image identified both the drawing and nickname of the plane: "Government Girl." The Mustang and Corsair stood as the crowning achievement of the Government Girls Warplane Campaign.

Although the *Post* and the federal government co-sponsored the fundraising drive, it was the Government Girls who conceived, organized, and operated the grassroots campaign. The idea came from Agnes Richardy, a representative at the Veterans Administrations, as a patriotic gesture (she was, appropriately enough, born on the Fourth of July). She wrote a letter to the newspaper suggesting that every government employee give one dollar to raise funds for the planes donated in their name.

Thousands of women answered the call. Ad hoc committees sprung up in each federal agency. Members identified themselves by wearing armbands and badges emblazoned with "Government Girl." Phyllis Grothjan, a nineteen-year-old clerk, won a contest to design the distinctive nose art. Women recruited volunteers, solicited donations, and managed the money. Interdepartmental leaders met after work hours to discuss fundraising strategies.

Competition between agencies heated up. Fundraising tallies appeared in the *Post* like sports statistics under the heading "Government Girl Box Score." Contributions continued to pour in after the $50,000 goal of the original two-week campaign was met, so the sponsors doubled the collection period. By the end of an intense month of canvassing, women raised over $157,000—more than enough money for two of the most glamorous and expensive fighter planes available.

Women at the dedication ceremony sported lapel pins identifying them as proud donors to the fund. The dollar offering also guaranteed their name would be published in the newspaper and added to a book the organizers hoped would be dropped by the warplanes on Berlin or Tokyo "along with tons of bombs."[3]

Eighty Government Girls had the added distinction of belonging to an Honor Guard representing their respective federal agencies. Chosen by their peers (based on popularity, beauty, money raised, patriotism, or random drawing depending on the bureau) they stood in formation as ceremonial custodians of the aircraft. Speeches from the *Washington Post*, Civil Service Commission, Army, and Navy officials and a congratulatory letter sent by President Roosevelt were broadcast to the crowd and live over the radio.

At the climactic moment of the event, the band struck up a fanfare as two Government Girls decked out in shoulder corsages and spotless white gloves stepped forward to grasp identical champagne bottles wrapped in thick, criss-crossing red, white and blue ribbons. "I now christen thee Government Girl," proclaimed Edith Disney as she smashed the bottle against the nose of the Corsair to riotous applause. "I now christen thee Government Girl," Irene Lefcheck repeated as she swung her bottle at the Mustang. But instead of releasing a bubbly shower, the bottle landed with a dull thud against the propeller knocking its protective guard to the ground. A quick adjustment to the blade and Irene's second attempt shattered the bottle on cue. She smiled with relief as the crowd cheered her success. The ceremony marked not only the capstone of the campaign, but also a public affirmation of Government Girls' importance to the war effort and their prominence in wartime Washington.

Almost 200,000 young women came to Washington to work for the government during World War II. They were young. Most were single. Many were shedding the economic restrictions of the Great Depression and the social restrictions of protective families and small town life. Joining this so-called "Lipstick Brigade" as a civilian or with the military offered women a break with the past and new prospects for the future. These Government Girls helped make D.C. a unique wartime environment by creating an active, vibrant, professional community of women.

The endearingly guileless image on display along with the warplanes was accurate but incomplete. It represented the earnest, inexperienced, excitable war worker eager to serve her country. But Government Girls were not one-dimensional, one-size-fits-all paragons of patriotic virtue. Some women were naïve, idealistic, and fun loving. Others were hard working and ambitious. Still others drank, smoked, and experimented with sex. But as the fundraising campaign demonstrates, regardless of a Government Girl's individual persona, as a group they became an integral, accomplished force for change in a wartime city that one frustrated taxi driver anointed, "the greatest goddamn insane asylum of the universe."[4]

At the height of the war, over 1,000 people arrived in Washington every day. The city operated as America's central command post for both overseas military action and domestic war production. Decisions made in the small, cramped government offices affected not only the entire nation but the whole world. The usually sedate capital turned into a rollicking boomtown. Yet, Government Girls dealt with as much frustration as fun.

Undercurrents of conflict and danger heightened wartime insecurities and often placed Government Girls at odds with locals, city officials, and federal agents. They battled overcrowding, housing shortages, discrimination, and workplace hazards along with the very real threat of contagious diseases, crime, rape, and murder. And Government Girls maneuvered through these unexpected perils while under close scrutiny of the press, which alternately lauded and condemned their patriotism, beauty, behavior, and impact on the nation's capital.

People tend to look back on the 1940s through a Hollywood induced haze of nostalgia for simpler times. The elegant men and women seem more sophisticated, better dressed, and artistically deft with a cigarette than subsequent generations. But Washington did not belong in a glossy movie still. The reality was grittier, tougher, frustrating, and sometimes disheartening.

From *Sister Carrie* to Carrie Bradshaw, the adventures of young, single women working in the big city have captured the imagination of generations of writers and their audiences. Washington's World War II

Government Girls lived more boldly, bravely, publicly, and influentially than any fictional archetype. *Lipstick Brigade* explores the captivating, surprising, and often moving stories of how these women experienced and confronted the challenges of war.

Notes

[1] Luther Huston, "Uncle Sam's Seminary for Girls" *New York Times Magazine*, December 6, 1942, 31.

[2] "City Poised for Patriotic Christening," *Washington Post*, May 8, 1943, 1.

[3] Jerry Kluttz, "Government Girl Plane Drive Starts Today in U.S. Agencies," *Washington Post*, April 7, 1943, 1-B.

[4] Man at the Microphone, *Washington Broadcast* (Garden City, New York: Doubleday, Doran & Co., 1944), 4.

1

Womanpower

arion Tompkins' life changed on a routine visit to the dentist. As she waited for her regularly scheduled cleaning in the same Albany office she had been visiting since she was a child, Marion absently flipped through magazines. Bored with her job as a secretary, in fact, bored with her life in general, the twenty-four-year-old mulled over her best friend's plea to leave New York and join her in the Navy. While it sounded just like the sort of adventure Marion had been craving, she was still hesitant to leave her parents, friends, and everything familiar for the unimagined rigors of the military. The military! She was a secretary, not a sailor. Even with her friend's assurances, Marion was uncertain the Navy would be better than the daily drudgery she already knew.

As Marion turned the pages of *Holiday* magazine, a full color photo of Coast Guard SPARS marching in formation wearing identical, chic white uniforms caught her attention. The accompanying article detailed the women's training at the luxurious Biltmore Hotel in sunny Palm Beach, Florida and their work at the Coast Guard headquarters in Washington, D.C., where the majority of SPARS were stationed during the war. Marion decided on the spot to leave her job and enlist in the SPARS. Within three weeks, she was drilling down the same oceanside street she saw in the magazine. After another six weeks of basic training, she was running one of the SPARS barracks across the street from the iconic monuments on the National Mall.

Marion regularly chuckled over and appreciated the fateful teeth cleaning that led to her joining the ranks of Washington's Lipstick Brigade. She fondly recalled, "[My mother] never had the opportunity to get out and be independent in her life and she wanted me to do that. It was wonderful... I felt so sorry for all my friends who stayed home and never got to go anywhere. Heavens, it was one of the few really good ideas I had in my life."[3]

Magazine stories enticed women like Marion with the excitement of living in the nation's capital. Recruiting posters appealed to their sense of patriotism. Hollywood movies promised the heady rush of wartime romance. Attracting workers to join the war effort followed the time honored sales pitch—work for the government, serve your country, and find adventure. The difference with this particular call to duty was its target: America's young women.

The federal government needed help. The massive bureaucratic demands of running a war required a clerical corps with numbers and skills only women could deliver. They comprised the largest available labor pool as men shipped out to the battlefronts and new jobs created by wartime agencies multiplied daily. The resulting administrative void provided career opportunities for hundreds of thousands of young women across the country.

The average Government Girl was twenty-two years old, unmarried, educated beyond high school in college or vocational training, and new to Washington. She came from a small town in the Midwest, Northeast, or South before joining the civil service or military. She spent her first decade of life in the culture of the Roaring Twenties and her second decade in that of the Great Depression. She had parents who lived through World War I and could have grandparents who lived through the Civil War.

A connection to that nineteenth century conflict seemed remote to Hope Nussbaum until she went home to Virginia with a fellow clerk at the War Production Board. During a family lunch, Hope's friend gently chided her grandmother for adding two tablespoons of sugar—a rationed and therefore precious commodity—to her iced tea. The grandmother waved off the concern over wartime supplies. "Honey child," she admonished, "let me tell you about Mr. Lee's War." Hope remained captivated by the impromptu history lesson that followed.[4]

Most young Government Girls would be considered sheltered by today's standards. Many had never traveled beyond their hometowns, met people with backgrounds different from theirs, or lived on their own. Kathryn Moffit is a prime example. She was twenty-one years old from North English, Iowa when she joined the Navy and became a Government Girl. Almost sixty years later, Kathryn reflected on her naiveté: "There were a lot of things we wish our parents had told us... As I look back on it I realize, I was thinking this the other day, how unprepared I was when I went in. It was something I wanted to do. It was definitely a challenge. But I was a small-town girl and things I thought I knew I learned quickly better."[5]

Everything in Washington moved quickly during the war. The government's urgency to mobilize people and resources allowed women to break through many conventions and restrictions that normally blocked their entry to federal employment. Government Girls existed before World War II. Women had held a small percentage of low-level government positions since the nineteenth century. But until the defense build-up to the Second World War, women's employment was mercurial at best.

In 1854 Clara Barton, who would later help establish the American Red Cross, was one of only three women working in D.C.'s Patent Office. "Lady" clerks and copyists—at different times Barton ranked as a recording clerk, copyist, and clerk-copyist—generally earned less money than men holding the same jobs and were sometimes required to work from home. But a federal salary was higher than those offered by most other jobs open to women. Yet, with every turnover in administration, opportunities for women grew or diminished depending on officials' beliefs regarding women's abilities and appropriateness in the workplace. Barton was demoted, fired, and reinstated at least three times before she left her job to become the "Angel of the Battlefield," a nickname bestowed on her by the soldiers and surgeons she helped with relief operations during the Civil War. Like many of the male government employees, she hired a substitute to do her work and hold her appointment until she returned.

Several federal agencies used female workers to fill the empty desk jobs left by men fighting in the Civil War. However, in 1865 James Harlan, a conservative senator from Iowa, became Secretary of the Interior, which, at the time, housed several departments including the Patent Office, Pension Bureau and Bureau of Education. Harlan launched a campaign to eliminate anyone he considered a disloyal, inefficient, or immoral employee. He fired bureau chiefs, clerks, Walt Whitman (Harlan found out that the Bureau of Indian Affairs clerk wrote *Leaves of Grass*, which he considered pornographic) and every female copyist under his command. Harlan believed that the mere presence of a woman in an office threatened the morals of her male colleagues.[6]

Even after the turn of the twentieth century, women's federal employment seesawed because it was dictated as much by opinion as by demand. The reason most often cited for not hiring "the weaker sex" was their inherent frailty. The War and Navy Departments refused to appoint qualified female language translators because authorities did not believe women had the strength to fulfill an important part of the job—climbing ladders to retrieve books. Frailty referred to character as well as physique. John C. Black, head of the Civil Service Commission in 1910, vowed to rid the government of female typists and stenographers because "the blondes are too frivolous; the brunettes too chatty."[7]

Women's employment in the military was equally inconsistent. American women had held support positions such as nurse, cook, and laundress since the Revolutionary War, but they were not hired en masse until the country entered World War I. The Army and Navy set up permanent nurse corps in 1901 and 1908 respectively. But the numbers of women called to duty remained low until nearly 34,000 nurses were needed both stateside and overseas during the First World War.[8] In addition to medical services, Secretary of the Navy Josephus Daniels advocated enlisting women in the Naval Reserve to handle the onslaught of clerical work involved with the war. Just over 11,000 Navy Yeoman (F) and 300 Marine Corps Marinettes served between 1917 and 1919, when they were released from active duty. About 2,000 of these women worked in Washington as office staff, draftsmen, recruiters, fingerprint experts, and even electricians.[9]

After evaluating the success of women serving with the British military, General John Pershing, head of America's ground forces in Europe, requested women as bilingual telephone operators. But the 223 "Hello Girls" who served overseas in the Army Signal Corps were classified as civilian contractors, even having to pay the $300-$500 cost of their mandatory uniforms.[10]

Federal agencies also sounded a "ringing call to every intelligent woman" to participate in the war effort. Approximately 20,000 women responded to work in Washington primarily as filing clerks, stenographers, telegraphers, typists, and telephone operators. Because they were in such high demand, the women's starting salary was $1,000-$1,200 per year at a time when the average American income was $800.[11] Even with financial incentives, the government scrambled to attract qualified women to fill administrative posts throughout the war.

The press dubbed the women "Government Girls" and detailed their recruitment, housing difficulties (at its worst three women to a bed and twenty-five cents to bathe at a nearby high school), and the public debate over the appropriateness of using female workers. Spunky twenty-year-old Josephine Lehman did not question her choice to become a Government Girl. She traded a reporter's hat in her Michigan hometown for the prospect of adventure as a clerk in the War Department. She found it in friends, social activities, and professional opportunities. With characteristic humor, Josephine wrote home that, for the time being, she was even giving up dating to focus on her career, "Well, which would YOU rather do, get married, scrub, wash, cook, sew, mend, make beds, sweep floors, spank babies, and when you wanted some money say, 'Oh, please Jimmy or Georgie can I have a quarter, I have to pay the coal man,' or be your own boss and haul in $55 every two weeks?"[12]

Josephine never returned to Michigan. She parlayed her wartime experience into writing jobs that allowed her to travel widely, meet her future husband, and settle in New Jersey. The numbers of the first Government Girls were relatively small and the duration of employment short, but the experience changed lives and the catchy label stuck.

Just over twenty years later, the United States officially entered the Second World War and began an even more extensive and aggressive campaign to attract women with "Star-Spangled Hearts" to serve their country. In 1940 almost twelve million American women already worked outside of the home.[13] The nation would require over six million more from what Secretary of War Henry Stimson called the "vast reserve of woman power" to aid the war effort—nearly one million in the federal government alone.

Government Girls are sometimes referred to as white-collar Rosie the Riveters. The fictional factory-working Rosie became a World War II icon of female strength and duty on the home front. But Government Girls were not simply defense workers wielding typewriters instead of rivet guns. They differed from Rosie the Riveters in several key ways.

First, Government Girls did not challenge traditionally accepted notions of women's work in the same manner as her industrial counterparts. As Rosies walked into war plants to build airplanes, ships, tanks, and bombs, they stepped over the boundaries of deeply entrenched attitudes concerning women's proper behavior and abilities. Although women typically worked in light manufacturing jobs like assembling shoes, clothes, and small appliances and service positions like waitressing and housekeeping, heavy industry was men's domain. Rosies often literally replaced men on the assembly line.

Government Girls, however, continued a trend started in the late nineteenth century of hiring women for office work. The modern techniques of stenography and typing developed at a time when an increasingly hierarchical business culture emerged. Instead of employing one clerk to handle every administrative duty within a single office, growing companies hired individual specialists for each duty. Top male executives viewed the new entry-level secretarial positions as a good fit for women because of the lower wages, limited advancement possibilities, and the more "natural" situation of taking orders from a man in authority.

By 1930 women made up ninety-five percent of all stenographers and typists. A decade later nearly one out of every three working women held a clerical or sales job. Women were not universally accepted in the office or necessarily encouraged to be there by the general public, but their entry into white-collar war work did not test the same boundaries of acceptable feminine behavior that Rosies did.[14] In fact, some viewed it as the beginning of a well-established career path. Independent Woman, which billed itself as "a magazine for business and professional women," advised potential Government Girls that, "Stenography is still a woman's greatest opening wedge. Of the 200 women who held the highest positions held by women under Civil Service, the greatest number began as secretarial assistants."[15] Government Girls did not simply replace men for the duration; they were part of a continuum in the fields of office work and public service.

Second, because most Government Girls were single, they did not have to contend with juggling family responsibilities and a demanding workload.

This meant that they had more free time and money than the older, married Rosies who made up the majority of women entering wartime defense work.[16] Government Girl Loretta Pattison used her hours off from clerking at a succession of federal agencies to earn a sociology degree at George Washington University. She attended classes at night and studied at the Library of Congress.[17] Many schools and colleges in Washington offered courses and schedules specially designed to accommodate Government Girls.

The young women could also spend personal time going out with friends and dates. One of the main complaints by the Washington establishment about Government Girls was their boundless pursuit of entertainment. A journalist described them as a group of unwanted, bothersome social butterflies: "The city is jammed with thousands of employees—clerical, stenographic, statistical, and legal—who do their shopping on Thursday night each week, swarm continuously into air-conditioned motion-picture theatres, and stare and titter and get in the way in the hotel cocktail rooms at the Mayflower, Shoreham, Carlton, Statler, Willard, Raleigh, and Wardman Park hotels."[18]

As most Government Girls were from smaller towns and cities, they had little previous opportunity to experience the kind of nightlife that the nation's capital could offer—particularly when it was teeming with servicemen, celebrities, international military and diplomatic visitors, and even royalty. Sighting a king or queen provided much dinner table conversation for awe-struck Government Girls. But the possibility of seeing or meeting favorite performers propelled throngs of women to attend bond rallies and concerts with Hollywood stars like Hedy Lamar, Abbott and Costello, James Cagney, and Bing Crosby. War Department clerk Mary Wright recalled being late for work because, just as she was ready to board her bus, an Army cavalcade drove by on Pennsylvania Avenue carrying Lucille Ball, Dick Powell, and the Marx Brothers to perform at the Stage Door Canteen in Lafayette Square. She was so star-struck, the bus pulled out before she could tear herself away from the spectacle.[19] Socialite and political insider Vera Bloom quipped about the city's nonstop joviality, "Even if Judgment Day is well advertised in advance, I'm quite sure there will be a party going on in Washington."[20]

In addition to the crowded public spaces, Washington's boarding houses, dorms, and group apartments ensured that Government Girls were rarely alone. While this often created other problems, it eliminated the feelings of social isolation that many Rosies reported. Going home at the end of a shift to care for kids or worry about a husband on foreign shores could be lonely. Even women who lived with family members often lacked the regular company of companions their own age after work hours.

Conversely, Washington's Government Girls were surrounded by young adults. One reporter observed, "The federal triangle at 5 o'clock in the afternoon looks more like a college campus after 3 o'clock classes than the center of the nation's capital."[21] The chaotic swirl of young men and women living, working, commuting, and socializing together, made quiet moments alone singular and rare. Helen Gunter, who worked at the Naval Photographic Lab in Anacostia, recorded in her journal, "I decided nothing could lure me out of my room Saturday evening or Sunday. I find I have a craving to be alone because I've never had to be around so many people so many hours of the day."[22]

Many women used the concentration of potential friends and colleagues to network. At the Meridian Hill Hotel, a D.C. dorm for Government Girls, Women's Army Corps (WAC) officers developed their own supportive clique. They exchanged necessary information on the best places to get uniforms cleaned, find a cheap meal, and the "scuttlebutt" about promotions.[23] Civilian and military women often lived and worked in the same quarters, which added another uniquely defining element to Government Girls' experiences.

Almost ten percent of all women serving in the U.S. military were assigned to Washington. After much debate, Congress approved the creation of the Women's Auxiliary Army Corps (WAAC) in May 1942. As in World War I, Army officials accepted the idea as a way to release men from noncombatant work. Women, they decided, could take over certain jobs such as switchboard operators, clerks, and dieticians with little disruption in the Army's normal routine. Securing their commitment as reservists rather than civilian employees would prevent women from resigning at will.

The Navy introduced a similar plan two months later. For reasons of discipline, security, and convenience, Navy officials chose to make their women's corps, the Women Accepted for Volunteer Emergency Service (WAVES), a full-fledged part of the Navy instead of an auxiliary branch.[24] Equal rights' advocates supported this move as evidence of a woman's right to all the responsibilities of citizenship. However, it was the reluctance of Congress to hinder the military in a time of national crisis that carried the legislation through. Following the Navy's precedent and after experiencing legal and practical difficulties in administering the corps as an auxiliary program, the War Department decided to grant female WAACs full Army status.

To signify this change, the WAAC amended its name to the Women's Army Corps (WAC) in June 1943. The Coast Guard admitted SPARS (constructed from their motto Semper Paratus-- always ready) in November 1942 and the Marine Corps accepted Women Reserves in February 1943. When asked why the enlisted women did not have a memorable acronym, General Thomas Holocomb, commandant of the Marine Corps responded, "They are Marines. They don't have a nickname and they don't need one."[25] Female representatives from each of these military branches served in Washington.[26] Civilian and military Government Girls worked side by side on many of the same wartime projects and goals.

Lastly, Government Girls did not disappear en masse from their wartime jobs like Rosies. While most women working in heavy manufacturing found employment in other industries after the war, they had to give up the wartime positions they trained for and mastered as men returned from the fronts.[27] The number of Government Girls shrank but public and private office work deemed suitable for women expanded in the postwar economy. Over half of all workers who came to wartime Washington stayed in the city. Barbara deFranceaux became friends with several Government Girls who rented rooms in her family's Spring Valley home. "They were intelligent people," Barbara said of the young women who were her own age. "And when they were exposed to new things, they learned and caught on. Many didn't want to go back. Once they came here they were exposed, they learned and went on and accomplished things."[28]

Even the Government Girls who served in the military did not entirely disappear. A drive to maintain women as a permanent part of the peacetime forces began towards the end of the war. Despite contentious infighting and heated opposition in Congress, the support of the highest ranking military leaders, including General Eisenhower (who worked with numerous WACs in Washington and abroad) led to the passage of the Women's Armed Services Integration Act in 1948. This opened up opportunities for women to serve on regular active duty. By the time the U.S. entered the Korean War two years later, the Army had identified 20,000 jobs that could be filled by women.[29]

Rosies and Government Girls participated in the same wartime workforce. Their experiences may have resulted in similar individual and cultural changes in attitudes and expectations about women's capabilities and importance to collective American achievement, but the two groups of female defense workers experienced the war and its aftermath in vastly different ways.

A large part of the difference was geography. Washington was the busiest and most important wartime city in the nation. When Eunice Wilson emerged from Union Station and caught her first view of the Capitol building, she stopped short and gasped. She came from Nebraska to serve in the Navy and thought, "Here is a country girl in this beautiful big city, the capital of our nation, and I must remember this all my life."[30] Her dramatic reaction—akin to Dorothy entering the Technicolor world of Oz—was hardly unique. But as women uncovered the excitement and treasures unique to Washington, they also pulled back the curtain on the struggles and perils of a wartime boomtown.

Notes

[1] Luther Huston, "Uncle Sam's Seminary for Girls," *New York Times Magazine*, December 6, 1942, 7.

[2] Beatrice Shield Collection (AFC/2001/001/4122), Veterans History Project, American Folklife Center, Library of Congress (VHP).

[3] Marion S. Tompkins Collection (AFC/2001/001/18663), VHP.

[4] Hope Ribbeck Nussbaum interview with author, August 8, 2004.

[5] Kathryn Kaufman Moffit Collection (AFC/2001/001/66978), VHP.

[6] Jerry Kluttz, "Many Letters Protest Women in Federal Jobs," *Washington Post*, January 10, 1947, 9; Robert Tate Allen, "Was 'Leaves of Grass' Subversive in 1865?: Anyway, Whitman Lost Job," *Washington Post*, November 16, 1947, B6.

[7] Kluttz, "Many Letters Protest Women in Federal Jobs," 9.

[8] Evelyn M. Monahan and Rosemary Neidel-Greenlee, *A Few Good Women: America's Military Women from World War I to the Wars in Iraq and Afghanistan* (New York: Alfred A. Knopf, 2010), 11-15.

[9] Jeanne Holm, *Women in the Military: An Unfinished Revolution* (Novato, California: Presidio Press, 1982), 9; Susan Zeiger, *In Uncle Sam's Service: Women Workers With The American Expeditionary Force, 1917-1919* (Ithaca: Cornell University Press, 1999), 81-2.

[10] The women eventually received military and veterans' status in 1979, which, for most, was a posthumous honor. Monahan and Neidel-Greenlee, *A Few Good Women*, 10.

[11] Carrie Brown, *Rosie's Mom: Forgotten Women Workers of the First World War* (Boston: Northeastern University Press, 2002), 134.

[12] Margaret Thomas Buchholz, "Josephine: The Washington Diary Of a War Worker, 1918-1919," *Washington History* 10, no. 2 (Fall/Winter 1998-99): 18.

[13] U.S. Bureau of the Census, *Statistical Abstract of the United States–1948* (Washington, D.C.: Government Printing Office, 1948), 174.

[14] Alice Kessler-Harris, *Out to Work: A History of Wage-Earning Women in the United States* (New York: Oxford University Press, 2003), 143; Sharon Hartman Strom, *Beyond the Typewriter: Gender, Class, and the Origins of Modern American Office Work, 1900-1930* (Urbana: University of Illinois Press, 1992), 172-226.

[15] Marjorie Barstow Greerbie, "Women Work With Uncle Sam," *Independent Woman* (March 1942): 74.

[16] Mary M. Schweitzer, "World War II and Female Labor Force Participation Rates," *The Journal of Economic History* XL, no. 1 (March 1980): 92-93.

[17] Loretta Pattison interview with author, June 25, 2004.

[18] The Man at the Microphone, *Washington Broadcast* (Garden City, New York: Double-day, Doran and Company, Inc., 1944), 295.

[19] Mary Herring Wright, *Far from Home: Memories of World War II and Afterward* (Washington, D.C.: Gallaudet University Press, 2005), 40.

[20] Vera Bloom, *There's No Place Like Washington* (New York: G.P. Putnam's Sons, 1944), 271.

[21] Sally Reston, "Girls' Town – Washington," *New York Times*, November 23, 1941, SM8, 9, 22

[22] Helen C. Gunter, *Navy Wave: Memories of World War II* (Fort Bragg CA: Cypress House Press, 1992), 82.

[23] Elna Hilliard Grahn, *In the Company of Wacs* (Manhattan, Kansas: Sunflower University Press, 1993), 15, 23.

[24] Vicki Friedl, *Women in the United States Military, 1901-1995: A Research Guide and Annotated Bibliography* (Westport, Connecticut and London: Greenwood Press, 1996), 5-6.

[25] "Women Marines," *Life* (March 27, 1944): 81.

[26] The Women Air Force Service Pilots (WASPs) and Women's Auxiliary Ferrying Squadron (WAFS) were organized in 1942 (and merged in 1943), flew over sixty million training and mission miles during the war, but were denied military status with the Army Air Force. An amendment to the 1977 GI Bill Improvement Act identified the World War II WASPs as de facto military personnel.

[27] Nancy F. Cott, ed., *No Small Courage: A History of Women in the United States* (New York: Oxford University Press, 2000), 479-493; Kessler-Harris, *Out to Work*, 278.

[28] Barbara deFranceaux interview with author August 6, 2003.

[29] Evelyn M. Monahan and Rosemary Neidel-Greenlee, *A Few Good Women: America's Military Women from World War I to the Wars in Iraq and Afghanistan* (New York: Alfred A. Knopf, 2010), 247.

[30] Eunice Wilson interview with Judy Bellefaire, April 28, 2003, Women in Military Service For America Oral History Collection (WIMSA).

2

Capital Chaos

It was a typical, lazy Sunday morning for high school sophomore and future Government Girl Elizabeth Delean. She finished breakfast and half-heartedly attempted a few chores around the three-story brownstone in Dupont Circle she shared with her family. Elizabeth's parents called for her when it was time to walk over to the Convent of the Sacred Heart for their regularly scheduled mass. December 7, 1941 promised to be an ordinary winter day.

While the Deleans lingered after the service to chat about the upcoming holidays over hot tea and pastries with friends and neighbors, a sudden buzz spread from group to group transforming the idle chatter into agitated concern. Where was Pearl Harbor? Did anyone know servicemen stationed in Hawaii? How bad were the Japanese attacks? What would President Roosevelt do? The speculation and brief radio bulletins did not satisfy Elizabeth's curiosity about the bombing. The Japanese Embassy was only about a mile from the church. Maybe they were issuing statements to the public.

Elizabeth hurried, trailed by her parents and sister, towards the Georgian revival mansion on Massachusetts Avenue. They weren't alone. A growing mob crushed together in front of the locked, guarded wrought-iron gates. Clouds of smoke drifted up from the consulate's formal gardens. Elizabeth watched at least a dozen Japanese men hustling boxes of documents, codebooks, and letters out of the stately white building onto the lawn. They fixed each box with a small package of powder and a long fuse before setting it on fire and running back into the embassy for more. Elizabeth gasped as one flame shot more than fifteen feet into the air. Every time a Japanese attaché drove in or out of the complex, she heard a loud chorus of boos and shouts of "Go home Japs!" erupt from the angry crowd. When it became clear that the embassy would not release any new information, the Deleans headed home. As Elizabeth turned away from the spectacle, something shiny caught her eye. She stopped to pick up the used flashbulb that had dropped from a reporter's camera. She has kept it for over seventy years as a tangible reminder of that unexpectedly momentous day. Neither Elizabeth nor anyone else in Washington could predict how the war would change their lives, but change itself seemed inevitable.[3]

Wartime Washington became, as one foreign visitor noted, "where the future of the world is being planned."[4] The administrative engine running the war consisted of the military and civilian agencies headquartered in the nation's capital. The magnitude of that planning spurred the city's largest and fastest expansion to date, leaving longtime residents like Elizabeth and her family fighting to keep pace. As existing agencies expanded and new ones formed overnight, staff requirements skyrocketed. At the height of the war, an estimated 1,000 workers a day flooded into the city—almost three-quarters of whom were women. Their numbers and needs would ultimately push Washington's infrastructure to the brink of collapse.

Government Girls arrived in a city already preparing for war. When Japanese bombers attacked Pearl Harbor, the federal government was in the midst of a decade-long administrative build-up. Between 1933 and 1937, the Roosevelt administration created a series of New Deal programs to provide economic relief and recovery from the country's Great Depression. This shifted much legislative and political power to Washington and brought in New Deal agency heads and expert consultants from cities and towns all over the U.S. In general, this group of well-educated, highly paid men (women made up only a small percentage of appointments) moved to Washington for relatively brief periods of time, often leaving their families back home. Military and diplomatic personnel receiving assignments to the area for short, fixed terms and support staff hired to assist them also added to the growing population. Between 1930 and 1940 the population of Washington grew by twenty-seven percent, increasing to a total of 663,091.[5]

An even more significant jump in population occurred after World War II began in Europe. President Roosevelt revived the National Defense Advisory Commission to analyze the nation's preparedness for war in 1940 and Congress passed the Lend-Lease Act, which authorized the United States to provide its allies with equipment and supplies, in March 1941. A new string of government agencies formed to coordinate these efforts and control the wartime economy. This created staffing needs that became urgent and extensive with America's full-scale military involvement in the war.

Over 231,000 people moved to the D.C. Metropolitan area between April 1940 and May 1942, making it the second fastest growing community in the nation behind Detroit (thanks to its assembly lines, which President Roosevelt famously dubbed the "great arsenal of democracy").[6] The dizzying pace of growth prompted a local observer to quip, "No one can say with exactitude how many persons are attached to the Federal Government pay roll at any one time in wartime Washington, as the number changes daily."[7] There is truth behind the remark. Personnel departments struggled both to fill demand and manage new hires.

In contrast to the New Deal build up, the majority of wartime entries to the city were women. By 1942 they made up six out of every ten incoming workers.[8] Virginia LeBouef was one of them. After finishing business school in Lexington, North Carolina, the twenty-one-year-old took the Civil Service exam and made her first trip to Washington to work as a clerk in the War Department. "It was an awe-inspiring time really," Virginia recalled. "Because having grown up in a really small town and getting through high school and graduation and all that and then going to the big city and as a little country girl and going in the Pentagon—mercy! There were others in the same boat I was in, that had come from small places and come up here to work."[9]

For women used to small town, Depression-era living, navigating through the bustling capital would require some major adjustments. Not everyone was able to make them as successfully as Virginia and many returned home to a more familiar pace. Conditions in the city changed almost daily. Even locals had to adjust their expectations--oftentimes watching familiar terrain, including famous landmarks, become unfamiliar territory.

President Roosevelt personally approved designs for tempos, or, as a *New York Times* reporter described them: "ugly structures thrown up hurriedly to house mushrooming war agencies."[10] The majority of tempos, short for temporary buildings, lined the monumental core of the city, the National Mall. FDR ordered architects to create flimsy, austere buildings that would fall apart within ten years. Several supposedly temporary concrete structures from World War I were still in use—notably the Main Navy and Munitions Buildings on Constitution Avenue. He wanted to make sure the new tempos would not permanently disfigure the Mall (despite the president's intentions some tempos remained standing through the second Nixon administration). Each building stretched about half a city block and was made with a concrete foundation and low cost, pre-fabricated cemesto (a composite of cement and asbestos) walls.[11] Wooden ramps and overpasses crisscrossed the Mall connecting the maze of offices and living quarters. Two enclosed bridges in front of the Lincoln Memorial allowed workers to save time by walking over, instead of around, the Reflecting Pool. By the end of the war, 30,000 government employees worked in tempos.[12]

After agencies filled every available office space in the city, they spilled over into the community. Wartime operations moved into basketball arenas, theaters, auditoriums, concert halls, old homes, new apartments, and even horse stables. Virginia Scagliarini worked for the Treasury Department at a roller skating rink in Foggy Bottom hastily outfitted with long rows of desks. Trains traveling past the rink on nearby railroad tracks perpetually covered the glass ceiling with black soot, which occasionally fell onto newly typed memos.[13]

When individual buildings failed to meet the government's needs, it bought entire complexes. Surveyors showed up unannounced at the twenty-acre campus of Mount Vernon Seminary and Junior College, a private girls' school on Ward Circle in Northwest Washington. The Navy announced it was taking immediate possession "in the interest of the war effort." It offered $800,000 for the property worth over $5 million, eventually agreeing to a $1.1 million purchase price. Over 5,000 codebreakers soon arrived to transform the school grounds into a Communications Annex.

When Mount Vernon students returned from their winter holidays, the girls were re-routed from their quaint, colonial campus to makeshift classrooms set up on the second floor of a recently built Garfinckel's department store. They rented rooms in houses throughout the adjacent Spring Valley neighborhood to substitute for dorms. Barbara deFranceaux, a junior in the high school program at the time, remembers famed Washington socialite Marjorie Merriweather Post helping to sort out the confusion. Marjorie and her daughters graduated from the Seminary. "They worked it out that one house was where we would all go for lunch. We would walk up the hill and... all go to Wagshal's [deli] to get food," Barbara recalled. Post, one of the wealthiest women in the world, also lent the school several of her luxury cars to help the girls commute between their new sleeping quarters and classrooms. Mount Vernon did not reopen on a new, permanent campus until a year after the war ended.[14] Displacement became the norm rather the exception during the war.

The rapid and widespread wartime expansion overwhelmed local utilities. The press praised companies for their "herculean" efforts to meet the "unparalleled" demands in the face of labor and material shortages. Companies invested almost $100 million over three years to expand services, equipment, and facilities to keep the city's infrastructure functioning. The Potomac Electric Power Company laid 445,000 miles of additional underground and overhead wire to keep up with D.C.'s increasing electricity needs. The volume of mail sorted through the capital's post offices rose eighty-eight percent above prewar totals. Capital Transit doubled its fleet of buses. And C&P Telephone was so inundated with demands for new phone lines that by 1944 it had already surpassed its projected business model for 1965. The switchboard at the new Pentagon building alone was larger than the one that used to serve the entire city. The company ran ads imploring people to make phone calls only when absolutely necessary in order to spare its overburdened switchboards and operators. The plea failed. Utility services strained to keep up with growth throughout the war years.[15]

In addition to bolstering its infrastructure, the city prepared to defend itself from possible enemy invasion. Military personnel stationed around the city guarded power grids, bridges, and landmarks. The Works Progress Authority erected miles of metal fencing to protect water lines at Cabin John, a Maryland suburb just outside the city. The Army mounted 40mm anti-aircraft guns and .50 caliber AA machine guns on dozens of rooftops around D.C., including the Government Printing Office, Department of Interior, Riggs Bank, and in front of the Smithsonian's Arts and Industries Building. They placed wooden replicas of the guns at each end of the Arlington Memorial Bridge to give the illusion that it was heavily protected without using precious resources.[16]

The military barricaded the sidewalk in front of the White House, closed its surrounding streets to unauthorized traffic, and turned away visitors. Before the war, the general public could stroll across the White House grounds, leave their calling cards for the president (an outdated custom elsewhere but still practiced in Washington), or enjoy the gardens.[17] "Secretaries from other office buildings downtown used to sit on the White House lawn and eat lunch," recalled Bryson Rash, an award-winning broadcast journalist who worked for NBC News at the time. "It was wide open," Rash remembered about the capital. "If you wanted to get from, say, Pennsylvania and West Executive Avenue to down around Pennsylvania and Fifteenth, you'd cut through the White House grounds."[18] That type of casual access to the president's headquarters would never return.

D.C. National Guardsmen began drilling under blackout conditions as early as July 1940. They turned out the lights in the Sixth Street Armory and used candles and flashlights to practice maneuvers. Vigorous debate in Congress over whether civilian blackout drills in Washington would aid defense or cause mass hysteria delayed the city's first air raid test until two weeks after the attack on Pearl Harbor.

In the meantime, dutifully prepared residents in Tenleytown built D.C.'s first air raid shelter in November 1941. Dozens of others soon sprang up around the city. The local Civil Defense Council scheduled drills once every three months and usually on a Sunday. Residents covered their doors and windows with store-bought or homemade black cloth to lightproof their homes during the practice air raids. Volunteer wardens policed neighborhoods during the blackouts. One Government Girl discovered that civilians approached defending their city as seriously as the professionals.

Hope Nussbaum, a native Washingtonian, was a twenty-year-old college student and typist at the War Production Board. She lived with her father in a Capitol Hill row house located next to a heavily used bus stop. During a practice air raid, the neighborhood warden pounded on their door because he noticed a sliver of light coming from Hope's tabletop Philco radio. While writing out the citation, the warden decided to designate the home's basement as a shelter for anybody waiting at the bus stop. Hope's father absolutely refused to have groups of strangers parading through his home. During the next drill, the same warden pounded on the door demanding to inspect their buckets of sand (for incendiary bombs). They had none. Another citation. "So the next practice air raid and another knock on the door. I kid you not," Hope recalled. "This time he requested to inspect the attic. The house had no attic. The warden said he could see the roof and windows of an attic. It took some convincing argument by father that what the warden saw was a fake façade." Though the warden eventually ran out of reasons to cite Hope's family, she retained a sense of dread whenever she heard those sirens. And it had nothing to do with potential enemy strikes.[19]

Plans to protect Washington's historic and artistic treasures against attack went more smoothly. Soon after the bombing raid on Pearl Harbor, Metropolitan Police Chief Edward J. Kelly ordered additional foot patrols along the Tidal Basin to protect the city's trademark cherry trees. Japan gifted the trees to the U.S. in 1912 as a token of friendship between the two nations. Angry vandals cut several down in reaction to the Japanese attack on Pearl Harbor in December 1941. The added protection worked. Although additional trees had to be sacrificed to make way for the Jefferson Memorial (despite activists who chained themselves to the trees in a city-wide protest called the "Cherry Tree Rebellion"), no others were harmed in retaliation during World War II.

One of the newest additions to the Mall, the National Gallery of Art, sent many of its most valuable pieces out of the city. Sixty-two paintings and seventeen sculptures were secretly stored at the rural Biltmore Estate in Asheville, North Carolina. The 175,000 square foot chateaux in the middle of 8,000 acres built and owned by the prominent Vanderbilt family was the largest private home in the country. Gilbert Stuart's iconic portrait of George Washington sat out the war behind steel doors and barred windows alongside artwork by masters such as Raphael, Rembrandt, Titian, Vermeer, and van Dyck.

Even the remote countryside was not secure enough for some of the nation's most revered documents. Under heavy guard, the Declaration of Independence, Constitution, and Bill of Rights traveled by train from the Library of Congress to a vault at the famously impenetrable Fort Knox in Kentucky. They were placed in a specially designed bronze container fastened with padlocks, which were then sealed with lead. The Declaration of Independence was briefly released for display at the dedication ceremony of the Jefferson Memorial in 1943 and permanently returned to Washington a year later when the military declared the danger of potential enemy attacks over.[20]

Not all of the safeguards made Washingtonians feel more secure. In September 1942 a rooftop gun on the National Mall accidentally fired and hit the Lincoln Memorial. It clipped off three small marble pieces from the cornice above the main entrance. The fourth round of spent ammunition was never found and authorities assumed (and no doubt hoped) it ended up in the Potomac.[21]

The Office of Civil Defense (OCD) nearly caused panic or worse in its initial zeal to keep the city safe. The night President Roosevelt declared war on Japan, the OCD ordered the National Park Service to immediately shut off the floodlights illuminating the Washington Monument. The Park Service complied and the tallest structure in the city went dark. A few minutes later the Civil Aeronautical Authority (CAA) anxiously demanded the Monument be relit. How were pilots flying planes loaded with passengers going to navigate into National Airport when one of their major landmarks had suddenly disappeared (radar use on commercial planes was still a few years away)? Lights went back on. The OCD immediately called to complain. The Park Service fielded angry phone calls from each agency until it finally gave up and demanded that the OCD talk directly with the CAA. They agreed to leave the lights on until every commercial and military pilot in the country had been warned of the upcoming blackout.[22]

The threat of potential invasion left many residents feeling vulnerable and apprehensive. "We were at war and we lived in Washington, D.C., which we thought was pretty vulnerable," Edith Brainerd remembered. After graduating from Sweetbriar College in 1942, Edith returned to live with her family in the capital. Her French major and Spanish minor helped her land a job as an analyst with the Office of Strategic Services (OSS). The city she came back to had a decidedly more anxious atmosphere from the one she'd left four years earlier. "It was scary. I mean this was serious business, no question about it."[23] Security measures offered Washingtonians piece of mind but also served as a reminder that the city was now fully involved with the business of war.

The outbreak of war instigated other changes around the city as well. Washington already ranked among the nation's most expensive places to live, but the wartime economy raised the cost of goods and services as much as four percent each month. The average yearly spending per person in Washington ($1485) was just shy of the average spending per family in the rest of the country ($1562).[24] Rents tripled. The cost of food went up almost thirty percent. At a time when movie tickets averaged $.25, the best seat on Broadway cost $3, and a two-bedroom apartment on the Upper West Side of Manhattan rented for $105 per month, Washingtonians paid $.44 cents for a movie, $3 for a back row seat at National Theater, and up to $40 per month for one room in a boarding house.[25] Local salaries did increase as much as forty percent during this time, but people still had a hard time keeping up with inflation. As more and more war workers arrived in the city, they drove the demand, and therefore prices, even higher.[26]

In an attempt to rein in D.C.'s increasingly expensive and scarce housing market, Congress passed a 1941 Rent Control Act establishing maximum rents and freezing housing and hotel room prices. This legislation provided some relief from price gouging, but did not help with the shortage of available living space.[27]

Washington experienced a building boom after the First World War as the federal government and D.C.'s business sector expanded during a period of economic and political growth throughout the 1920s. Housing followed suit. Over fifty percent of Washington's population lived in apartments, the fastest growing sector of the industry (Washington's distinctive rowhouses still dominated the single family home market). The market dried up with the Great Depression and construction virtually stopped until the New Deal staffers moved to town and found nothing to rent. Because of the demand, prices increased by twenty-five percent in 1935. Many families moved further out of the city and private developers invested millions in new construction. But even this didn't offer enough space to keep up with increasing demand. By the time Government Girls arrived in the city, the housing crunch was already oppressive. Their numbers pushed an overloaded market into a full-scale crisis.[28]

Virginia Durr's story epitomized the unconventional arrangements that often resulted from this housing shortage. She moved to Washington from Alabama when her husband Clifford was appointed to the Federal Communications Commission. The Durrs had such difficulty finding a place to live that, once they were settled, they offered to help others. Virginia recounted her ever-increasing household: "So we had an English refugee [Decca Romilly, Winston Churchill's niece by marriage], an amazing person, and her baby. My mother had come to live with us. I had four children and another on the way. And Mr. Tamasaki. He was Lowell Mellett's Japanese butler. Lowell was a member of the President's staff, with a hot line to the White House. The authorities didn't want a Japanese butler answerin' the phone. We found a job for him with a general, who wasn't scared of him a bit. He brought with him a wife and baby. We had a household of thirteen, fourteen people. There was a problem of food and ration books."[29] Virginia found amusement in the absurdity of the multi-family, multinational situation that sounds like the set-up for a Marx Brothers movie. Not everyone did. Forced, cramped living arrangements with strangers created at least as many clashes as it did lifelong friends. Local families already living in Washington generally had control over who shared their homes. Most Government Girls didn't have the time, money, or options to be as picky. But no matter who you were or where you lived in the city, personal space was at a premium. And the lack of it wasn't limited to housing.

"Tragicomic overcrowding" is how Vera Bloom, author, composer, and daughter of Congressman Sol Bloom, described Washington's wartime scene. In her 1944 book *There's No Place Like Washington*, Bloom lamented that with the influx of new government workers, "Washington was acquiring a perpetual convention-city atmosphere. And for the first time in capital history it became a conversational tidbit to boast that you had been able to get a drug store sandwich in less than an hour."[30] Crowds, lines, and traffic made up the holy trinity of dependable wartime frustrations. The problem was not simply that there were too many people. It was also the city's inability to absorb so many people so quickly. The number of federal employees *tripled* between 1939 and 1943.[31]

The *Washington Post* created a special Sunday column called "Crowds Are Fun" for readers to share their grievances, because, "Crowds may not always be fun, but they're most always funny."[32] Frustrations ran high as carrying out even the most basic tasks became difficult and time-consuming. Local resident Virginia Michael wrote in to the Crowds Editor about an incident she witnessed. Virginia saw a weary young Government Girl pressed into the back of a packed streetcar. She managed to pull the cord above the window to signal the driver of her upcoming stop. But by the time she pushed her way through the uncooperative mob, the car was already several blocks past her street. The woman paused as she finally stepped off the trolley, turned a menacing eye towards those who clogged her path, and very slowly spit out: "I'm...going...back...to...Kansas...and...you...all...can...go...to...HELL."[33] It's hard to imagine that this woman found her experience as fun or funny as Virginia apparently did, but the column offered a place for people to commiserate, if not chuckle, over their circumstances. There was not much else they could do except go back to Kansas or wherever else they called home.

This is exactly what another Midwestern Government Girl did after complaining: "I have to stand in line in the morning to clean my teeth, stand in line to get my breakfast, stand in line to get the bus, stand in line for lunch, stand in line for the movies, stand in line to be helped in the stores and stand in line to get a bus or trolley home."[34] Long, snaking queues became a symbol of the wartime city as exasperated Washingtonians spent countless hours waiting for day-to-day essentials. Freda Segal, a Veterans Administration stenographer, recalled, "When we saw a line we'd get into without knowing what we were signing up for."[35] Freda just assumed it would be for something she needed. It always was.

Union Station boasted the longest lines and most relentlessly congested space in the city. The elaborate Beaux Arts terminal served as the principal gateway into and out of Washington for both civilians and military personnel. National Airport opened in 1941 and soon became the second busiest in the country. But commercial air travel was relatively new and expensive (in its first year, 2.9 million people visited the airport as a tourist attraction but only 600,000 people traveled through it). People generally relied on trains and buses to move around the country. Union Station held the dubious wartime distinction of being the busiest depot in the country.[36]

At the height of the war, additional ticket windows divided into "Coach Only" and "Pullman Only" (sleeper cars) were installed to break up the seemingly endless lines. Conductors added train cars to squeeze more riders into each trip and lengthened platforms to accommodate waiting passengers. "I used to take the train on occasion and that was something to go through," remembered Dorothe Stream, a WAVE radioman at Anacostia Naval Air Station during the war. She traveled home to Connecticut when she had leave, and neither her military status nor gender helped her wrangle a seat. "We used to have to ride standing up or sitting on bags of luggage from Washington, D.C. up to New York City... they were crammed. Always crammed. It was really tough."[37]

John Milton Morris, award-winning artist for the Associated Press, drew a wartime cartoon called "Union Depot, Bedlamburg" depicting vignettes and pieces of conversation among the mob of passengers at Union Station. One character working at the newsstand asks a customer, who is balancing a tall stack of magazines from hip to chin, "Can you read all those magazines between here and St. Louis?" The man exclaims, "Read 'em? I'm going to sit on 'em!"

Information clerks answered 80,000 questions from the approximately 200,000 travelers passing through Union Station every day. The 24-hour USO canteen averaged three million servicemen and servicewomen per year. James "Doc" Carter started working as a Red Cap in 1942. The young porter witnessed some of the tricks passengers used to make their trains. "People used to bribe me to put them in wheelchairs so they could get to the trains in front of the crowds," he remembered. The Christmas crunch in Doc's first year literally shut down the station. Servicemen jumped gates and flooded the platforms so that incoming passengers couldn't open the train doors to get out against the crush of people. Army Sergeant George Timko was on his way home after being wounded at the front in Germany. The crowd trampled the injured soldier and broke one of his legs. Station Master W.H. Marks closed and locked the depot for the better part of two days in order to gain some control and clear out the mob.[38]

Both U.S. train travel and Washington's Union Station reached its peak number of passengers during World War II as gas and rubber shortages, military transports, and work migrations made people dependent on the railways. The station's main concourse, the largest room under one roof in the world when it was built in 1907, remained barely controlled chaos throughout the entirety of the war.

Such problems were not just an annoyance. They could hurt the war effort. Staffing federal agencies depended on attracting women workers into the city. Washington's overcrowding became a national joke and fodder for plays, movies, and comedians. The promotional poster for the film *Standing Room Only* shows movie stars Paulette Goddard and Fred MacMurray huddling under a statue near the Capitol building trying to sleep in the pouring rain. The tagline suggestively reads: "The hilarious story of what a secretary will do to get a bed... for her boss in Washington!" A radio journalist labeled wartime Washington, "a bewildering bedlam." A local resident quipped, "If the war lasts much longer, Washington is going to bust right out of its pants."[39] And in the summer of 1943, Ringling Brothers-Barnum and Bailey's Circus extended its Washington booking by four days, claiming it took that long for the troupe to make its presence known amidst so much pandemonium.[40]

Since the federal government was in competition with other war industries and private businesses around the country for the pool of clerical workers, a reputation for disorder and danger (both physical and moral) could drive women to other, more enticing cities. Local officials, federal representatives, and congressional committees all worked quickly to find solutions. They developed housing projects, staggered work schedules, lifted zoning restrictions, changed the starting time for schools, extended shopping hours, and built "war wagons" to supplement buses in transporting people around town. Individually, these fixes did little to control the chaos. But added together they succeeded in keeping the city functioning and workers flowing in. By the end of 1943, the incessant battle for space had fallen into a manageable routine.

The city's perennial overcrowding also exacerbated limitations created by mandatory rationing. Once the Office of Price Administration (OPA) began restricting access to certain consumer products and materials in 1942, shoppers spent hours searching for goods, more often than not walking away empty-handed. Attorney James Grafton Rogers kept a diary while working in intelligence for the Office of Strategic Services, the wartime precursor to the Central Intelligence Agency. He recorded his struggle to find basic necessities from D.C. stores that were "getting bare like Mother Hubbard's shelves."[41]

Finding a way around the rationing—especially for favored items like meat and gasoline—became a duration pastime. Some, like Elizabeth Watkins and her family, relied on knowing the right people. The eighteen-year-old ran errands with her mother and saw the many benefits of having good connections. "Mother had a very close personal relationship with the butcher at the A&P," Elizabeth later remembered. "There were long lines at the meat counter to get anything. He would always have the meat packaged for her under the counter and just hand it to her when she arrived. We only had meat for the Sunday roast. It was always pot roast. My older sister was courting at the time and he always came for Sunday dinner. The marriage was built on pot roast."[42]

Others resorted to the illegal but widespread black market. Alice Marriott and her husband John owned the Hot Shoppes restaurant chain during the war (and started the Marriott Corporation after it). Even with their access to food distributors, they had to resort to underground means for their personal shopping. Alice recalled, "We had a grocery store right close by that had all the black-market stuff in town. We could get anything we wanted from those people. We paid through the nose. If we wanted a roast of meat, we had to buy two cases of canned goods, but they had it. They only gave it to their charge customers, and we would get a bill at the end of the month. We bought all kinds of stuff we didn't need just because we needed to get a little meat."[43] Black markets became subject to several congressional investigations and exposés but thrived throughout the country and lasted as long as OPA controls stayed in in place.

Joanne Lichty was in high school during the war and remembered how some of her friends got around the gasoline restrictions, even though they didn't have money to buy things on the black market. But that was not going to stop them from enjoying their all-important social lives. The teens would pick a neighborhood, meet in the middle of the night, and, as quickly and quietly as possible, siphon a little bit of fuel from each of several parked cars. The guys would then take turns using the gas to drive their girlfriends to dinner or the movies on the week-ends. Their plan required them to sacrifice sleep but never the chance at a hot date.[44]

Charlotte Carter took circumventing rationing to an extreme. She left Pennsylvania for Washington when she joined the civil service as a typist. After about a year, the twenty-two-year-old heard about the latest OPA restriction and decided she'd had enough. As Charlotte tells it: "One Sunday morning I was coming down the stairs [of her boarding house] and the news said shoe rationing. You could have two pairs of shoes a year. I said, 'Oh no, no, no, no. I'll just join a service.' I'm telling you all my patriotic reasons. I was serious about this. *NO* way. Two pairs of shoes a year? I joined the Navy because I look better in Navy blue than I do khaki."[45] Enlisting in the military provided Charlotte with other lifestyle restrictions, but she no longer had to worry about tracking down new pairs of shoes.

Other women came up with equally creative solutions to what *Business Week* called the "Stocking Panic." OPA routed silk and then nylon to the military for use in making parachutes, tents, and tires. At a time when most women wore skirts and dresses, stockings were considered a feminine necessity, especially for those in the workplace like Government Girls. Substitutions made from heavy rayon, fishnet, or lisle cotton were uncomfortable, twisted and bagged around the thighs and ankles (one-piece pantyhose were not available until the 1960s), and tended to be an unbecoming shade of purple-gray. Katharyn Rice Sockolov wore the "service-weight" hosiery to her job in the Photographic Science Lab at D.C.'s Anacostia Naval Station, but the young, fashion-conscious WAVE refused to wear them for special events like dates. One Thanksgiving, a gentleman took her to Annapolis, Maryland where they stopped into an Episcopal Church service that nearly caused her to panic. "I had one pair of nylon stockings and they were very, very dear," Katharyn explained. "During the ceremony they do a lot of kneeling, somewhat like the Catholics, I guess. So, all through the service he would kneel, and I just sat there." She spent an anxious hour thinking her date or the deacon would question or criticize her behavior, but she still wasn't willing to ruin her prized nylons over it.[46]

Some women chose to go without stockings altogether. Norma Clark, a civilian stenographer with the War Production Board, and her friends tried a temporary and rather faulty alternative: "We painted our legs with leg makeup. In those days they always had a seam up the back.

We'd use an eyebrow pencil up the back of the leg. Then when it rained, it went like mascara. It just melted away. So it wasn't really the best way to do it."[47] Cosmetic companies marketed the makeup Norma used as "birthday stockings," but the brown liquid was messy, runny, and often rubbed off on clothes and furniture even without rain.

Hope Nussbaum and Elizabeth Delean admitted they were among the many women who opted for another popular solution to wearing thick cotton stockings during the hot, humid Washington summers. They mixed baby oil with iodine, slathered it on their legs, and sat out in the sun to give them a reddish-brown tan that approximated the look of nylons.[48] Hope found the mixture tricky to apply for an even tan, but streaky legs were still preferable to the rough, itchy hose. The stocking-free trend had its detractors, both male and female. First Lady Eleanor Roosevelt publicly disapproved of women who didn't wear stockings or did wear pants. A female reporter writing about Government Girls' fashion choices remarked: "After the first thousand bare legs you agree with the lieutenant who commented: 'Best sight in Washington are the straight seams of the WAVES, the WACs and the girl marines.'"[49] The military not only disapproved of bare legs, it forbade them.

In addition to loosening fashion etiquette, Government Girls and wartime conditions also initiated the loosening of rigid social protocol in Washington. The capital's social scene had a reputation as a conservative and clearly defined class system. In 1934 Hope Ridings Miller, long-time society editor for the *Washington Post*—equal parts Emily Post and diplomatic doyenne—explained: "All Washington social life, like Gaul, is divided into three parts."[50]

She categorized people into groups of descending importance and influence: national and international political officials, descendants of longtime residents (known as "cave dwellers"), and those who worked outside of politics but managed a profitable and culturally significant living (preferably in artistic, scientific, or academic arenas). These divisions rarely intersected and precedence flowed up as well as down the hierarchy. Miller advised newcomers to present letters of introduction and then do nothing but wait. "First calls" must only come from the established in-crowd. She counseled that crowd to wait for introductions and then call upon the newcomers before issuing invitations to tea or other engagements. However, no one should approach a top tier official except for another top tier official. Miller did not explain what catastrophe would occur if these rules were broken, but a denouncement of bad manners and social ostracism would surely follow. The middle and working classes lived in Washington, but they were not part of the population that mattered to society pages.

Eleanor Davies Tydings Ditzen belonged to two of Miller's divisions that did matter. She grew up in the rarefied world of inherited wealth from both sides of her family and political connections from her father's work as a presidential advisor, first chairman of the Federal Trade Commission, and later ambassador to several countries. She became a senate wife when she married Milyard Tydings in late 1935. Even Ditzen was surprised at the rigidity of entrenched traditions once she began her role as an official hostess. She wrote in her memoirs, "I soon became acquainted with Washington's strict official protocol. It wasn't long before I saw the reason for it. Senators and ambassadors, cabinet ministers, justices, generals, or admirals, or their wives might (and sometimes did) actually refuse to sit down at a dinner party where they were not properly placed according to their rank!"[51]

Five years later, when Lindy Boggs, wife of Louisiana Representative Hale Boggs (and later the first congresswoman elected from that state), arrived in the city for the first time, other congressional wives helped steer her through the arcane customs. She learned, for example, that political wives adhered to the Victorian tradition of calling on each other every afternoon and having weekly "at-homes," or designated days and times to receive visitors. Women followed a specific order for the visits, depending upon the official post their husbands held (i.e., wives of U.S. Supreme Court justices accepted visitors on Mondays, wives of cabinet members on Tuesdays, and so on).[52] The custom of calling remained in Washington even after it disappeared elsewhere because title and political clout served as social currency much the same way wealth and heredity did in Boston and New York. Visiting reinforced rank and status.

The war started to crack this previously impenetrable shell surrounding Washington's social caste system. The growing number and revolving assignments of government appointees sent hostesses scrambling to include the new and unknown names on their guests lists lest they inadvertently exclude important wartime officials or relocated elites from other cities (or a combination of the two). This, along with a significant increase in parties, dinners, and receptions, helped relax protocol and expand the boundaries of whom and how many were included in those traditionally defined social circles.

Entertaining in wartime Washington mushroomed into a frenzied race to keep up with the latest news, invitations, trends, and people. So much so that people across the country became alarmed at stories of how, "Capital society fiddled while Bataan burned." Hope Ridings Miller defended what she notably termed "parties for a purpose" and tried to explain to uninitiated readers around the country that the business of the federal government, and specifically of the war, was conducted under the cover of these gatherings. But the appearance of Washingtonians' patriotism was just as important as the reality of it, so Miller promised to change the focus of her column from the white glove circuit to the current wave of residents. "For the duration—and probably longer—we are finished with society-as-such," she boldly declared. Patricia Grady, another society reporter, dared to follow suit. She changed the name of her column from "Top Hats and Tiaras" to "Now is the Time." The press needed new topics of local and national interest. "Particularly," Miller explained, "are we interested in persons who are making contributions of time and energy to the war effort."[53] Government Girls became a popular subject for articles, photos, and editorials.

Where people socialized also changed. While Washington could never compete with New York or Los Angeles for exciting nightlife, the wartime boom revved up its after-hours operations. Local reporter Emily Towe observed, "In a city noted before the war as a place where people entertained in their homes, the glittering lights of night clubs are having uniformed visitors as well as civilians employed in war jobs."[54] New clubs ranged from inexpensive to elegant in order to appeal to both the young workers with limited means and "oldsters" looking for an upscale night out. And the lowly cocktail party, once deemed unsophisticated and gauche by the A-listers, became "an omnipresent form of entertainment" on the Washington social scene.[55] These developments expanded avenues for interaction between classes and created a more fluid and accessible entry into society. A popular raconteur summed up the melting pot effect: "Society in wartime Washington is a whirling of many waters—like splashing together in a gigantic soup tureen a Manhattan, a martini, a scotch and soda, rye with water on the side, a straight gin, bourbon with ginger ale, and Bacardi rum."[56]

This effect did not extend to African Americans. Nineteen-forties Washington was a divided city. Although D.C. had no Jim Crow laws on the books (something that would prove decisive in future legal challenges of discrimination), de facto segregation was enforced in public accommodations (restaurants, theaters, pools, etc.), schools, federal offices, and housing. Congressional oversight of the city brought ideas about race relations from other parts of the country to bear on the residents of Washington. The ebb and flow of rights and restrictions changed along with administrations and congressional committee members. A prime example is President Wilson's administration defending and extending segregation in D.C.'s government offices (including separate windows for white and black customers in post offices) and President Franklin Roosevelt's administration desegregating national parks and monuments. The varying local and federal policies and practices could be confusing for residents and newcomers alike.

In 1932 Clara Sharon Taylor and her family moved from North Carolina into Georgetown's then-thriving working-class, black community. Even as a seven-year-old, she was aware of restrictions limiting her access to the city: "We were separate and knew we were separate. We could use the libraries but we could not try on clothes or hats in stores. Because you were black you could stand on the bridge, but not sit on the steps to listen to concerts or watch fireworks near the Capitol. In 1933 you could listen to the concerts, but not sit on the steps."[57] Clara's experience shows the strangely schizophrenic nature of access to public spaces in Washington.

Yet, there was no universal African-American experience in the city. Mary Brown grew up in Foggy Bottom during the Depression years and rarely felt restricted by segregation. Although she knew there were places in the city she, her parents, and thirteen brothers and sisters were not allowed to go, her immediate neighborhood, across the street from where the Watergate complex now stands, was inclusive and multiethnic. Mary explained, "We had a few Italian, Greek, Jewish, Spanish... we had French on F Street, we had a mix. Actually, a lot of Germans. Because you see the [Heurich] Brewery was there and they worked at the Brewery. I'd say it was sort of a mixed neighborhood. Everyone would socialize with each other all day long and then go home to wherever they lived. It was good. Actually, it was sort of like: if you need this, I have it. You can use it or you can have it, regardless of the color. My mother fed everybody up and down the street." Mary felt the economic restrictions of the era more keenly than the racial ones. Most accommodations prohibited to her because of race were already out of reach because of price.[58]

Even people in the same family experienced the city's racial divide differently. Georgia Herron spent her childhood living on the only street of African-American families in her area of Kenilworth. Yet, for her, segregation was not a clearly defined concept. One of her white neighbors worked at the adjacent Aquatic Gardens and let Georgia and her siblings play in the racially restricted park, so she viewed color barriers as more permeable than permanent. "I knew it [discrimination] and didn't know it," Georgia recounted. "I had to walk all the way across the tracks to be at [my] school and pass the white school, Kenilworth Elementary School. And I knew that but it didn't mean anything to me. I just knew I couldn't go to that school. And after the fact I said, 'Well, that was because of segregation.' I remember having to go past that school for seven years. I had to walk an extra half a mile because I couldn't go to the school right around the corner from me. But it turned out well."

This attitude was not shared by every member of her household. Georgia was somewhat insulated as the self-described "baby girl" of eight kids and scholar of the family, whose focus and energy were geared towards studying. "I had one older brother and sister—they resented it. They barely stayed on the right side of the law because they were so angry. See, I didn't have that kind of anger," she reflected. The sting of the city's racial barriers and institutionalized prejudice affected individuals in deeply personal and varied ways.[59]

Many African Americans living in Washington felt the same sense of injustice as Georgia's brother and sister. By World War II the city's large middle and upper-middle class, well-educated black population was organizing mass economic and legal resistance to discriminatory race policies. One of the earliest and most successful groups was the New Negro Alliance, which initiated campaigns such as "Don't Buy Where You Can't Work" and won the 1938 landmark U.S. Supreme Court case New Negro Alliance v. Sanitary Grocery Co., which protected their right to boycott and helped spur similar campaigns in other cities. In 1944 law student Pauli Murray led about fifty of her fellow students from Howard University (the country's preeminent African-American institution of higher learning) in a successful sit-in at the white only Thompson's cafeteria- sixteen years before the more widely known summer of sit-ins organized by college students.[60] Murray's group held up signs asking "Are You for HITLER'S Way (Race Supremacy) or the AMERICAN Way (Equality)? Make Up Your Mind!" Management eventually served the students the day of the protest, but once direct pressure let up, the cafeteria returned to its segregated practices that same week.[61] Civil rights activism revealed the capital's underlying racial tensions and added to its atmosphere of wartime turmoil.

Newcomers quickly lost any naiveté about Washington's uneasy and conflicted relationship with African-Americans. Twenty-year-old WAVE Specialist Franke Burke grew up in Glendale, California and had not considered the racial situation she'd be encountering when she arrived in D.C. to work at the Naval Code Lab. Franke remembered: "I was stunned by segregation. I didn't know a thing about it. I couldn't understand it. Sometimes on weekends we would take off and visit the countryside. We'd go to North Carolina or Williamsburg [VA]. When we were on the train, of course the black people were sitting in closed off areas on the train. I wasn't really aware of that until we got close to Washington, D.C., and as one group all of the black people got up and moved into the section where we were sitting. It was a gesture that they were making. They were now in Washington, D.C. and they were not going to be segregated there. So, I assumed there was no segregation going on in Washington, D.C. That's the only thing I could think about. I was very, very upset about it because there were black girls in the WAVES. We'd talk about this sometimes. They were hurt, but they were used to it. I remember thinking I'm so glad I don't have to endure that... I was *stunned* by segregation having been in a protected environment in Southern California. It was amazing to me."[62]

Transportation issues were even more amazing and confusing to Mary Wright. She grew up in rural Iron Mine, North Carolina and, as an African-American living in the south, understood legalized discrimination first hand. Mary initially came to Washington in 1942 to consult a hearing specialist. Although her deafness proved untreatable, she decided to stay and take the civil service exam. Mary roomed in Washington with relatives and worked as a clerk at the Pentagon in nearby northern Virginia. One night she caught the bus for her ride home and sat near the front. The driver ordered her to move to the back. Mary refused. She'd been riding the buses and trolleys in the city and knew they weren't segregated. Mary was arrested. All buses in Virginia, even in neighborhoods separated from Washington by the short span of a bridge, were legally partitioned.

The opposite situation also created problems. A white Government Girl commuting home from Virginia chose to sit towards the back of a bus. The impatient driver refused to pull away until she switched seats. When the Midwestern woman, unused to and offended by such regulations, protested, other passengers explained the driver's dilemma. If she did not move, black passengers would have to stand crammed in behind her because no African-American could legally sit in front of a white person in that state.[63] As with so much in wartime Washington, race relations, expectations, and codes were challenged by the growing population, questioned by new arrivals, and reconsidered by longtime residents.

Elizabeth Watkins was eighteen when the war broke out. She remembered the comparative calm of her adolescent years: "Before the war Washington was a small Southern town. We lived in Bethesda, which is ten miles out. All of our dentists and doctors were there on Farragut Square. We did our shopping at Woodward and Lothrop down on F and G Streets. We went to the big movie palaces on F and G Streets... Traffic was so much easier. My mother would make two or three trips into the heart of Washington, D.C. from Bethesda and think nothing of it in a day."[64] Elizabeth left Washington for Pennsylvania to start her freshman year at Bryn Mawr. She came back for breaks every few months and had the chance to watch the city transform over the course of the war. "Pearl Harbor changed everything," she observed. "It was, 'This is something that we're all in together. What can we do?' There was a great feeling of fear. It was not a fear of invasion. It was a fear of what was going to happen to the people we loved. Then what can we as an individual do?" Elizabeth found the answer to her question. She graduated from college and, like her mother and two sisters, joined the Lipstick Brigade.

Notes

[1] Jessie Fant Evans, "War Time Washington, New Wonder of the Western World." in *Confidential from Washington* (Washington, D.C.: The George Washington Victory Council, August 1945), 1.

[2] Milton Mayer, "Washington Goes to War," *Life*, January 5, 1942, 57.

[3] Elizabeth Delean Cozad, interview with author, June 14, 2004; "Heavy Guard Thrown Around Capital's Most Vital Spots," *Washington Post*, December 8, 1941, 3; Frederick R. Barkley, "Winter and War Fall on Capital," *New York Times*, December 8, 1941, 16.

[4] Amalia de Sotela, "City of the Future," *Washington Post*, September 14,1942, B4.

[5] Campbell Gibson and Kay Jung, "Historical Census Statistics on Population Totals By Race, 1790 to 1990, and By Hispanic Origin, 1970 to 1990, For The United States, Regions, Divisions, and States," Working Paper Series No. 56 (Washington, D.C.: U.S. Bureau of the Census, September 2002), Table 23.

[6] "Capital Area's Population Soars Past the Million Mark," *Washington Times-Herald*, December 2, 1942, Statistics, Comparative, 1800-1959 Folder, DC Public Library, Washingtoniana Division (DCPL).

[7] Man at the Microphone, *Washington Broadcast* (Garden City, New York: Doubleday, Doran and Company, Inc., 1944), 5.

[8] Luther Huston, "Uncle Sam's Seminary for Girls" *New York Times Magazine*, December 6, 1942, 7.

[9] Virginia LeBoeff Collection (AFC/2001/001/50566), VHP.

[10] Luther Huston, "Washington- A Summer Portrait," *New York Times*, July 25, 1943, SM12.

[11] Antoinette Josephine Lee, *Architects to the Nation: The Rise and Decline of the Supervising Architect's Office* (New York: Oxford University Press, 2000), 283.

[12] Paul K. Williams, *Washington, D.C.: The World War II Years* (Charleston, South Carolina: Arcadia Publishing, 2004), 100; James E. Goode, *Capital Losses: A Cultural History of Washington's Destroyed Buildings* (Washington, D.C.: Smithsonian Books, 2003), 485; David Brinkley, *Washington Goes to War* (New York: Alfred A. Knopf, 1988), 120.

[13] Virginia Scagliarini interview with author, May 8, 2013.

[14] Mount Vernon became part of George Washington University in 1999. Barbara deFranceaux interview with author, August 6, 2003; Brinkley, *Washington Goes to War*, 109, 116-7.

[15] John F. Gerrity, "Utility Firms Do Herculean Job for Wartime Washington," *Washington Post*, August 26, 1945, B3; "District Business Barometers," *Washington Evening Star*, July 24, 1944; Brinkley, *Washington Goes to War*, 119-120; "Factual Survey of Washington," *Real Estate Board News*, March 1945, 8; "Washington Facts and Figures," 1943, Statistics Vertical Files, Statistics, Comparative Folder 1800-1959 #1, DCPL; "Facts About Washington," *Washington Evening Star*, April 1941, 3.

[16] David L. Lewis, *A History of the District of Columbia, Unit IV*, Washington, D.C.: "The Fight for Freedom at Home and Abroad, 1940-1953" (Washington, D.C.: Associates for Renewal in Education, Inc., 1980), 5; Huston, "Washington—a Summer Portrait," SM12.

[17] William Seale, *The President's House*, Volume II (Washington, D.C.: The White House Historical Association, 1986), 977.

[18] Bryson Rash interview in Roy Hoopes, *Americans Remember the Home Front: An Oral Narrative of the World War II Years in America* (New York: Berkley Books, 2002), 54.

[19] Hope Ribbeck Nussbaum interview with author, August 8, 2004.

[20] Milton Mayer, "Washington Goes to War," *Life,* January 2, 1942, 63.

[21] "Lincoln Shrine Hit By Accidental Machinegun Fire," *Washington Post*, September 4, 1942, 1.

[22] Mayer, "Washington Goes to War," 62.

[23] Edith Brainerd Walter Collection (AFC/2001/001/57582), VHP.

[24] "Sales Index of Department Stores," Statistics Vertical Files, Statistics, Comparative Folder 1800-1959 #2, DCPL; Brinkley, *Washington Goes to War*, 119-120.

[25] *Monthly Labor Review* 54, no. 1 (January 1942): 144; "Washington in Wartime: It is Terrible Place to Live," *Life,* January 4, 1943, 47-50; *Monthly Labor Review* 59, no. 5 (November 1944): 1070; "Buying Power in D.C. Again Leads Nation," *Washington Post*, April 12, 1942; James B. Reston, "L'Enfant's Capital and Boomtown, Too," *New York Times*, June 1, 1941, SM7.

[26] *Monthly Labor Review* 59, no. 5 (November 1944): 1050, Anne Hagner, "New Government Girls' Hotel—Home of 1942-Style Miss Washington," *Washington Post*, August 13, 1942, 20.

[27] *Monthly Labor Review* 54, no. 1 (January 1942): 145; Charles Mercer, "How Rent Control Bill Will Affect Landlord and Tenant; Law Becomes Effective January 1," *Washington Post*, December 3, 1941, 4; "D.C. Newcomers Told to Study Rent Control," *Washington Post*, February 20, 1942, 27; "End Rent Control," *Washington Post*, September 7, 1945, 8.

[28] For more on the development of D.C.'s housing and neighborhoods, see Richard Longstreth, ed., *Housing Washington: Two Centuries of Residential Development and Planning in the National Capitol Area* (Chicago: Center for American Places at Columbia College, 2010) and James M. Goode, *Best Addresses: A Century of Washington's Distinguished Apartment Houses* (Washington, D.C.: Smithsonian Books, 1988).

[29] The Durrs became key figures in the Civil Rights Movement, notably befriending and helping to bail out Rosa Parks when she was arrested in Montgomery, Alabama in 1955. Virginia Durr interview in Studs Terkel, *"The Good War," An Oral History of World War II* (New York: The New Press, 1984), 334.

[30] Vera Bloom, *There's No Place Like Washington* (New York: G.P. Putnam's Sons, 1944), 271.

[31] Gladys M. Kammerer, "An Evaluation of Wartime Personnel Administration," *Journal of Politics* 10, no. 1 (February 1948): 53.

[32] "Not a Contest, Just a Few Laughs," *Washington Post*, June 27, 1943, L1.

[33] "Crowds Are Fun," *Washington Post*, July 11, 1943, L1.

[34] Ann Cottrell, "Government Girls Wait in Line: All Services Slow in Capital," *Washington Post*, April 9, 1943, 3B.

[35] Freda Segal Collection (AFC/2001/001/30833), VHP.

[36] Edward T. Folliard, "Capital Now 2d in U.S. Air Traffic," *Washington Post*, December 5, 1941, 25; "Heavy Travel Taxes Air, Bus, Rail Units," *Washington Post*, June 1, 1942, 13.

[37] Dorothe Stream Collection (AFC/2001/001/46541), VHP.

[38] Carol M. Highsmith and Ted Landphair. *Union Station: A History of Washington's Grand Terminal* (Washington, D.C.: Chelsea Publishing, Inc., 1988), 39.

[39] "Washington in Wartime: It is Terrible Place to Live," 47.

[40] Man at the Microphone, *Washington Broadcast*, 4.

[41] Thomas F. Troy, ed., *Wartime Washington: The Secret OSS Journal of James Grafton Rogers 1942-1943* (Frederick, Maryland: University Publications of America, 1987), 61.

[42] Elizabeth Law Watkins Collection (AFC/2001/001/5869), VHP.

[43] Alice Marriott interview in Hoopes, *Americans Remember the Home Front*, 279.

[44] Joanne Lichty interview with author, July 29, 2004.

[45] Charlotte Carter Collection (AFC/2001/001/67868), VHP.

[46] Katharyn Rice Sockolov Collection (AFC/2001/001/10028), VHP.

[47] Norma Clark Collection (AFC/2001/001/32761), VHP.

[48] Nussbaum interview, August 8, 2004; Cozad interview, June 14, 2004.

[49] Ruth Mac Kay, "White Collar Girl," *Chicago Daily Tribune*, July 7, 1944.

[50] Hope Ridings Miller, "Social Life Here Divided Into 3 Parts: Official, Unofficial and Artistic," *Washington Post*, October 14, 1934, S9.

[51] Eleanor Davies Tydings Ditzen, *My Golden Spoon: Memoirs of a Capital Lady* (New York: Madison Books, 1997), 88.

[52] Burt Solomon, *The Washington Century: Three Families and The Shaping of the Nation's Capital* (New York: William Morrow, 2004), 46.

[53] Hope Ridings Miller, "This Changing Whirl," *Washington Post*, July 21, 1942, 12.

[54] Emily Towe, "We're Making Up for Lost Time," *Washington Post*, October 3, 1943, L1.

[55] Lewis, *A History of the District of Columbia*, 4; Stuart A. Kallen, *World War II: The War at Home* (San Diego: Lucent Books, 2000), 97; Troy, *Wartime Washington*, 169.

[56] Man at the Microphone, *Washington Broadcast*, 164.

[57] Clara Sharon Taylor in Jill Connors, ed., *Growing Up in Washington: An Oral History* (Charleston, South Carolina: Arcadia Publishing, 2001), 31.

[58] Mary Brown interview with author, March 25, 2011.

[59] Georgia Herron interview with author, March 31, 2011.

[60] This same eatery was later targeted by civil rights activists and involved in the landmark 1953 Supreme Court case "District of Columbia v. John R. Thompson Co." that upheld Washington's nineteenth-century anti-discrimination laws.

[61] Constance McLaughlin Green *The Secret City: A History of Race Relations in the Nation's Capital* (Princeton, New Jersey: Princeton University Press, 1967), 254-255; Pauli Murray, *Song in a Weary Throat* (New York: Harper & Row, 1987), 220-231.

[62] Franke Burke Collection (AFC/2001/001/18447), VHP.

[63] Mary Herring Wright, *Far from Home: Memories of World War II and Afterward* (Washington, D.C.: Gallaudet University Press, 2005), 92-3.

[64] Watkins, interview.

U.S. Government propaganda poster encouraging women to join the
war effort.

Treasury Department employees at the turn of the twentieth century.

Department of Commerce Government Girls in the early 1940s.

Florence Paul, a Government Girl from Illinois, visits the Washington Monument for the first time.

"Tempos" surrounding the Lincoln Memorial Reflecting Pool.

Office desks with pull-out typewriter tables squeezed Government Girls into every available space—in this case, a converted stable.

The Gilded Age ballroom of Dupont Circle's Leiter mansion became a rare, upscale government workplace. Metal from the home's wine cellar doors, Turkish baths, chandeliers, and fence were donated to the war effort.

Navy WAVES mark their second anniversary with a rally on the
National Mall.

Coast Guard SPARS march in formation past the Capitol.

War wagon trailers used special "stand-sits" to ferry defense workers around the city.

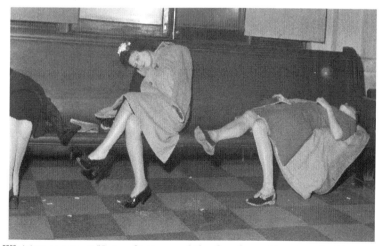

Waiting rooms at Union Station and the Greyhound bus terminal became makeshift hotels for weary travelers.

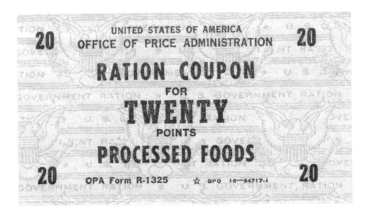

The OPA issued ration books filled with coupons that could be used to buy restricted items such as food, gas, and shoes.

Thursday night shopping, started by downtown stores to accommodate Government Girls' long working hours, became especially popular during the holidays.

Streetcars and buses were the main forms of transportation in D.C. The Metrorail system would not exist for another thirty-five years.

Washington's population reached a wartime peak of 891,000 in 1943.

Elizabeth Delean in Washington during the war.

Street photographers sold Government Girls souvenirs to send back home.

Pepsi-Cola canteen at 13th and G Streets, NW.

A typical wartime scene at Union Station.

Government Girl Marian Norby quipped, "If you could tell the difference between a typewriter and a washing machine, the government would hire you because they were so desperate for secretaries."

Over 24,000 servicewomen were stationed in the Washington area.

Arlington Farms in Northern Virginia housed 8,000 civilian and military Government Girls.

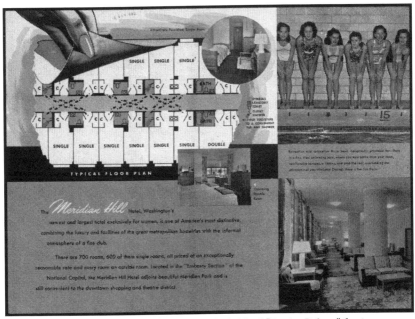

Brochure for the Meridian Hill Hotel, dubbed "Purity Palace" for its hundreds of single, female residents.

SPARS barracks on Independence Avenue across from the Smithsonian.

WAVES enjoy the small but comfortable bedrooms at Quarters D.

Servicewomen living in federal housing were lucky enough to enjoy the
generous portions of mess hall food.

Washington-area Army WACs lived in efficient if sparse barracks.

The Army made one decorating concession for WACs—window coverings
for privacy.

Union Plaza dorms built for World War I Government Girls.

Idaho Hall, the first residence built at Arlington Farms.

Lucy Slowe Hall housed African-American workers at U & 3rd Streets, NW.

The 150 classified "slums" that existed in Washington during the early 1940s spurred public heath concerns in Congress.

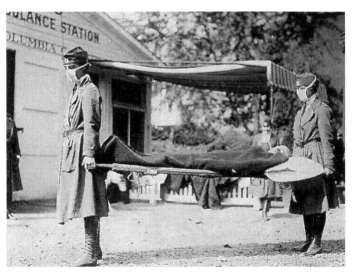

Red Cross volunteers helped care for the nearly 33,000 D.C. residents sickened by the Spanish Flu pandemic during the First World War.

Sleep and privacy were at a premium in the capital's boarding houses.

Having to wait in line for the bathroom was a common complaint among Government Girls renting rooms in private homes.

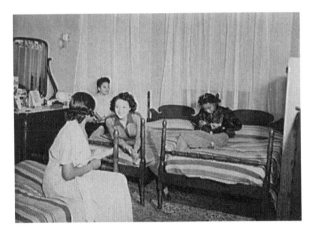

Federal dorms offered single or shared rooms that were nicer and more affordable than other housing options for Government Girls.

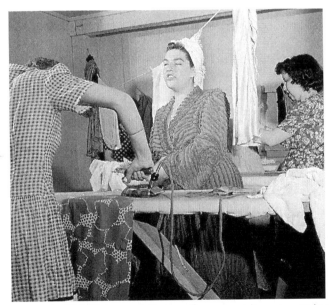

Government Girls living at Arlington Farms rent irons to use in the communal laundry rooms.

Betty McIntosh was a reporter for Scripps Howard before joining the OSS.

Chief Yeoman Elizabeth "Betty" Splaine

WAC Second Lieutenant Martha Putney

3

Secretaries of War

It was interesting. It was harrowing. It could be boring to tears. It could be so exciting you could go crazy.
  ~KATY SLUKA, OFFICE OF THE CHIEF OF NAVAL OPERATIONS[1]

My desk was located right under the crack in the ceiling and we were on the first floor. And I can remember periodically two men would come in, one would stand on my desk and measure the crack. The problem being that the safe upstairs was over the crack. Some of the joys of a temporary building! Happily the safe never did come down on me.
  ~EDITH WALTER, OFFICE OF STRATEGIC SERVICES[2]

argery Updegraff hated rainy days. Her normal commute was bad enough. Every day the twenty-eight-year-old clerk squeezed her tiny frame onto the jam-packed buses with 14,000 other D.C. workers riding back and forth to northern Virginia. But on wet, clammy mornings, the added nuisance of dripping umbrellas left soggy imprints against Margery's freshly pressed suits. Yet, even worse than her damp skirt was the ankle-deep mud clogging the unpaved roads stretching a quarter mile from the bus stop to her office in the partially completed

Pentagon. Margery survived those messy, seemingly endless treks but several pairs of her fashionable pumps did not.

Conditions inside the mammoth building during that spring of 1942 were not much better. Margery had recently earned an architecture degree from Carnegie Melon University, but even she had trouble finding her way around what was basically an enormous construction site. The Pentagon's official opening was still nine months away and building crews outnumbered War Department employees. Completing over six million square feet within seventeen months meant that carpenters, concrete mixers, painters, movers, pipefitters, and other workers focused more on speed than the comfort of the first occupants.[3]

Margery's office at the Army Ordnance Bureau had no interior walls. In fact, the entire floor lacked dry wall or dividers of any kind. The agency made do with a floor, a roof, and desks. In order to avoid getting lost in the cavernous and confusing maze of hallways every time they ventured to the bathroom, Margery and the women in her office devised their own system. They tied a rope around the leg of a desk, stretched it along the corridor to the nearest restroom, and attached it to one of the sinks. Women followed this modern, makeshift version of Ariadne's mythical thread to and from the bathroom until the interiors took shape.

The nearly 17.5 miles of corridors (and 280 bathrooms) in the completed Pentagon accommodated up to 40,000 employees. Margery and other Government Girls who weathered the building's transitional phase eventually found unprecedented workplace opportunities to shop, bank, eat, run daily errands, visit the beauty parlor, or even see a doctor in the mini-mall lining a massive concourse. And, best of all, its state-of-the-art air conditioning—rare for government offices—made the Pentagon "closely akin to heaven" during Washington's brutally hot summers. Margery felt her war work was important enough to compensate for the initial physical discomfort. After a year of working for the Army, Margery decided to take her patriotic commitment one step further and enlisted as one of World War II's 100,000 Navy WAVES.[4]

Newly commissioned Government Girls arrived in Washington with little idea of what to expect. Work environments, hours, co-workers, and expectations varied drastically. Women like Margery were thrown into rigorous, often confusing, and sometimes precarious situations. Wartime work offered Government Girls greater access to jobs and training, exposure to a wider scope of people, places, and activities, and a chance to use or develop skills that many of them didn't even know they possessed. These women provided the only feasible solution to the federal government's severe wartime labor shortage. Less than a century earlier, the U.S. government refused to employ women. During World War II, federal agencies simply could not function without them. As a young stenographer bragged to the *New York Times*, "Men may have made this war but the women are running it."[5] In one sense, she was right. By the end of the war, women made up nearly sixty percent of Washington's federal workers.[6] Wartime Government Girls helped establish the city's first significant female workforce.

So what made a young woman choose to leave her friends and family for the bedlam of Washington? A sense of patriotism definitely played a part. But millions of women chose to aid the war effort without leaving home. The primary incentive for most Government Girls proved to be money and job opportunity. The average yearly income for an American woman in 1940 was $592 but occupation and location determined her earning potential. A waitress in Alabama could earn $725 a year and a beautician in New York might pull in $1040. A Government Girl's starting salary of $1440 outweighed potential difficulties for many women.[7]

The comparatively high income attracted Elizabeth Watkins back to Washington. As a senior at Bryn Mawr, Elizabeth hoped to use her English degree and experience on the college newspaper to launch a writing career. She applied to publishing companies in Philadelphia but wartime wage restrictions kept entry-level salaries low. Elizabeth next investigated working for a newspaper, but found, "I'd have to start as a copy girl and again start at $25 a week. The government jobs in Washington really paid. I mean they paid two thousand something or other a year, so they were great salaries. Since I came from Bethesda, Maryland and the Washington area, that's when I began looking for a government job."[8]

Elizabeth used her writing and editing skills to help prepare intelligence reports for the Joint Army Navy Board. Her father's contact with a former Yale classmate secured the position. Elizabeth's job made federal work a family affair. Her two sisters worked for the Office of Strategic Services (OSS), the precursor to the Central Intelligence Agency, and her mother for the Treasury Department.

Economic advantages also led to a near exodus from the tiny town of Alma, Arkansas. Not only did a quarter of the women in the 1944 high school graduating class sign up to leave for Washington, but several teachers left their lower paying jobs to go with them.[9] Women's departure from teaching for defense work became so rampant that states were forced to issue emergency teaching certificates to people, mostly housewives, who would not normally qualify. Nearly 97,000 certificates were issued in 1943.[10]

The chance to forge new professional and personal opportunities drew many other women to Washington. Betty Allen found the prospect of relocating to the nation's capital from upstate New York, "infinitely preferable and certainly more exciting than a teacher's life in some small town high school." Facing the prospect of remaining at home with her parents, teaching math to local teenagers, and settling down in the insular community in which she was raised, the twenty-one-year-old saw being a Government Girl as a way to broaden her experiences. "My mother, having a rather adventurous nature herself, secretly encouraged me to follow my own desire," she fondly recalled. "After filling out many forms and passing a preliminary interview and security check, I was told to appear at Arlington Hall [the Northern Virginia headquarters of the Army Signal Corps] for a job at $1500 a year. I snapped it up although I really had no idea what I'd be doing." Betty took an overnight train to Washington and discovered that as a cryptanalyst she would be attempting to break enemy codes—worlds away from high school math class.[11]

Women like Betty felt that becoming a Government Girl was likely their one chance in life to find and afford the adventure they so craved.

The Civil Service Commission capitalized on women's willingness to take a risk for their careers or their country. This federal agency maintained central command for recruiting Government Girls. Teams of agents traversed the country selling the idea of working for Uncle Sam. Representatives contacted employment agencies, placed ads in newspapers, magazines, and on the radio, and held open recruiting drives in town squares, post offices, and movie theaters. Alice Randall made her first scouting trip for the Labor Department in 1943. She toured Illinois for three months enticing groups of business school students to take the civil service exam and helping convince doubtful parents to let their daughters relocate to D.C. Part of Alice's pitch to women in Cairo, Illinois came from her own experience as a recent college graduate who moved from the Midwest to the nation's capital. "Certainly you'll be homesick," she empathized. "But although homesickness is uncomfortable, like a cold, you *do* get over it!"[12]

Another recruiter found twenty-year-old New Yorker Pauline Menes on campus at Hunter College in the Bronx. She started her senior year as a geography and economics major unclear as to what she would do after graduation. She briefly considered joining the Army WACs, but a presentation by a federal agent convinced her to interview for a civilian position instead. The hustle and bustle of wartime Washington sounded exciting and knowing she would use her degree was appealing. As soon as she graduated, Pauline started as an economist in the Quartermaster General's office.[13] Colleges and business schools served as prime talent pools for finding women already trained to fit government personnel needs.

As the labor crunch in Washington became more severe in late 1942 and early 1943, the Civil Service Commission began to relax some of its more stringent regulations. It waived longstanding requirements to consider three applicants for every available job, lowered the eligibility age from eighteen- to sixteen-years-old, and accepted women for entry-level clerical appointments after only two years of high school. This helped fill vacancies quickly, as very few open positions required any college experience. Even at the height of the war, less than one percent of civilian office jobs required a college degree.[14]

For those without specialized degrees or training, the government relied on entrance exams. An applicant spent several hours answering written questions targeted towards a specific job (stenographer, typist, clerk, cartographer, etc.). The pressure of the day-long process and performing against the clock under the watchful eyes of a proctor could prove nerve wracking for novice candidates. Mary Wright, a recent graduate of North Carolina School for Black Deaf and Blind Students, could barely focus enough to take the test. "My hands were shaking, and my mind was a total blank," she recounted. She had the added burden of not being able to hear the instructions from the local examiner. But it was the actual test material that made her really nervous. The proctor gave her the exam for keypunch operators, a position she had never heard of before. Her results arrived in the mail a few days later. Although Mary scored well, no war agencies needed additional keypunch operators. The Commission suggested that she return and take the exam for junior clerks. After another arduous round of testing and waiting for results, Mary was thrilled and flustered to receive a telegram from the Navy giving her the standard forty-eight hours notice to report to Washington.[15]

Testing standards also became more flexible as the war progressed. The Commission set aside its rule of making an applicant wait six months before retaking a failed exam. And a failed test did not necessarily disqualify potential Government Girls. Sophomore Margaret Crook arrived home in D.C. for her summer break from Ursiline College with no thoughts of working for the government and even fewer clerical skills. A local friend pestered her to take the civil service exam so Margaret could join her at the Department of Economic Warfare where they desperately needed a typist. But Margaret couldn't type. She had no desire to embarrass herself, but finally gave in and indulged her friend.

Margaret watched the proctor grade her test and scribble "ineligible" across the top of the paper. Without missing a beat, the examiner turned to Margaret and asked the astonished young woman to start work immediately.[16] Hope Nusbaum had a similar experience when the Commission gave a typing test to her class at George Washington University. Hope failed the exam but found that "if you could identify a spare tire from a typewriter, you were classified as a typist." She began work at the War Production Board as soon as the spring semester ended.[17]

Thousands of other women became Government Girls by joining the military. Their individual reasons for joining varied as widely as those of civilian women. Some had brothers, cousins, or boyfriends in the service and wanted to feel like they were also contributing. Others didn't have any male relatives in the war and wanted to represent their families in the national emergency. Wilda Beeby had a mission when she decided to leave her home in Kalamazoo, Michigan and enlist in the Navy. Even decades later the drive and emotion remained fresh: "I was widowed and I wanted to get in the service. I had no children and I wanted to join the service because of what had happened to my husband... I was staying with them [her in-laws] at the time and between the two of us, we were both so unhappy, I had to get away. That was the first thought I had was to go in the service. And to get even. I had to get even."

Joining the WAVES gave Wilda some control back over her life after her husband's Army Air Corps plane was shot down. It helped the twenty-nine-year-old escape the remnants of her grief and lost dreams for a family life and create a fresh start. She felt important working in the Motor Corps driving military officials around Washington. As time went on her work became less about revenge and more about finding a new sense of belonging. "Most of the girls were in their twenties, and I became mom and mother to the lot of them," she recalled.[18]

Crystal Theodore was also looking for a new beginning. She was determined to join the service to expand her career options. Her job teaching college art courses was eliminated because of Depression related financial cutbacks. She eventually found work at the Tennessee Valley

Authority as an engineering draftsman making maps. She figured the war effort could use her skills and she could gain valuable experience. Crystal checked out her options and decided, "I wanted to go into the Marine Corps possibly because it was the hardest branch of the service to get into and I've always felt challenged to do whatever was hardest." Crystal needed that determination to make it past the recruiters: "They didn't think they needed me to win the war and I thought they did. I had a broken nose, I was nearsighted, I was too thin, I had a tricky back, but I didn't see that any of that would necessarily interfere with what women were doing in service. I tried three times before I got in. I went to the recruiting office in Columbia, South Carolina. I think they got a little tired of seeing me coming and finally they decided they would give me the examination, a written examination, just to see how I would do. I was lucky enough to make the highest average in that naval district. That sort of settled matters. I was accepted with waivers."[19]

The wiry brunette with the thick glasses and unwavering spirit quickly proved her mettle through basic training and was assigned to the Division of Plans and Policies, part of the Corps' intelligence service. Although women had uniquely personal reasons for becoming Government Girls, a distinct theme in their decision-making was the chance to change and improve some aspect of their lives.

As Crystal found out, each branch of the military developed slightly different eligibility requirements. These changed over the course of the war to reflect the rise and fall of willing recruits and gradual acceptance for enlisting married women and then mothers. In general, an enlistee had to be a U.S. citizen, between twenty-one- and thirty-five-years-old, at least five feet tall and one hundred pounds, have completed a minimum of two years of high school, and have no children under age eighteen at home.[20] Officer candidates had to have a college degree or two years of college and two years of work experience.

Regulations could be confusing and recruiters often gave women contradictory information. The weight standards seemed to be especially misleading. A common snafu involved women rejected by a recruiter for being too thin, stuffing themselves for a few weeks—often choking down as many bananas as possible on weigh-in day for added bulk and then told by a different recruiter at the same office that their initial weight was fine. Any extra pounds tended to melt away with the countless hours of drilling during boot camp.

Before servicewomen could report for duty in Washington, they, like their male counterparts, completed basic training. Training Centers opened on bases, at colleges, and in hotels around the country. The typical route to D.C. for enlisted WAVES included six to eight weeks of boot camp at the Bronx branch of Hunter College in New York City followed by twelve weeks of yeoman school to develop administrative skills at Oklahoma A&M College.[21] WAVE officers trained in Massachusetts at Smith College with specialized communications school set up at Mt. Holyoke College. WACs generally came from training on a converted cavalry post at Fort Des Moines, Iowa. Coast Guard SPARS and Marines initially shared Navy facilities but soon developed their own centers at the ritzy Palm Beach Biltmore Hotel in Florida and barracks at Camp Lejeune, North Carolina respectively (not surprisingly, SPARS seemed to enjoy boot camp more than Marines).

For military Government Girls, the surest route to Washington was to put in a request *not* to go there. Anita Galofaro's experience in the WAVES was typical for the Navy as well as the other branches of service. "Of course, they told us when we joined that we'd have three choices of where we wanted to go," Anita recalled. "So I put down California because I'd never been there, and I don't remember the other place I wanted, and then I said any place but Washington, D.C. And guess where they sent me? Washington, D.C. I was very disappointed. I had an aunt that lived there and we had often visited her. I just didn't like it. It was a big city. It was hard to get around. Anyway, I went. I was lucky. That's where I met my husband, so I guess that was meant to be."[22]

Chaos and big city life were just a few reasons women didn't want a post to Washington. Wilma Wilson worked as a cryptographer at the Navy Communications Annex near Ward Circle during her time in the

WAVES. She explained her initial reservations: "We hadn't wanted to be sent to Washington because we heard there were so many women. But it was wonderful!"[23] Regardless of whether or not they hoped to end up in Washington, approximately 24,000 military Government Girls served in the capital during the war—20,000 WAVES, 2,100 WACs, 1,000 Marines, and 900 SPARS.[24]

They performed a wide range of administrative work depending on their education, training, and rank. Women with previous work experience or professional degrees generally received assignments in their specialized fields, such as law, physics, engineering, meteorology, graphic design, or photography.[25] However, the majority of servicewomen provided clerical support to the various war departments operating under the military.

A few hundred British WRNS (Women's Royal Naval Service), Canadian CWACS (Canadian Women's Army Corps), and French women enlisted with the American WAC also served in Washington. Published diagrams matching pictures of women in uniform to their corresponding military branch served as a sort of field guide to help locals master the "awesome alphabetical code" of women taking over the city's streets.[26]

Civilian Government Girls far outnumbered those in uniform even though the military paid more for similar work. For example, the lowest paid Navy WAVE earned $1698 per year compared to the lowest paid civilian worker starting at $1440 per year. But legislation mandated quotas for female enlistment and federal agencies limited how many female employees they would release to the military (and insisted on sixty days notice). Plus, the military's lifestyle restrictions and commitment (duration plus six months) made a civilian job appealing to a greater number of women.

Although they were colleagues, tension between the two groups sometimes crept into the workplace. Civilians complained that they had to pick up the slack when servicewomen received time off for military drills and other institutional requirements. Elizabeth Watkins listed some of her grievances against the women in her department at the Joint Army Navy Board: "We worked six days a week. We didn't have Saturdays off. We civilians had to scramble to get the grocery shopping done, to get to the cleaners, and we just had the one day of rest during the week. Whereas all the military had Wednesday afternoons off because they were supposed to go and do rigorous exercise or further training or something. They weren't supposed to be just goofing off but they usually did just goof off."[27]

Conversely, military women often grumbled that civilian Government Girls took advantage of the looser parameters governing their behavior. Mary Bliss, a telegrapher first class working at the Naval Communications Headquarters, offered an example of an indolent woman who worked for the Captain in charge of her office: "We WAVES resented his civilian secretary. On the early watch, we arrived at 7 a.m. She came in at nine. We had half hour for lunch; she took as long as she wanted, many times going department store shopping afterward, and sometimes not coming back at all in the afternoon."[28] The discord rarely evolved into more than a case of simple annoyance or work envy. Since military and civilian women often lived and socialized together, the two factions of Government Girls developed greater bonds than divisions.

Job assignments dictated more than who sat at the next desk. It also determined Government Girls' working conditions. Because government agencies often operated out of cramped, improvised, or hastily constructed sites, physical circumstances varied widely. Stenographers for the National Advisory Committee on Aeronautics sat at rows of well-equipped desks lined up in the elaborate ballroom of the neoclassical white brick Leiter mansion in Dupont Circle, considered the finest home in the city when it was built in 1891. Government and military workers stationed at the four-story Navy Annex in Northern Virginia passed through two well-armed Marines, barbed wire fencing, and roof-mounted guns on their way to drab but secure offices.[29] Clandestine agent trainees at the OSS practiced throwing fake grenades on the golf course at the posh Congressional Country Club and "shadowing" targets along Peacock Alley at the elegant Willard Hotel.[30] Army cryptologists and operational personnel worked out of quarters at Arlington Hall Station, a complex set up on the rolling green hills of former women's junior college.[31] Government Girls assigned to un-air conditioned, concrete tempos constructed along the National Mall sweated so profusely throughout the summer that supervisors placed salt tablets near the water fountains to prevent them from fainting.[32] Margaret Bundick worked in a tempo at the War Production Board. "They were like little cracker boxes out in the sun," she remembered. "Fans were at a premium because they weren't making electric fans for civilian use. If you left your office and you had one, you didn't dare leave it unattended because someone would swipe the fan. My boss had a bright idea. He brought in a lock and chain and chained his to the radiator."[33] And one typist who was evicted from her Dupont Circle apartment so the building could be turned over to a war agency ended up working at that agency in an office constructed from what used to be her bathroom.[34] Government Girls adapted to unusual and often disruptive workplace situations.

A new career in the nation's capital sounded glamorous and exciting, but many Government Girls faced what the press called "crushing disappointment" at the reality of the tedious and repetitive work necessary for the day-to-day operations of running a war. Assignments could include typing twenty copies of a single report or filling out thirty forms each for hundreds of production requests—all done by hand. Carbon paper and mimeograph machines served as the high tech office equipment of the time.[35] Clerks at the Treasury Department spent whole days doing nothing but writing down individual savings bond serial numbers into enormous leather-bound ledgers. In 1944 alone the Treasury sold twenty-seven million of the popular Series E war bonds.[36] Navy Department employees clocked up to ten hours a day carefully comparing the names on monthly muster rolls for accuracy.[37] Telegrapher Mary Bliss at the Naval Communications Headquarters took incoming radio messages, verified and prioritized each, and assigned them to the appropriate departments. The volume overwhelmed her. One week the telegraphers counted how many messages they handled. They stopped when they reached 43,000.[38] Even at the OSS, which hired the greatest number of college educated women of any government agency, most Government Girls spent their time analyzing and cataloging reams of incoming intelligence material in order to forward them to the appropriate offices.[39] The one dependable aspect of wartime work was the endless shuffling of paperwork.

War agencies hired women in anticipation of growing workloads. During World War I, the federal government continually struggled to fill clerical positions. It remained understaffed throughout the comparatively short mobilization period, issuing desperate pleas for stenographers as late as November 1918. War departments hoped to avoid similar problems by hiring more Government Girls than they needed at any given time. This resulted in difficulties coordinating the number of workers with the amount of work, leaving some women idle and others simply confused.

Hope Nusbaum and her fellow clerks at the War Production Board arrived at their temporary office building on the National Mall one Monday morning to find that someone had removed all of the typewriters over the weekend. The head of the department quickly reassigned the workers to another unit, but the women sat around for three days waiting for new orders. After the third full day with nothing to do, a supervisor walked into the room and informed Hope and her shocked colleagues that he needed them to stay and work overtime.[40] Elizabeth Delean encountered similar bureaucratic logic. She was hired to fill out supply forms for the federal court system. Elizabeth usually finished her requisitions by the middle of the day. Because her supervisor couldn't find more work for her to do and yet insisted she remain for the full shift, Elizabeth spent her afternoons reading the newspaper. The supervisor balked at this. She demanded that Elizabeth look busy and told her to count paper clips instead.[41]

Other Government Girls sat idle because of a lack of training or necessary skills to complete their jobs. Boyd Dennison, Jr., a senior engineer with the Navy Department, filed numerous complaints about Government Girls being assigned to work in his department who not only had no engineering background but barely understood what an engineer did.[42] These women had little choice but to wait for assignments that they knew how to complete or to be transferred to another department. Tales spread of women who sewed complete wedding trousseaux during unused office time and Government Girls who fled Washington after two weeks because they felt bored and underutilized in their jobs.[43]

Employee turnover became a serious issue for federal agencies. In July 1942 the Civil Service Commission placed 23,000 employees with government departments but netted an increase of only 5,600 workers. Officials estimated that two out of every three workers filled vacancies rather than new positions.[44] *Life* magazine ran a feature story about why Government Girls quit. The article profiled several women: clerk Miriam Glassman got tired of commuting from Baltimore because she could not afford rent in Washington; stenographer Adrianne Young felt the government offices were poorly managed; junior clerk Helen Tucker got discouraged by the lack of boyfriends and was afraid the government would freeze her in her entry-level job for the duration; clerk-typist Carol Todd relocated to a Seattle war plant for more money; and Darlene Lindley found D.C. so expensive she ended up having to work nights in a drugstore just to make ends meet.[45]

By the beginning of 1943, approximately 1,000 Government Girls quit each month. Several agencies hired counselors to conduct what they newly termed "exit interviews" to try to keep women from fleeing. Employees could air their grievances about problems such as superiors they felt unfairly threatened to fire them or penalized them by putting them on night shifts at the more geographically remote agencies. Counselors solved many cases through transfers to other departments.[46] However, Government Girl resignations remained high throughout the war and affected recruiting efforts. *Independent Woman* magazine reported that, because of the city's reputation as a difficult working environment, "50 percent of the eligible stenographers are refusing appointment to Washington."[47] That was likely an exaggeration, but it did take a certain fortitude to stick it out in Washington. Government Girls who stayed did so out of a sense of duty (including a legal one to the military), because it advanced their careers, or the personal and professional opportunities in D.C.—no matter how difficult the circumstances—were still better than those back home.

One aspect of that stressful work environment derived from a shift in the use of private secretaries to the "secretarial pool." This new division of labor worked like an office assembly line. Government Girls performed a single, specialized task for several bosses or an entire department instead of handling virtually all office duties for one single boss. The system was efficient, but many women found it hard to adjust to long days of repetitive work.[48] A few agencies tried to relieve the tediousness of clerks' assignments by alternating one week at the typewriter with one week of work on other office machines. Claire Shrivener felt that her work in a Navy Department secretarial pool was a "comedown" from her prewar job as a private secretary in Wisconsin. She considered going back home, but decided to stay when she found a more challenging position with a D.C. engineering firm.[49] By the 1930s, a workplace culture existed which prized and respected private secretaries and office managers above clerks and jobs such as typists and stenographers that utilized office machines. The professional skill set needed by secretaries and managers was deemed more complex and demanding and were generally held by women with further education and from a higher social class (those two factors were usually connected). The secretarial pool challenged this hierarchy. Private secretaries were not eliminated from the federal government, but they were limited and reserved for high-ranking officials.

For women like Claire who wanted to use their experience and training outside of the government, Washington's private sector offered plenty of options. Thousands worked in stores, hotels, restaurants, and other businesses as the city's growing population increased the need for additional services. Much of the extra labor came from the regional population. By the end of the war, forty-five percent of area women earned a paycheck. For instance, local young women not yet old enough or experienced enough to work in government agencies supplied much of the seasonal help in retail stores. Retail clerks earned an average of $1250 per year, about $200 less than a starting government salary. Private industry jobs added even more women to Washington's total workforce. In 1944 they made up forty-one percent of all full time workers.[50]

Monotonous war work could be draining or demeaning, but certain assignments exhausted women's emotions rather than their intellect. A pivotal scene in the movie *Saving Private Ryan* revolved around one of these jobs. It shows a Government Girl dutifully typing as part of a large secretarial pool. As she works her way through a massive pile of official condolence letters, she notices she has typed the same name three times and brings it to her supervisor. This propels the plot of the film (to bring back the family's one remaining son) but does not show the toll such work could take on the women who did it.

Dealing with death notices all day every day was a constant reminder of the human cost of war and the danger loved ones were surely facing. When Yeoman Second Class Christine Weyandt received her duty assignment to the Bureau of Naval Personnel, the WAVE thought she'd be doing "something exciting and fun." But she was placed in the casualty notification section. "The war became very real to me then because these were people with families, loved ones, who were going to miss them," Christine recalled. "If they were missing in action, they would worry about them. I knew what my mother was like [about her brother who was drafted]. It was real hard for me for a while to get to a place where I could really do the job, I thought, efficiently. Well, I won't say efficient, I think I was efficient all the time because I took it very seriously, but it was very hard for a while."[51]

Bonita Bailey found no levity in her work either. She was eighteen years old and away from her home in the Ozark region of Missouri for

the first time. She was assigned to work with an Army Major who handled that branch's suicide cases. Thinking back on her eight hours a day
delving into the reasons for, methods, and aftermath of men killing
themselves, Bonita sighed, "You learn the facts of life pretty soon after
that." She heard that another department needed Government Girls for
work preparing telegrams notifying survivors about servicemen killed in
action, missing in action or held as prisoners of war. She applied for a
transfer. She felt it couldn't be worse than what she was already doing.
However, Bonita discovered, "It was a very depressing job and they just
couldn't keep people who wanted to do the work. I got there about the
time the Battle of the Bulge started, shortly before. And when that started, we would have rooms full, I don't mean just one room, I mean *rooms*
full of mail pouches of casualty reports. And this is why it was a 24-hour
operation. This is why you worked the long hours that you did. Many
times it was very depressing. We had one young woman in our department who found her husband's death report, killed in action. Needless to
say that wasn't a pleasant day in the department. She was reassigned to
another department. She didn't come back because it was such a devas-
tating thing... I was in the department for a year and a half... We sent
out not just thousands but hundreds of thousands of telegrams per day.
It was a 24-hour process."[52]

Government Girls came across names of people they knew more often than seemed plausible given the sheer volume they handled. WAVE
Katy Sluka worked in Communications at the Office of the Chief of Naval Operations. She became good friends with the other women in the
office, which is why her worst memory of that time relates to one of
them: "Mary Francis was sitting next to me when we were both a little
higher [in office seniority], reading messages when they came in and
correcting them before the girls typed them up to distribute. Mary Francis began to cry. She handed over her message, said, 'Excuse me,' and
headed for the ladies room. Her fiancé had just been shot down. How
awful, sick luck to have the message come to Mary Francis. It shattered
the whole office. But it was war. And we all knew that. We had some

other disappointments when it was a neighbor or friend that you knew who had met with a disaster of some sort. But you had to try. It's terrible that you wished it was strangers that you read about. But it was better than reading about your friends."[53] These type of incidents occurred enough times in notifications offices that several agencies asked Government Girls for the names and service numbers of close family and friends so the records could be flagged.

Such a precaution wouldn't have eased Freda Segal's heartbreak. Although she didn't lose a loved one, the unexpected news of a soldier's death hit hard: "There was one fellow. He was married, but whenever I went to Fort Belvoir, we always managed to spend a lot of time together dancing. Then he disappeared from sight. We never wrote. One of the ladies who came in to apply for death benefits was his wife. I was so upset. I remember being so upset that after I finished with her I just had to go home. This fellow did not die in action. He died of some disease in Hawaii she said. That was an awful moment… I remember having a hard time saying when did your husband die. I tried to phrase it when did your husband leave us?"[54] Attempting to maintain the emotional distance women found necessary to turn daily contact with grief and pain into routine business caused many Government Girls to burn out quickly and transfer out of those departments.

Racism created another kind of emotional strain for Washington's Government Girls. The growth in the number of female government workers did not necessarily mean greater career opportunities for African-American women. While the nation-wide number of black female federal clerical workers increased from 60,000 in 1940 to 200,000 in 1944, the majority of black workers remained barred from higher-level jobs.[55] Executive Order 8802 banned racial discrimination in defense industries and civil service jobs in June 1941, but the policy was never stringently enforced and African-American employment opportunities were hindered in part because of employers' and co-workers' racist attitudes.[56]

Martha Putney struggled with such prejudice. Martha earned a master's degree in history at Howard University before taking a job as a statistical clerk for the War Manpower Commission. She felt ostracized and ignored by her white co-workers and was passed over for choice assignments despite excellent performance reviews. Supervisors told Martha not to expect promotions within the agency because of her race. She resigned out of frustration and enlisted in the WAC, where she hoped to find greater career prospects.[57]

Although African-American women trained and, for the most part, worked in separate, all-black units of the Army, it offered them their greatest wartime military opportunities. Congress mandated that the Army enroll enough black women to equal up to 10.6 percent of the auxiliary's strength—roughly equal to the proportion of African Americans in the total U.S. population.[58] Forty black women ranked among the first 440 female Army trainees in July 1942. All but one group of the 6,520 women who served in the Army during World War II (not including the 512 working in the Nurse Corps) remained stateside. The WAVES and SPARS didn't enlist African Americans until late 1944. Because the war was almost over and recruiting severely scaled back, fewer than eighty black women served in the Navy. And, while the Marine Corps did not officially restrict black women from enlisting, it did not recruit them either. The first black female recruit joined the Marines in September 1949. No African-American military units served in the D.C. area, but individual servicewomen did work in integrated departments.[59]

Regardless of whether black women worked in government offices as servicewomen or civilians, they faced similar experiences of racism. In her study of black female wartime workers, historian Karen Anderson found that white women frequently showed hostility in an effort "to maintain social distance" from African Americans at work. They often objected to sharing space based on fatuous and prejudicial beliefs like black women never bathed or carried diseases.[60]

Some women also had trouble getting past their long-held cultural intolerance. Marine Lieutenant Bernice Berry counseled a subordinate who broke down in tears after her first day of work in Washington. She came to Bernice in hysterics because she had been assigned to an African-American civilian supervisor. The woman did nothing to upset the Marine and, in fact, helped her navigate through the day's procedures. But the idea of working for a black person offended the southern-born Marine. Bernice counseled the woman to get past her prejudices and see the supervisor as an individual but, at the very least, respect her as the boss.[61]

Yeoman Third Class Lillie Mae Colombo received a similar response to her initial complaint, but later found help from a more sympathetic official. The twenty-seven-year-old West Virginia native was the only WAVE working at the Navy Department's Bureau of Ships. Among the civilian workers were twenty or so African-American men and women set up in one corner of the massive room making copies on a Photostat machine. Thinking back on the experience, Lillie Mae was embarrassed by her reaction: "From where my desk was I could look down this room and see all these black people. And I thought, 'What am I doing here with all these black people?' Now that is ignorance. It just got to me. And I went down to the Bureau of Ships and asked for a transfer." When she told the officer the truth about why she wanted a new assignment, the woman sternly replied, "As far as I'm concerned, as long as you are in the Navy, you will stay right where you are." Lillie Mae felt devastated but returned to her job. A few days later the Commander in charge of the department called her into his office. He knew about her request and asked Lillie Mae to replace his civilian secretary when she left to get married. She avoided interacting with the other workers and retained her bigoted views until years later when she was forced to work alongside African Americans back in West Virginia and got to know her peers as individual women instead of an impersonal and stereotyped racial group.[62]

Just because Government Girls came together for the war effort did not mean that prewar racial attitudes disappeared. The workplace became a space for women to negotiate an understanding of each other and determine the measure of animosity or acceptance that would make up the office culture. The restrooms at Mary Wright's job with the Navy became a source of contention rather than negotiation. White women in the department claimed the largest and nicest lounge as the meeting spot for their breaks. When Mary and the other black workers walked into the bathroom, they received scathing looks and clipped directives to use the smaller restrooms further down the hall. Mary and others ignored the women's comments and continued to use the lounge even though they dreaded the daily confrontations. They felt justified and relieved when officials eventually posted signs declaring facilities open to all federal employees regardless of race, color, or creed.[63] A widespread discrepancy still existed between racial policy and practice.

A poem called "Civil Service" printed in *The Crisis*, a magazine published by the National Association for the Advancement of Colored People (NAACP), expressed black women's disappointment with their treatment in Washington's government offices. The last few lines reveal the hypocrisy of the white women who work to rid the world of oppression but themselves perpetuate racism:

> You send your memos on a metal tray,
> And coldly kill each overture I've tried.
> Why hope to rid charred continents of gloom
> 'Till *we* have learned to smile across a room?[64]

By 1945 black workers held nineteen percent of all federal jobs in D.C.[65] The frustration of breaking through the professional barrier of getting hired by the government only to hit up against another barrier of inclusion and acceptance in the office plagued African-American women throughout the war.

Workplace racism ran so deeply in federal agencies that white Government Girls could also be subject to discrimination by association.

When Loretta Pattison, who worked downtown at the Commerce Department, enjoyed lunch in the building's cafeteria with several of her African-American peers, all four received nasty looks and derogatory comments from Loretta's white colleagues.[66] Economist Pauline Menes received urgent hushed warnings from white co-workers at the Quartermaster General's Office after she began carpooling with three African-American women who worked in her building. They told Pauline how other people assumed she must be black, even though she was fair-skinned, because she rode to work with black women. They were concerned that the misunderstanding would lead to social and professional suicide. Pauline shrugged off their suggestions to find another ride. She came from a racially diverse neighborhood in New York City and felt strongly about keeping her new friendships despite other people's prejudices.[67] These women and others attempted to cross the racial divide on a personal level, even if they couldn't bridge it on an institutional one.

In addition to conflicts over race, Government Girls dealt with workplace friction over their gender. Many servicewomen faced hostile male reactions starting in basic training. Lieutenant Phyllis Paxton shied away from dealing with high-ranking officials while working at the Naval Communications Annex because of her experience during WAVES officer's school: "The captain that we had at Northampton [Smith College] was awful. He hated WAVES... He talked at our graduation. He said he thought it was a terrible mistake to let women in the Navy and he knew we'd never amount to anything, literally."[68] The derisive commencement address intimidated Phyllis but also made her determined to prove herself in her work.

SPAR Betty Splaine's boot camp drill instructor Danny, a Marine injured at Guadalcanal who felt degraded at having to work stateside with women, unleashed an even more inappropriate display of animosity. As Betty's unit marched in formation, instead of the traditional chorus of, "Left, left, left right left," Danny shouted out, "Rape, rape, allow rape rape." Betty and the other apprentice seamen discussed reporting him, but couldn't figure out whom to tell and decided it would probably only make matters worse.[69]

Such resentment often followed servicewomen into the office. Betty's first boss, a Naval officer, took his disdain so far as to rearrange the desks in their office so he wouldn't have to look at her. And when another newly commissioned SPAR reported for work, her commanding officer exclaimed, "Good God, first horses, then dogs, now women![70] Elizabeth Marsh, who worked with other WAVES at the Bureau of Naval Personnel, observed: "Most of the stress came from the old Navy men who bitterly resented us. Or the sailors who came in and knew they were going to be sent to sea as they saw us come in. Yes, we took a lot of guff. We were called all kinds of names and suggested we were simply there, shall we say, to service the male personnel. A lot of them were not very nice to us. We ignored it. Just got up and left."[71]

Civilian Government Girls also fought chauvinism simply to get into the workplace. A forty-two-year-old lawyer aced her civil service exams for government jobs that required knowledge of the law, including Deputy U.S. Marshal. But when she called to set up the job interviews, an agent informed her they wouldn't accept women for any of those positions. The lawyer recalled being told, "if I were still in my 20s and a good stenographer I could be used, but that no employer wanted an 'old woman past thirty.'"[72] None of the twenty-three women who passed the 1941 D.C. bar felt optimistic about attaining successful government careers. One new lawyer summed up the government's endemic gender bias: "The Federal Government has very little use for women with brains. Women in the Federal service are not classified by training. If they advance, likely as not it is because they have looks, not brains. It's the price they pay for being women."[73]

This was not a new complaint. Two years earlier Louisiana Senator Allen Ellender declared he was making an official study of the fact that "a shapely turn of the ankle is often more effective in helping a girl get a good job than is the skillful twist of the wrist that makes her rival a superlative stenographer."[74] The investigation came under his committee work looking into personnel issues within the government. He discovered beauty beat out brains every time. The problem, he concluded, was simple. Most government officials were men and men liked pretty girls. And there wasn't much to be done about that. So they did nothing.

Even in the OSS, many women with doctorates, high-level administrative experience, and tenured professorial backgrounds ended up working for much younger, inexperienced men who lacked advanced degrees. Only about eighteen percent of the college-educated women in the department held jobs other than filing clerk, librarian, or secretary.[75] Successful career women faced perception as well as hiring difficulties. Government recruiters turned away Priscilla Crane, a saleswoman used to earning upwards of $5,000 per year. The men told her that their employers "do not want women who are used to large salaries."[76]

WAVE Lieutenant Margaret Riordan had a theory as to why all Government Girls hit up against such resistance. Men, she believed, "had no idea how efficient, intelligent, easy to work with women were. Even though after the war they started taking women in wholesale. They had *no* idea we were that bright, that cooperative."[77] Navy photographer Stephen Kanyusik's experience reinforced Margaret's hypothesis. He eventually became convinced of women's professional capabilities. Stephen admired the Government Girls' work ethic he witnessed while posted at the Anacostia Naval Air Station Photographic Lab and felt that during the war other men "became aware that [women] were not lesser—even if you didn't admit it publicly. You knew they were competent."[78]

Occasionally men crossed the line from hostility or admiration to what today would be defined as sexual harassment but at the time was accepted as the price of being a career woman. While working at Naval Communications Headquarters, Mary Bliss became the target of unwanted romantic attention. Her youth, inexperience with men, and common but coincidental first name caught the fancy of one of her bosses. "I had a chief who fell in love with me," she recalled matter-of-factly. "I didn't like him at all. He had been married, his wife had died, and her name was Mary. He thought 'Mary Pure' was the one for him. He kept writing notes to me. Sweet, hard words. When it came time for the cleanup Sunday nights [when WAVES on duty cleaned the office], he tried to assign me to a desk job so I wouldn't have to work. I said everyone is taking notice of that, and I want to do just what the other people did. He finally decided to have me wash and wax the desk tops."[79] Mary stayed in the uncomfortable situation because she liked her work. But she continued to fend of his advances throughout her time there.

One infamous case of harassment turned deadly. Rosemary Sidley, a former Chicago socialite who worked as a stenographer at the OSS, met William Chandler at the office. He was one of her supervisors. Once Rosemary learned he was married with two sons, she tried to maintain a purely professional relationship with him. But William, a professor of literature before joining the OSS, barraged Rosemary with long, flowery letters and interoffice memos expressing his desire and torment over her. One note included the foreboding passage: "I have said horrid things in anger, but not in hate: I have done still more horrible things. But the only important emotion—however different its manifestations—that has guided me for six months now Rosemary, has been love of you." Office culture in the 1940s allowed for a wide range of acceptable flirtations. There was no protocol to deal with these types of incidents, so Rosemary confided her troubles and concerns to her roommates but not to her supervisors.

On a midsummer's evening in 1943, one of those roommates, Elizabeth Maguire, let William inside their rented Georgetown townhouse to wait for Rosemary to come home. He had called earlier and convinced a leery Elizabeth that he merely wanted to say goodbye before being transferred out of Washington for good. A short time later Rosemary arrived and, seemingly uncomfortable but not particularly alarmed, went into the parlor to talk to William. Elizabeth hurried upstairs to give the two some privacy. Minutes later, she heard gunshots explode over her friend's terrified screams. William shot Rosemary three times before turning the .32 caliber automatic pistol on himself. Police found Rosemary's body with a lit cigarette still dangling between her fingers.[80]

Author Roald Dahl worked for British intelligence in Washington and knew Rosemary and some of her roommates. When the writer heard one of them say she never wanted to set foot in the house again, he campaigned to rent the spacious townhouse. Once inside Dahl noticed the bloodstained carpet and bullet holes were still in the parlor. He decided to find another place to live.[81]

The sensational murder-suicide did not change Government Girls' relationships or conditions at the office. Rosemary became one more tragedy in a period of ongoing wartime drama. With so many potential emotional stressors, how did Government Girls cope? Some didn't. Dr. Winfred Overholser, superintendent of D.C.'s St. Elizabeths psychiatric hospital, complained that "many girls coming to Washington have become unstable, discontented and have gone off on a tangent" because of work-related strain.[82] Cecilia Campbell wrote home about one of those women. The WAC detailed the intense and competitive environment she experienced working with Army codes at the Pentagon. Like most Government Girls, they worked six days a week and up to twelve hours a day. Not everyone could handle the stress and the schedule, Cecilia told her parents. "One of the girls went off the beam last night at work," she wrote on a postcard. "Nervous breakdown, technically, and she was sent to North Post [at Virginia's Fort Myer] to the hospital."[83] Women diagnosed with a breakdown or nervous exhaustion were either sent home or allowed to take sick leave, recuperate, and return to work.

Kathleen Huff's uncle suggested she do just that—take a break from her work as a file clerk in the Adjutant General's Office. Dr. Huff noticed his twenty-three-year-old niece seemed strained and exhausted. He often checked in at her downtown apartment from his home nearby in Maryland. Kathleen had previously lived away from her immediate family in Denver in order to attend Woodbury College in Los Angeles. But her studies never distressed her the way working in Washington did. On a Friday night in September, Kathleen left two partially completed notes and leaped to her death from the window of her fourth-floor apartment. "Concentrate on your copy being typed. You simply cannot concentrate if you allow your thoughts to go wool gathering," she admonished herself in one of the notes.[84] It was typewritten.

Kathleen's reaction represents the extreme minority, but Washington's wartime suicide rate among women hit only ten fewer than its all-time high during the Great Depression. Dr. A. Magruder MacDonald, D.C.'s Coroner and the one who signed Kathleen's death certificate, attributed the number of suicides to the vague malady "war fatigue," an umbrella term for aches, pains, depression, anxiety, stress, exhaustion, and any other mental or physical symptom that appeared during the war years but which doctors could not attribute to a specific cause (which is different from "battle fatigue" which equates in modern terms to post traumatic stress disorder).[85] Neither the suicides nor the war fatigue were limited to Government Girls. But since many women had no ties to the city, and therefore no built-in community or family support, they were at increased risk of feeling alienated and overwhelmed.

Overly simplistic solutions by federal officials for Government Girls to exercise, such as having a nice swim in order to "take the kinks out of taught nerves," may have kept them trim but did little to ease daily pressures.[86] The women who were most successful at handling both work and wartime tensions were the ones who turned to each other for support, advice, and encouragement.

Joanne Lichty, a teenage clerk in the Treasury Department, relied on more experienced, older workers to help navigate the bureaucratic challenges and professional demands of the job. Joanne found mentors in a group of women who had been working for the government since World War I. "I was this young kid and they treated me so nicely," Joanne remembered fondly. "There was a feeling of camaraderie."[87] Resentment over the invasion of newcomers rarely surfaced. Permanent employees tended to view war workers as temporary, so Government Girls did not necessarily threaten their status or promotion potential. Joanne did not plan on a career in the government. Her long-term goals focused on teaching. But the women offered her more than workplace guidance. They gave Joanne confidence in her own abilities. The professionalism and generosity of the women in Joanne's department allowed her to successfully maneuver through the heightened wartime pace and expectations.

Betty Allan also felt like she was part of a supportive female team at Arlington Hall, headquarters for the Army's Signal Intelligence Service. Betty's recent math-related degree from New York State Teacher's College helped her land a civilian job as a code breaker. Although each woman worked independently, the group shared in one another's triumphs and setbacks. Betty recalled, "If we found what we thought could be a slight breakthrough we took it right up to our supervisor. She was a very bright gal. And when she'd see something she thought offered some possibility, she'd yell, 'Hot spit!' And everyone would gather around."[88] The group formed an ethos based on the principle that what was good for one was good for all, since that meant deciphering Japanese codes and helping to protect American troops. The sense of belonging to a group, especially a group with a shared purpose deemed noble and effective, kept Government Girls motivated at work and willing to endure the often difficult circumstances.

Developing that connection to other women at the office impacted how Government Girls felt about their work and their attitude in general. Ellenora Spratt Barker worked at the Navy Barracks as a WAVES Specialist unscrambling messages to and from top Naval officers. Her memories of the day-to-day operations revolve around the women she worked with as much as the duties she performed as a cryptographer. "I was the luckiest person I have ever known in my opinion," she enthused. "My assignment was to be in with the Officers Communications Department and unscramble these messages that would come in. I met some of the nicest girls in that department... There were six of us who became real close friends, and we did everything as a group."[89] Having allies to turn to when problems arose, to share complaints with, and confide in, eased much of the stress inherent in learning a new job, skills, and government system all at the same time. Ellenora's success at creating friends in the office to laugh and socialize with gave her an added reason to go to work each morning.

Bonita Bailey enjoyed the women she met as friends, but also as a chance to broaden her knowledge and understanding of life in general. "The people I worked with were very nice people," she recalled. "They were from all over the country. You learn about lifestyles, all shapes, sizes, and colors. It was my first time working with people of different nationalities. When I grew up here, we were simply Missouri hillbillies, and we were all white. There I learned working with the various nationalities. There were even two women of Russian ancestry who worked in our department."[90] Bonita found something besides her departmental duties to keep her interested and involved. She may not have had a lot in common with the women around her, but her willingness to reach out and bridge those differences gave her the connections she needed to cope with the monotony and intensity of working for the notifications divisions.

A local reporter sardonically commented, "Washington is the biggest 'company town' in the world. All of its people either work for Uncle Sam or work for someone who works for Uncle Sam."[91] When the number of Uncle Sam's workers in Washington hit a peak of almost 300,00 in 1943, Government Girls made up nearly forty percent of that "company." And they would reach a majority of it by the end of the war.[92] These women came from all over the country, every conceivable background, and for widely varying reasons. Yet, each one knew that moving to wartime Washington would be an adventure they couldn't quite conceive and probably wouldn't forget.

First Lady Eleanor Roosevelt warned parents not to allow their daughters to come to the city "unprepared" for the fast pace and potential problems they would encounter.[93] Even though the difficult working and living conditions were publicly discussed and known throughout the country, most Government Girls never imagined the personal and professional challenges that lay ahead. These serious, sometimes deadly serious, circumstances contradicted the smiling, carefree images widely promoted by federal agents and government recruiting posters. Many Government Girls quit and returned home or found less chaotic jobs in other businesses or cities. But the ones who remained developed coping techniques and a network of other women for support and encouragement. Bonita Bailey, who typed hundreds of death, MIA, and POW notification letters every day, made it through the emotional strains with a progressive attitude, newfound allies, and one absolute certainty. She knew that what she was doing mattered—both to her and her country. "I know that I had a greater and deeper understanding and love of country. Understanding of what these men went through to protect my freedom," Bonita reflected. "I learned there too, since it was really my first job. I learned the importance of doing a job well. Doing my best at what I was involved in. Because I knew what I was doing was important in Washington, very important."[94]

Notes

[1] Katy Sluka Collection (AFC/2001/001/26420), VHP.

[2] Edith Brainerd Walter Collection (AFC/2001/001/57582), VHP.

[3] Steve Vogel, *The Pentagon: A History* (New York: Random House, 2007), 213, 217.

[4] Margery Updegraff interview with Wanda Driver and Ardith Kramer, November 19, 2003, WIMSA.

[5] Sally Reston, "Girls' Town – Washington," *New York Times Magazine*, November 23, 1941, SM8, 9.

[6] Margaret C. Rung, "Paternalism and Pink Collars: Gender and Federal Employee Relations, 1941-50," *Business History Review* 71 (Autumn 1997): 383.

[7] U.S. Department of Labor, Women's Bureau, *Women Workers in Ten War Production Areas and Their Postwar Employment Plans* (Washington, D.C.: Government Printing Office, 1946), 44; U.S. Department of Labor, Women's Bureau, *Handbook of Facts on Women Workers* (Washington, D.C.: Government Printing Office, 1946), 5; Susan H. Godson, *Serving Proudly: A History of Women in the U.S. Navy* (Annapolis: Naval Institute Press, 2001), 121; "Changes in Women's Employment During the War," *Monthly Labor Review* (November 1944): 1029.

[8] Elizabeth Law Watkins Collection (AFC/2001/001/5869), VHP.

[9] David Brinkley, *Washington Goes to War* (New York: Alfred A. Knopf, 1988), 243.

[10] "OWI Report Franklin-2994," 1944, 14, Records of Natalie Davisen, Program Manager for Homefront Campaigns, 1943-5, RG208, Box 7, National Archives (NARA).

[11] Betty E. Allen Collection (AFC/2001/001/34265), VHP.

[12] Frances T. Cahn, *Federal Employees in War and Peace; Selection, Placement, and Removal* (Washington, D.C.: The Brookings Institute, 1949), 33, 35, Ruth Mac Kay, "White Collar Girl," *Chicago Daily Tribune*, April 1, 1946, 23.

[13] Pauline Menes interview with author, May 11, 2006.

[14] Cahn, *Federal Employees in War and Peace*, 67-8.

[15] Mary Herring Wright, *Far from Home: Memories of World War II and Afterward* (Washington, D.C.: Gallaudet University Press, 2005), 205.

[16] Margaret and Jim Crook interview with author, May 27, 2005.

[17] Hope Ribbeck Nusbaum interview with author, August 8, 2004.

[18] Wilda Beeby Collection (AFC/2001/001/9304), VHP.

[19] Crystal Theodore Collection (AFC/2001/001/16136), VHP.

[20] Pilots with the Women Airforce Service Pilots (WASP) always needed a high school diploma. Martha S. Putney, *When the Nation was in Need: Blacks in the Women's Army Corps during World War II* (Metuchen New Jersey: Scarecrow Press, 1992), 28; D'Ann Campbell, "Women in Uniform: The World War II Experiment," *Military Affairs* 51, no. 3 (July 1987): 138.

[21] The Bronx branch of Hunter College is now Lehman College and Oklahoma A&M College became Oklahoma State University.

[22] Anita Galofaro Collection (AFC/2001/001/33632), VHP.

[23] Wilma Leota Martin Wilson Collection (AFC/2001/001/24747), VHP.

[24] Jerry Kluttz, "Uniformed Girls in D.C. To Disappear Shortly," *Washington Post*, November 2, 1945, 12.

[25] "Training Received by WAVES Prepares Them for Postwar Life," *Washington Post*, January 14, 1944, B4.

[26] Patricia Grady, "A Few Pointers on Knowing Who is Which About These Women in Uniform," *Washington Post*, May 31, 1942, 14; Commandant M.H. Fletcher CBE, *The WRNS: A History of the Women's Royal Naval Service* (Annapolis: Naval Institute Press, 1989), 41.

[27] Watkins, interview.

[28] Mary Merick Bliss Collection (AFC/2001/001/33087), VHP.

[29] Wright, *Far from Home*, 42-43.

[30] Elizabeth McIntosh interview in "Government Girls of World War II" (The History Project, 2004); Elizabeth P. McIntosh, *Sisterhood of Spies: The Women of The OSS* (Annapolis: Naval Institute Press, 1998), 53.

[31] James L. Gilbert and John P. Finnegan, eds., *U.S. Army Signals Intelligence in World War II: A Documentary History* (Washington, D.C.: Center of Military History United States Army, 1993).

[32] Crook, interview.

[33] Margaret Bundick Collection (AFC/2001/001/5891), VHP.

[34] Bob Levey and Jane Freundel Levey, *Washington Album: A Pictorial History of the Nation's Capital* (Washington, D.C.: Washington Post Books, 2000), 107.

[35] Doris Weatherford, *History of Women in America: American Women and Word War II* (New York and Oxford: Facts On File, Inc., 1990), 193.

[36] Paul K. Williams, *Washington, D.C.: The World War II Years* (Charleston, South Carolina: Arcadia Publishing, 2004), 93.

[37] Wright, *Far from Home*, 137.

[38] Bliss, interview.

[39] McIntosh, *Sisterhood of Spies*, 43.

[40] Nussbaum, interview.

[41] Elizabeth Delean Cozad interview with author, June 14, 2004.

[42] Dorothy Dennison interview with author, July 19, 2004; Peter A. Soderbergh, *Women Marines: The World War II Era* (Westport, Connecticut: Praeger, 1992), 65.

[43] Selden Menefee, *Assignment U.S.A.* (New York: Reynal & Hitchcock, Inc., 1943), 34-5.

[44] Jerry Kluttz, "CSC Hopes to Stop Mass Resignations," *Washington Post*, September 16, 1942, B1.

[45] "Washington in Wartime: It is Terrible Place to Live," *Life,* January 4, 1943, 47-50.

[46] Zenas L. Potter, "Government Employe [sic] Turnover," Letters To The Editor, *Washington Post*, September 27, 1942.

[47] Marjorie Barstow Greerbie, "Women Work With Uncle Sam," *Independent Woman* (March 1942): 74.

[48] Reston, "Girls' Town," SM22.

[49] Claire Shrivener interview with author, June 4, 2004.

[50] Washington Board of Trade, *Postwar Plans of Metropolitan Washington Residents* (Washington, D.C.: Washington Board of Trade, February 19, 1945), A-2, A-7.

[51] Christine Weyandt Collection (AFC/2001/001/43153), VHP.

[52] Bonita Orr Bailey Collection (AFC/2001/001/19375), VHP.

[53] Sluka, interview.

[54] Freda Segal Collection (AFC/2001/001/30833), VHP.

[55] Martha S. Putney, *When the Nation Was in Need: Blacks in the Women's Army Corps During World War II* (Metuchen, New Jersey: Scarecrow Press, 1992), 3.

[56] Karen Tucker Anderson, "Last Hired, First Fired: Black Women Workers During World War II," *Journal of American History* 69, no. 1 (June 1982): 84-86; Maureen Honey,

ed., *Bitter Fruit: African American Women in World War II* (Columbia, Missouri: University of Missouri Press, 1999), 36-7.

[57] Martha Putney interview with Kate Scott, March 26, 2004, WIMSA; Tom Brokaw, *The Greatest Generation* (New York: Random House, 1998), 187.

[58] U.S. Department of Labor, Women's Bureau, *Negro Women War Workers* (Washington, D.C.:, 1945), 14-15.

[59] Kathryn Sheldon, "A Brief History of Black Women in the Military" (Washington, D.C.: WIMSA, 1996), 4; Susan H. Godson, *Serving Proudly: A History of Women in the U.S. Navy* (Annapolis: Naval Institute Press, 2001), 116; Kathi Jackson, *They Called Them Angels: American Military Nurses of World War II* (Westport, Connecticut: Praeger, 2000), 166.

[60] Anderson, "Last Hired, First Fired," 86.

[61] Peter A. Soderbergh, *Women Marines: The World War II Era* (Westport, Connecticut: Praeger, 1992), 73.

[62] Lillian Colombo Collection (AFC/2001/001/28436), VHP.

[63] Wright, *Far From Home*, 63-4.

[64] Constance C. Nichols, "Civil Service," *The Crisis*, April 1945, 106.

[65] Jerry Kluttz, "Negroes Holding 19.2% of U.S. Jobs in Capital," *Washington Post*, February 21, 1945, 3.

[66] Loretta Pattison interview with author, June 25, 2004.

[67] Pauline Menes interview with author, May 11, 2006.

[68] Phyllis Paxton Collection (AFC/2001/001/64009), VHP.

[69] Elizabeth F. Splaine interview with Kate Scott, April 16, 2004, WIMSA.

[70] Ibid.

[71] Elizabeth Marsh Collection (AFC/2001/001/37368), VHP.

[72] Weatherford, *History of Women in America*, 180-181.

[73] "Uncle Sam Favors Beauty Over Brains, They Charge," *Washington Post*, February 27, 1941, 17.

[74] "On Capitol Hill," *Washington Post*, May 13, 1939, 2.

[75] Robin W. Winks, "Getting the Right Stuff: FDR, Donovan, and the Quest for Professional Intelligence" in George Chalou, ed., *The Secrets War: The Office of Strategic Services in World War II* (Washington, D.C.: National Archives and Records Administration, 1992), 24; Nusbaum, interview.

[76] Weatherford, *History of Women in America*, 181.

[77] Margaret Riordan Collection (AFC/2001/001/15730), VHP.

[78] Stephen Kanyusik interview with author, August 3, 2004.

[79] Bliss, interview.

[80] "Coroner's Finding of Murder Ends Probe of Sidley Death," *Washington Post*, July 14, 1943, B1; "Stenographer Slain by Supervisor When She Repulsed Advances Was Social-

ite-Heiress," *Washington Post*, July 15, 1943, 16; "How Rejected Suitor Killed Chicago Ex-Deb," *Chicago Daily Tribune*, July 15, 1943, 3.

[81] Jennet Conant, *The Irregulars: Roald Dahl and the British Spy Ring in Wartime Washington* (New York: Simon & Schuster, 2008), 171-2.

[82] "'Nervous Girls' Are Advised Not to Come to Washington," *Washington Post*, May 9, 1942, 1.

[83] Cecilia Campbell interview with Wanda C. Driver and Fran Richardson, November 7, 2003, WIMSA.

[84] "Government Girl Suicide Laid to Strain of Life in D.C.," *Washington Post*, September 19, 1942, B11; Obituary, *Washington Post*, September 19, 1942, B7.

[85] "District Suicides Rose 28% in 1945, Coroner's Report Says," *Washington Evening Star*, March 10, 1946, Statistics, Comparative, 1800-1959 #2 Folder, DCPL.

[86] Genevieve Reynolds, "Swimming Advised for 'War' Nerves," *Washington Post*, January 14, 1942, X11.

[87] Joanne Lichty interview with author, July 29, 2004.

[88] Betty Allan Collection (AFC/2001/001/34265), VHP.

[89] Ellenora Barker Collection (AFC/2001/001/65181), VHP.

[90] Bailey, interview.

[91] "Girl in a Mob," *American Magazine* 134 (October 1942): 33; Menefee, *Assignment USA*, 38.

[92] Rung, "Paternalism and Pink Collars," 382; "Women in Federal Defense Activities," *Monthly Labor Review* 54, no. 3 (March 1942): 640; "Scarcity of Manpower Puts Dent in Employment, But Payrolls Exceed 1942," Washington Facts and Figures, October 1943, Statistics, Comparative, 1800-1959 #1 Folder, DCPL; Washington Board of Trade, "The Bulletin," January 15, 1944, 3, Gelman Library Special Collections, George Washington University (GWU).

[93] "Girls on the Loose," *Washington Post*, October 14, 1944, 4.

[94] Bailey, interview.

4

No Room of Their Own

If the housing of war workers in Washington can be regarded as a sample of our ability to meet an emergency, it must cause great rejoicing in Japan.
~*WASHINGTON POST*, FEBRUARY 1943[1]

The water bugs came out at night, some very huge. I would run up the stairs, skipping over them, jump onto the bed and cover my head with a pillow, while [my roommate] Berdie killed them. We encountered only one mouse.
~MARY BLISS, BOARDING HOUSE RESIDENT[2]

Washington's housing crunch placed Betty McIntosh in a compromising position. She moved to the nation's capital from her home in Hawaii to work as a journalist for Scripps Howard news service. Her coverage of the Japanese attack on Pearl Harbor earned her the reassignment. Betty felt especially lucky in avoiding the notoriously mind and body-numbing search for a place to live in D.C. Her aunt and uncle offered her the third floor of their modest Georgetown home. The seemingly ideal situation worked well enough while Betty hustled around town as a reporter. She could even walk to her office. But after she took a job with the Office of Strategic Services (OSS), the wartime intelligence agency, the arrangements became much more complicated.

Betty was sworn to secrecy about her work spreading disinformation to the Japanese. Her unusual hours, furtive comings and goings, and new group of tight-lipped acquaintances unsettled her staid, older aunt and uncle. And then there was the problem of the key. The couple did not trust Betty with a key to the house. They still thought of the twenty-six-year-old as their young, inexperienced niece.

When Betty arrived after the household retired for the night, her only option was to enter by way of a discretely unlatched window on the ground floor. One evening a male friend—who happened to be a Navy admiral— walked Betty home and offered to help her get inside by hoisting her over the bushes onto the window sill leading into the living room. After a few awkward attempts, with Betty stepping all over the admiral's perfectly pressed uniform, she made it onto the ledge. While she balanced precariously on her stomach, her legs and bottom still dangling outside, a policeman walked by and demanded an explanation. Betty tumbled forward into the darkened house leaving the admiral to make a hasty excuse that would keep his reputation intact and her work under wraps. The next morning she joined the legions of Government Girls looking for another place to live.[3]

Betty's experience epitomized the housing crisis in wartime Washington—inconvenient, nomadic, filled with unexpected complications, and rife with conflict. It was common for Government Girls to move three, four, even five times throughout the duration. Sometimes this was by choice but more often it was by necessity—economic or, as in Betty's case, otherwise.

Population growth in Washington far outpaced available living space. The city's Defense Housing Registry processed up to 10,000 requests every month, often more than 300 women a day. Government Girls received V-cards ("V" for Victory) signaling priority status as war workers.[4] But this was America's central command post. Almost everyone coming into the city had priority status. And gender bias often trumped patriotism. One study revealed that while eighty percent of new arrivals were women, seventy percent of the landlords wanted male tenants only.[5] Men, they insisted, were less trouble than women. Such fierce competition for rooms spurred a renaissance in boarding houses, building projects, and a challenge to prewar notions of comfort and privacy. As Mary Tinder, an Office of Price Administration secretary, warned: "Wartime Washington is not the place for people with weak backbones who came here just to find out if they could take it."[6]

A recently hired Government Girl dashed off a frantic letter to the Housing Registry asking: "Does it take all your wages just to live? I never believe hearsay, but I would like an informal opinion. I am anxious."[7] She had good reason to be. The $24 a month she paid to rent a large, plushly furnished single room with equipment to cook her own meals would not go nearly as far in Washington as it had in the Midwest. One infamously nefarious landlady rented out the same single bed to nine girls for $40 a month each. The women worked on separate, consecutive shifts and took turns sleeping three at a time on the tiny mattress—sideways, the only way they could all fit on it together.

Overcrowding and economics often made for strange bedfellows. A woman needed to earn at least $2,000 a year in order to afford living in a relatively safe, clean room of her own. Government Girls' starting salary of $1,440 usually made doubling or tripling up a financial necessity, especially as many women also sent money home to help their families.[8] At the height of the war, housing inspectors found that four to ten people living in a single room was the rule, not the exception.[9]

Sharing intimate space with virtual strangers would become a hallmark of World War II Washington. "Newcomers Discover Private Baths Went Out With Hitler," newspaper headlines warned Government Girls.[10] Unlike today's young women who tend to leave home in their late teens to live in college dorms, rent apartments with friends, or find roommates online, the average Government Girl had never lived away from home. Social customs and a decade of economic depression kept most women with their families at least until marriage, even if they attended school or worked full time.

Many women enjoyed the chance to venture beyond the people and places they knew and others felt overwhelmed by the drastic change in lifestyle. Anna Fogelman experienced a little bit of both at leaving her comfortable Wilmington, Delaware home to become one of Washington's Navy WAVES. "I truly don't know why I decided to enlist, but it was the wisest decision I ever made in my life. Because I was, oh, a little bit reserved. I had not traveled much. Probably not more than twenty-five miles from home," she reminisced. "I don't remember being too scared. I was a little apprehensive, timid... You had the chance to really get to know people and learn how to be a friend. Of course some didn't. One of the things I remember is how disappointed and hurt I was that someone we thought was a friend, this individual, who ended up being the one who stole our hose. That's not small. I never knew people did things like this. It hit me, it really did."[11] A Government Girl's roommates and housing circumstances were two of the most important factors in determining how happy she was with her wartime experience.

A room-hunter's frustration level and likelihood of success depended greatly on timing, contacts, and money. Since newly trained Army WACs and Navy WAVES did not start arriving in Washington until late 1942, civilian women were first on the wartime scene. Those who arrived during the defense build-up and early years of the war had few choices. Apartments were expensive and usually reserved for families. Hotels offered a short-term solution but restricted the number of overnight stays because of demand. And government dorms were still in the planning stages. The most practical and affordable option was to rent a room in a private home or a boarding house. In an effort to meet the new demands, D.C. passed emergency measures lifting zoning restrictions and amending regulations to allow more residential homes to take in boarders.[12] Six months after the bombing at Pearl Harbor, an estimated 12,000 rooming houses of varying sizes, quality, and questionable legality operated in the District.

The press anointed boarding houses, "God's gift to the Government Girl."[13] For some women they were. Charlotte Carter found a haven in the 18th Street boarding house she shared with six other Government Girls, the Lindsey family who ran it, and a maid who lived in the basement. The twenty-one-year-old, who left her home in Greensburg, Pennsylvania to become a typist for the Signal Corps, felt overwhelmed at being "thrown into Washington, D.C." as she had "never been out of my town of 20,000 people." The home she shared proved an important bridge in the transition to her new life. The women turned over their food ration stamps to Mrs. Lindsey and the hard-working maid shopped for, prepared, and served them breakfast and dinner. Charlotte reveled in the meals and camaraderie after the hardships her family suffered through the Great Depression. "I had never eaten so well because I hadn't eaten well for ten years," she recalled. "I had never used a napkin before or anything like that. We had nice dinner talk. [Mrs. Lindsey] advised me on things my mother didn't even talk to me about. She wanted us to be proper. I had never been proper in my life up to that point. She was a good teacher to me."[14]

Charlotte lucked out. Many other Government Girls did not. "I have shivered in winter, melted indoors in summer. I've resided with those little brown bugs that work only on the night shift. I've hated and fought cockroaches. I've rented a first-floor apartment where the landlady sent her small son outside to look in at the windows and if he reported lights burning in more than one room at a time, she came in without knocking and turned off what she considered superfluous,"[15] one harried and exhausted Government Girl complained. Jean Ashby Sims, a twenty-year-old WAVE from West Virginia, was relieved to find a decent room in a private home relatively close to downtown. But she gave it up after a few months because she could no longer bear living with the eccentric owner. "The landlady was a clueless socialite who bemoaned the fact that I had to forage and told me about her terminated pregnancy which had occurred twenty years before when she was nineteen. She talked incessantly. I never saw her husband. Foraging was her word for eating in restaurants but she never asked me to dine with her," Jean recalled.[16]

Unhappy renters joined newcomers in the competition for potential rooms.

City housing officials investigated complaints about unsafe and unsanitary properties. They shut down houses like the one they found with nineteen government workers living in squalor among peeling paint, sagging stairs, and an infestation of rats and roaches. Two men slept in the bare concrete cellar and the seventeen others piled into bedrooms created with makeshift dividers.[17] Only the most desperate renters put up with such conditions. Some women arrived in the city with almost no money until their paychecks started, some didn't have the time to look for better housing (the government usually gave women forty-eight hours to report for work no matter how far away they lived), and still others trusted the wrong people.

The Washington Housing Association, a local advocacy group, worried about "ruthlessly commercial lodging house keepers" who swindled Government Girls by charging application fees, taking deposits for non-existent rooms, using illegal evictions to move in new, higher-paying tenants, and pulling bait and switch operations.[18] This last ploy was especially common. Owners listed rooms with the Housing Registry that easily passed inspection. But, when women arrived at the given address, landlords apologetically explained that the advertised room had recently rented. The weary house hunter—often with suitcase in hand and a job starting the next morning—was then directed to a different, substandard property and convinced she would find nothing better in the crowded city. District housing agencies and Traveler's Aid sent representatives to meet new arrivals at Union Station and the Greyhound bus terminal to warn them about getting caught in such "harrowing situations."[19]

A more pervasive problem for Government Girls lay in disgruntled rather than deceitful locals. "You ought to thank your stars that people, no matter how far out, are opening up their homes to you Government Girls. They're just doing it out of patriotism. They don't have to rent, you know. Most rooms are in neighborhoods where they weren't allowed to rent until the war boom came. You ought to be grateful for anything you get," vented one perturbed resident.[20] The barrage of complaints about renters focused specifically on women. Newspaper articles such as "Girl Tenants Not Desired" and "Just Because You Rent a Room, You're No Angel!" exposed the extent of public antagonism. Owners preferred men because they could charge more for the room (due to men's higher salaries) and young women upset the order of the house. They supposedly took long baths; made so much noise that the neighbors complained; raided the refrigerator for midnight snacks; stayed home evenings, which used extra electricity; and pasted pictures of Nelson Eddy and other movie stars on the bedroom walls. A particularly rowdy group of Government Girls shocked their landlady's sensibilities and upended her carefully outfitted home. "They laid wet towels on a beautiful chenille bedspread, sprinkled their clothes on a $50 gateleg table, threw chicken bones on the living room floor, threw meat and chewing gum on the kitchen floor. They mashed up furniture and broke dishes," she griped.[21]

Yet, the most popular reason given for not renting rooms to women involved underwear. A reporter explained, "The fact that girls wash their undies and hose in the bathroom and boys don't is creating one of the biggest bottlenecks in the Washington housing situation."[22] At a time when the majority of homes had only one bathroom, the time it took a group of women to wash their delicates as well as bathe proved too much for most homeowners. Investigators cited one overcrowded household in which twenty-four people shared a single sink and tub.[23] It was more appealing to support the war effort by buying bonds than putting up with female boarders

Locals did not hesitate to voice their opinions to Government Girls in person as well as in the papers. Navy Specialist Franke Burke shared a room with another WAVE in Chevy Chase, Maryland an upscale residential section on the outskirts of the city. The roommates developed a sense of humor about the looks and remarks they received from neighbors while waiting at the bus stop. "Once or twice some very genteel older ladies came up to us and said, 'You are ruining our neighborhood.

When will this all be over with? I wish you would just leave.' I thought that was hilarious," Franke laughingly remembered.[24] Wearing a military uniform did not separate or elevate them from the rest of the bothersome Government Girls.

Federal officials encouraged camaraderie over contention. In the government booklet *Boarding Homes for Women War Workers*, landlords were reminded to: "Let [female tenants] feel through your personal attitude your genuine interest in their well-being and happiness. Those young workers who are away from their homes, perhaps for the first time, will be grateful always for your thoughtfulness."[25] It's doubtful that many homeowners went out of their way to request the book, especially since letting the government know they rented rooms also meant paying taxes on that income. Yet, some knowingly or unknowingly followed its advice. "My husband and I are only 28 years old so we can really get together with these folks and have lots of fun," an enthusiastic young landlady insisted.[26] "It is my pleasure to speak up in defense of Washington's Government Girl *'room dwellers*,'" one motherly homeowner asserted. "My girls are no trouble at all. There is no conflict over the use of household accommodations. Each girl follows the routine best suited to her hours of work."[27] Another local appealed to her fellow residents' sense of civic duty in supporting Government Girls against the public tide of distrust and impatience. She encouraged detractors to look past the inconveniences and remember why the housing situation existed to begin with: "These girls are taking the place of men who are fighting. If we don't get places for them, there can't be any war."[28]

She made an important point. If potential Government Girls were worried about how and where they would live, they could not be convinced to leave their homes and accept positions in Washington. A Civil Service Commission officer warned the Tolan Committee, a Congressional task force examining defense issues,[29] "Recently, an effort was made to lure twelve stenographers to the city with the promise of a house near the Capitol, where they could live together. But it was soon realized that this was an impossibility—there are no empty houses for rent." In another Committee hearing, a War Department official testified that of "3,346 applications sent out to try to get employees to come to Washington to work in the War Department, 1,227 accepted. Of those 1,227, 70 per cent came to Washington and stayed an average of 2 days and then left [due to lack of housing]."[30]

These concerns echoed the ones voiced in Congress just over two decades earlier. Federal agencies never filled their need for Government Girls during World War I and lack of available housing was the main culprit. At that time, Congress debated where, how much, and for whom to build temporary government dorms and acted too late to make an impact on Washington's wartime labor needs. The first of the thirteen Union Plaza Dormitories for Government Girls built between Union Station and the Capitol was completed a month *after* the armistice ending the war. These "government hotels" were repurposed to house post-war government workers serving a growing federal bureaucracy. Some were later refurbished as office space. But within four years of their opening, citizen associations launched a campaign to raze the "ugly and shoddy" stucco and frame buildings to make way for a park. Demolition began in 1930. None of the Georgian Revival hotels remained by the outbreak of World War II when Government Girls again searched for affordable and available rooms.[31]

Pressure grew for the federal government to increase the budget and speed up the timetable for its Washington-area construction projects. But major struggles developed between federal and local agencies over financial responsibility; neighborhoods and developers over diminishing open space and whether to use temporary or permanent structures; and competing housing agencies which were "deeply immersed in confusion, conflicting authorities, and petty jealousies" to carry out effective policies.[32] Adding to the hold-up, private builders hesitated to invest in housing projects amidst fears that wartime restrictions on materials, locations, and costs for new construction would make the units obsolete and unprofitable after the war.

Congress made several decisions that helped break the construction stalemate. It officially declared Washington a war zone, which made the city eligible for emergency housing funds through the Lanham Act of 1940, consolidated authority under the Federal Public Housing Agency, and placed local precedence on public projects. But building still ran behind schedule. In 1942 only 14,000 out of the planned 32,000 house, apartment, and dormitory units were completed. Only two government dorms for women war workers opened that year. A moderate, apartment-style building off Dupont Circle and a larger complex near Meridian Hill housed less than 1,000 Government Girls between them and generated never-ending waiting lists.

These two government "hotels" were also limited to workers who had recently arrived in Washington. Government Girls already living in the city could not apply. Housing advocates criticized the dorms for charging more than low-income workers could afford. Rents started at $30 per month. Editorial cartoonist Jack Demoreland lampooned the situation in the *Washington Daily News* with a drawing of a uniformed chauffeur holding open the door to a stretch limo as a smartly dressed young woman orders, "To the dormitory, James."

A major turning point for Government Girls occurred in March 1943 when Arlington Farms, the largest government campus in the Washington area, opened its first residence hall. The complex eventually housed 8,000 women on property adjacent to Arlington National Cemetery on the Virginia side of the Potomac River. The Navy assigned Helen Griffen to the development because she worked nearby in the Marine Quartermaster General's office. The WAVE from Boston arrived at her dorm to find "a lovely big lobby such as you'd find at a hotel and off of that ran wings which contained individual rooms each with a comfortable bed and a chair, a vanity, a chest with drawers, and a closet."[33] A fresh coat of pale peach, yellow, green, or blue paint helped the living areas feel more like home and less like an institution. The simple, clean, functional rooms with matching curtains and upholstery alleviat-

ed guesswork, legwork, and anxiety for women relocating to an unfamiliar city.

Though only twenty-years-old, Ellen Stiles had already tried war
work as a welder in Minnesota and a federal secretary in Utah before
taking a clerical job with the Army Air Force at the Pentagon. After
hearing the housing horror stories about Washington, she was relieved
to snag a spot at Arlington Farms. She lived in Idaho Hall, one of ten
"neat but not flossy" two-story buildings all named after U.S. states.[34]
Ellen rented a single room for $24.50 a month, which was over twenty
percent less than she would have paid to share a room at a boarding
house. The federally subsidized rents were priced to accommodate Government Girls starting salaries. Double rooms cost an even more affordable $16.50 a month. Ellen slept alone but shared all other amenities. A
communal bathroom served the dozens of women on Ellen's floor, the
dining room served the entire building, and recreation areas were open
to the whole community. "We also shared a laundry room as we did
hand washing and dried our clothes on indoor clothes lines," she remembered. "We'd rent an iron to iron our clothes. We didn't have drip
dry clothes, so it was harder to take care of."[35] Ellen cleaned her own
wardrobe but had help maintaining her room. Her rent included weekly
maid service and twice weekly linen delivery.

The price and living conditions helped make Arlington Farms one of
the most desirable addresses in the area. The perks made it one of the
most enviable. Government Girls enjoyed an on-site post office, beauty
salon, library, bowling alley, soda fountain, swimming pool, movie theaters, and convenience stores. The compound functioned similar to a military post in that it offered women with little free time and disposable
income easy access to and affordable amenities. Federal agencies used
the promise of a room at Arlington Farms to attract workers to Washington. Yet, even with such resources, a resident from Arkansas
quipped, "We all live on the piggy bank just before payday."[36]

A *Reader's Digest* article flippantly referred to Arlington Farms as
"Girl Town" and depicted it as a raucous, exciting "combination of sum-

mer resort, girls' school and New York World's Fair." It gleefully reported that the "slick chicks and bobby soxers" consumed about 4,000 hot
dogs and 3,600 pies, cakes, and donuts every day while experiencing
"grown-up life and responsibility" for the first time.[37] Government Girls
like Helen and Ellen who came to Washington with work experience
and intent to serve their country did not view Arlington Farms as an
outlet for slumber parties and sock hops. The opportunity to relax, shop,
and eat without having to travel back over the Memorial Bridge into
downtown Washington was a relief after working up to sixty hours per
week behind a desk and typewriter. Yet, Arlington Farms was not a
panacea. Only about 18,000 women out of the hundreds of thousands
who came to Washington found rooms in government dorms during
the war.[38]

Several privately owned specialty hotels aimed to fill another segment of the housing void. Twenty-year-old Magdalene Maria Nuttall
moved with her best friend from Omaha into Scotts Hotel after they
"packed up these really big trunks with all our clothes and all our personal things and took the train to Washington, D.C." Maria's father was
friends with a relative of the Scott family and was able to pull a few
strings to secure the women a room in the highly coveted club.

Entrepreneur Maggie Scott opened her first boarding house in 1916
and built the business to include twenty brownstones along 21st and P
streets, NW. Scott's sons Ralph and Harry added to the family's holdings
during World War II by opening an additional six-story "residence club"
for 250 Government Girls. Months before its opening (at which Eleanor
Roosevelt cut the ceremonial ribbon) the hotel had twice as many applicants as available rooms. The comparably steep $34.50 a month rent was
still about $10 lower than other Scott residence clubs thanks to a build-
ing loan by the federally funded Reconstruction Finance Corporation,
which capped prices. Final selection of the first residents was based on
personal interviews to determine character and suitability. After long
days of work at her administrative job at the Pentagon, Maria looked
forward to coming home because, "we socialized with all these people

who were working, and they were from all over the country. It was very interesting living there and we were right in the center of Washington near Dupont Circle."[39]

Life magazine ran a photo spread on Scotts highlighting its "collegiate atmosphere of a university sorority." Residents called themselves "Scotties" and some women wore Scottie dog pins on their sweaters as a symbol of their membership. They relaxed on a private sun deck, roasted marshmallows in the rooftop fireplace, and self-published *The Wash*, whose motto, "We dish up the dirt and it all comes out in *The Wash*," fit the newsletter's attitude towards revealing the latest in-house gossip.

Fodder for *The Wash* came in part from the hotel's "beau parlors," partially curtained alcoves off the main lobby set up as small individual living rooms equipped with loveseats. The parlors were named after legendary lovers, with "Romeo and Juliet," "Dante and Beatrice,'" and "Anthony [sic] and Cleopatra" emblazoned over their entryways. It's doubtful that either the women or management realized the irony of celebrating romance with infamously doomed couples.[40]

In an attempt to cultivate the "Scotties" professional as well as personal lives, the hotel offered "office etiquette" courses in a penthouse classroom. Instructors imparted dubiously helpful suggestions such as imploring secretaries to remain "passive on the outside, wholly alert on the inside" and "cuddling with employer while taking dictation is not suggested." The courses were not designed to prepare women for a climb up the corporate ladder, but rather smooth the transition for novice war workers into Washington's clerical corps. This outlook was also reflected in its policy to only accept young women who worked at war agencies. For women with the financial means, Scotts Hotel offered a ready-made social clique and sense of belonging in a city full of strangers. If Washington served as a metaphorical college campus, Scotts was its elite sorority.

Dissin's Guest House targeted an even narrower segment of the market. One main building in a former Embassy Row mansion and two smaller row houses under the same name catered to Jewish war workers, both men and women. Esther Bubley, a photographer for the Office of War Information, took a series of shots at Dissin's to record war life in Washington. The pictures reveal cramped rooms filed with personal mementos and exhausted women enduring long waits for bathrooms, telephones, and moments of privacy. They also show a comfortable intimacy between roommates as well as between the men and women. It was not unusual for boarding houses to rent to both genders. Fraternization rules varied from place to place, but according to a *Rooming and Boarding House Manual* issued by D.C.'s Board of Commissioners, managers had to be "morally qualified" and rooms segregated by sex.

Anne Dissin had the reputation for being a strict housemother— eagle-eyed for men sneaking onto the upper floors reserved for women and refusing to allow women to leave the house wearing shorts or pants, which she considered unseemly and unfeminine. Yet, she also encouraged her tenants to socialize with each other over her kosher dinners and to attend Friday night services at Washington Hebrew Congregation. Roslyn Dresbold Silverman, who relocated to Washington from Portsmouth, Virginia to work for the Navy Department's Travel Section, remembered, "There was plenty of dating, but no co-habitation. I met my husband at Dissin's and several of my friends met their spouses there, too."[41] Roslyn went with her future husband and friends to Chinatown, concerts, theater, and the Jewish Community Center, which held daytime dances for night shift workers and nighttime programs for government and service personnel. A base government salary did not easily cover the $35 monthly rent at Dissin's Guest House, so it, like Scotts Hotel, filled little more than a niche of Washington's housing need.

That need was exacerbated once the thousands of servicewomen came to town. The military guaranteed women a place to live. It did not, however, make promises as to the location, comfort, or duration of those quarters. Army WACs, Navy WAVES, Coast Guard SPARS and female Marines moved around as often and in as many types of housing as their civilian counterparts. WACs started trickling into the city in

December 1942. The Army had not yet made permanent arrangements for WACs posted to Washington. Women stayed in temporary quarters or had to find their own space in the crowded city.

WAC officer Elna Hilliard Grahn did both. The Army placed her at the Burlington Hotel downtown, but, because management had overbooked, Elna was kicked out after only two nights. She followed several empty leads before finally finding a room at the government run Meridian Hill Hotel. The government called the Meridian an "Exclusive Hotel for Women," but locals sarcastically dubbed it "Purity Palace," for the almost 800 young, single women living there. The Army provided women a subsistence allowance of $45 a month for rent and $21 a month for food. But at $2.50 per night, the hotel room cost more than both allowances combined. Elna found that "it was common, and necessary, for us to send home for money."[42] Even in the Army, timing and money determined a woman's housing experience in Washington.

WACs eventually bunked at nearby Army bases in hastily built or renovated quarters. A *Washington Post* reporter noted, "The WACs in Washington, generally speaking, live more as do their masculine compatriots than any other women's branch of service."[43] That living started with a daily routine of a 5:30 a.m. wake-up call, 6 a.m. reveille, exercise, chores, 8 a.m. breakfast, and then reporting for duty.

"Life With 'Uncle [Sam]'" at Bolling Field, Fort Washington, Fort Myer and other installations included barracks with open floor plans, wooden bunk beds, footlockers for storage, and a single clothing rod. Open windows offered the only relief from hot weather and coal-fed potbellied stoves served as the heating system. Not only did WACs bear responsibility for stoking the temperamental stoves both day and night, but the women issued bunks closest to the grates roasted from the overwhelming heat, while those farthest away froze throughout the winter. Out of a sense of propriety, the Army made two concessions to its female recruits: curtains for the windows and separate shower stalls. Otherwise, WACs' barracks offered the women little privacy and even less sleep.[44]

Cecilia Campbell was stationed at Fort Myer in northern Virginia. She and her fellow bunkmates walked back and forth to work at the Pentagon for round-the-clock shifts lasting nine hours each six days a week. The constant commotion of women coming and going based on their disjointed schedules left the entire barrack in an unremitting state of sleep deprivation. After a few months of living in such conditions, Cecilia fell into bed each night and passed out from exhaustion. "It was just awful... It wasn't like sleeping," she recalled. "It's like you were drugged." The former high school teacher from Oklahoma wrote a post-card home to her parents lamenting, "The life of a WAC is not all glamorous. Far from it."[45]

At nearly 20,000 strong, WAVES made up the largest contingency of military women in Washington. There was no one place large enough to house them all. Women were placed in government dorms, temporary barracks on the Mall, specially-built WAVE quarters, or given subsistence pay to go "on the beach," the term used for finding their own housing. Margery Updegraff arrived in Washington from boot camp with no immediate room assignment. She invited a few other newly transferred WAVES to split the cost of living. Her house-hunting strategy was morbid but effective: "We paid attention to the death notices in the paper to see if we could find a place to live. In fact, that's the way I got an apartment. A lady died."[46]

Yeoman Elvera Schwartz Feltes spent her first six weeks in D.C. billeted at the Continental Hotel across from Union Station surprised to find Marine guards on each floor. Staying in a hotel was not what the former secretary from Illinois expected when she joined the Navy but also felt "sure this isn't what the Marines had planned to do either in the Marine Corps." Elvera and about 5,000 other lucky women soon moved to Quarters D, the first and largest installation in the country built exclusively for WAVES. The thirty-eight-building complex covered forty acres of land on Ward Circle in Northwest D.C.[47]

The women slept in bunk beds like the WACs, but that's where the similarities ended. Special features included a lounge decorated with furniture from the glamorous French ocean liner *Normandie*,[48] a photographic darkroom, bakery, thousand-seat auditorium, beauty shop, dry cleaners, and gift-wrapping room for the holidays. And bathtubs. Rumor had it that Eleanor Roosevelt toured the barracks before it opened and insisted to the Naval officers that ladies need bathtubs. WAVE Jean Ashby Sims from West Virginia discovered another luxury item in the bathroom at Quarters D. "In the head one of the stalls contained a bidet," she recalled. "Sometimes a disconcerted WAVE who had never before encountered a bidet would rush out of the stall. I had never seen one either, but since I had read French literature and studied French Civilization, I figured out what it was."[49]

WAVES in Quarters D had minor housekeeping responsibilities in return for these comparative luxuries. Elvera Feltes recalled, "You took care of your own bunk. If you wanted to change those sheets on that bunk every day you went down to the laundry room and picked up fresh sheets. Same thing with towels." Retrieving their own linens was the extent of the women's chores. Sailors, not WAVES, did KP [kitchen] duties in the mess hall and an outside service was hired to clean the barracks. The women also ate well. A journalist invited to try the food found it surprisingly good. "The lunch served in the mess is savory and satisfying. For example, we had a delicious vegetable soup, asparagus, cole slaw, potatoes, and meat balls, hot cocoa, bread, butter, and raisin pie," she reported.[50] The food was so popular that Government Girls working across the street at the Naval Communications Annex jammed the cafeteria at meal times until administrators restricted how often non-residents could eat there.

Elvera recognized the benefits of living in the Navy's flagship quarters: "We were one of the fortunate women's groups."[51] That luck did not always last. Assignments to Quarters D tended to be short-term, sometimes as short as one month. Each new group of WAVES arriving in D.C. pushed one of the previous groups out to another location, usually Arlington Farms, Anacostia Naval Station, the smaller and less lavish Quarters B downtown on Constitution Avenue, or "on the beach."

Betty Splaine was never sent to sea with the Coast Guard but she was sent just about everywhere else in Washington. Her unit originally resided in an apartment building on 16th Street near the Meridian Hill Hotel, but, after a fire destroyed the property, it was moved to the Plaza Hotel near Union Station on the other side of town. After a few months, the unit was shuffled to the administration building at American University across from WAVES Quarters D. Although now in yet another part of the city, Betty enjoyed the open, green space of the campus. But this assignment was also temporary. Betty, and almost half of all SPARS in D.C., eventually ended up in specially built barracks across from the Smithsonian Castle on Independence Avenue.[52]

Marion Tompkins served as a SPARS boatswain at one these residences. During basic training, she lobbied for the chance to run a barracks instead of a typewriter. While visiting Norfolk, Virginia on leave, Marion saw the "old men's barracks" used for WAVES, so she was relieved to get a look at the buildings she would manage in Washington. She discovered that "they had an interior decorator in there. Everything was blue and gold. They had lounges. Everything was gorgeous. Instead of being in a long row like barracks, we had cabins. Two girls to a cabin. They had bunk beds, a couple of easy chairs and closets and whatnots. Everything was lovely. So comfortable. You had your privacy."[53]

As an enlisted Marine, Crystal Theodore "had no privacy" at Henderson Hall Marine barracks. "That was one of things you just accept. I accepted it. I didn't care too much one way or the other," she said. What Crystal did care for were the stray cats that lived amongst the female and male Marines sharing the Northern Virginia Headquarters Battalion, which butted up against the southern edge of Arlington National Cemetery. "I adored those cats," she recalled. "They were a great sort of release valve for the hard work that we did and the required routines which could be kind of tedious at times to one of my temperament. So the cats helped." Once Crystal earned a commission, she was required to leave the barracks. In general, officers had to make their own living arrangements. She moved into a walk-up studio apartment in a row house that "seemed to go on forever when you were climbing stairs." Crystal turned to painting, another of her passions, for stress relief, but still missed her transitory pets.[54]

Margaret Mary Reese, another of the 1,000 female Marines stationed in Washington, had already lived in a private apartment and at Arlington Farms by the time she was assigned to Henderson Hall. Several months later, "the barracks got full so we were all moved out into subsistence again and this went on three different times. I was moved back and moved out." This was especially frustrating since the twenty-one-year-old worked as a secretary at the Navy Annex within walking distance of the base. After a year and a half of constant shuffling, Margaret learned of yet another impending reassignment. But she discovered that married women could keep their military jobs and live with their husbands. Already planning an April wedding, she moved it up by a month figuring it was easier to change her marriage plans than her address one more time.[55]

No matter where they were assigned to live or which branch they served, military Government Girls could all find respite at the Pepsi-Cola canteen downtown at 13th and G streets, NW. This proved a life-saver for women on subsistence allowances. The Navy assigned Joan Dunlap's unit to a government dorm that had no cafeteria. The WAVES provided funds for food, but officers warned Joan before she left boot camp that the first allowance might take a long time to come through. "We had to watch our money very closely," she recalled. Since servicewomen did not receive ration stamps and the cost of living in Washington was at an all-time high, after a few weeks, "it was getting pretty thin but we vowed and determined—a bunch of us—that we would not send home for money. We were living on a pint of milk for breakfast, no lunch, and we'd walk... into town to go to work and then while we were in there we'd go to the Pepsi-Cola canteen and they had hamburgers for a nickel and then we'd fill up on Pepsi the rest of the way and that's all we'd have all day." The canteen offered five cent sandwiches and unlimited drinks to all men and women in uniform.

Joan found the Pepsi-Cola canteen more reliable than the hospitality at the United Service Organization (USO). The USO centers provided military personnel with a "home away from home," a place to rest, play cards, read books and magazines, celebrate holidays or attend organized social events. One Saturday Joan and several other hungry WAVES went to a USO club near the White House. They ravenously devoured cookies and cupcakes stocked on the shelves because "none of us could remember when we had a good meal." The women felt energized enough to stay for a dance or two. They soon caught the enticing aroma of dinner wafting through the room. However, without explanation "the loud speaker came on and said, 'Would the women please leave.' The men got to eat and we had to leave." They snuck a few extra cupcakes as they were herded out the door in protest to the unfair, though not unusual, difference in how they were treated.[56]

In addition to cheap, reliable meals, the Pepsi-Cola canteen offered Friday night dances, reading rooms, stationary and desks for letter writing, and a studio to record greetings for loved ones back home. WAC Demaris Black Schebig made a record saying, "Here I am in the Pepsi Center!" for her parents in Webster, Indiana. Her mother, who wrote a poem called "Tears on My Pillow at Night" when Demaris joined the Army, and her father, who proudly referred to his daughter as a "Wacie," were so pleased after hearing their daughter's voice they recorded a song on the reverse side to send back to her.[57]

Not everyone was welcome at the canteen. Although Pepsi-Cola ran several integrated canteens during the war, Washington's segregationist policies kept African-Americans from visiting the one in the nation's capital. Segregation was even more evident in the city's residential neighborhoods. Racially restrictive covenants eliminated entire sections of the city as potential living quarters for both current black residents and incoming war workers. If finding suitable housing proved difficult for white women entering the city, it seemed Herculean for African Americans.

The Phyllis Wheatley YWCA in the predominately African-American Shaw neighborhood offered women one potential solution. Like most YWCAs it offered housing in addition to recreational and employment programs. The organization had also adopted the elimination of racism as one of its missions in the late 1800s. Dorothy Height, who would later spend forty-one years as head of the National Council of Negro Women and become a leading civil rights advocate, served as the facility's executive director from 1939 to 1944. Height managed the influx of young, anxious women who showed up day and night ready to work for the federal agencies.

Alice Allison Dunnigan was one of them. She arrived for her job as a typist at the Labor Department without a "single friend or acquaintance." So Alice nearly panicked upon reading the application requirement to provide three "reputable" local character references. She listed names of prominent speakers, including famed educator Mary McLeod Bethune, whom she briefly met during college and her years as a schoolteacher in Kentucky. The ploy worked and Alice lived at the YWCA for nearly a year until she found an available room.[58]

Alice had plenty of company in her search. Most boarding houses, the "gift to Government Girls," refused to accept black tenants. Dorothy Height reported the increasingly difficult situation to local and federal housing agencies but was rebuked. Authorities told Height that black women did not need government help because Washington's African-American community could be counted on to take care of its own.[59] This disregard for the welfare of black workers forced incoming Government Girls to squeeze even more tightly into every available space.

Mary Wright initially came from North Carolina to treat her hearing loss and then returned to work as a Government Girl. Her older cousin lived in Northeast Washington and let Mary live at her two-story red brick row house on N Street. The long, crowded commute to and from Mary's job as a junior clerk at the Pentagon was nothing compared to the crunch at home. In addition to her cousin, Mary shared quarters with her cousin's husband, their seven children, two other relatives, sev-

eral male boarders, and two female tenants.[60] Misguided housing authorities were right about one thing. When forced by circumstances,
D.C.'s black community did make room for the displaced newcomers as
much as possible.

In mid-1943 the federal government finally relieved over-burdened
locals and opened the first dorms for African-American women. Midway Hall and Langston Stadium Hall (two dorms) in Northeast and Lucy
Slowe Hall in Northwest housed up to 300 Government Girls each.
Women paid $28 per month for a single and $24 for a double (compared
with $24.50 for a single at Arlington Farms).[61] The buildings followed
similar floor plans and furnishings to white-only dorms but lacked the
impressive amenities of the larger complexes. Eleanor Roosevelt attended the opening of Langston Hall, but unlike the fanfare that accompanied the openings of federal residences for white women (receptions
with congressmen and local housing officials), dorms for black women
generally celebrated by simply opening their doors for business on an
appointed day and time.[62] African-American women occupied four out
of the twenty-two area residence halls constructed during the war. But
the relatively high price kept many women searching for cheaper alternatives within the overcrowded community.[63]

Finding housing was one major problem for all Government Girls.
Staying healthy once they found it was another. A 1943 congressional
subcommittee conducted hearings on Washington's overcrowded and
unhealthy condition. After three months of research, the committee declared inadequate housing for Government Girls a major contributor to
the threat of an epidemic of typhoid fever and other contagious diseases
and the overall poor sanitation of the city. The subcommittee concluded:
"We believe that an epidemic of major proportions in what has become
the 'capital of the world' would be such a disastrous event that the War
Production Board should be compelled to recognize the needs of this
community and give its approval to the use of essential material for this
purpose as a war measure." Congressman Charles Plumely from Ver-
mont went so far as to call conditions "absolutely shocking" and a "dan-

gerous menace." He criticized D.C. Commissioners for ignoring the situation. Sanitation problems included sewage back-ups in hastily constructed housing developments and filth from overused, rickety outhouses leaking out onto the sidewalks and oozing down the streets. "Are we trying to commit mass murder down here or suicide by sewage?" Plumley demanded.[64]

Outhouses in 1940s Washington seems incongruous. But close to 20,000 people, ninety-five percent of whom were African-American, still lived in alleys, often without electricity or indoor plumbing.[65] With so many boarding houses opening in residential neighborhoods, Government Girls sometimes witnessed these conditions. SPARS boatswain Marion Tompkins "was never so amazed [as] to find the slums right behind the White House... Right behind the White House in that area! Pennsylvania Avenue all gorgeous and in the background were these terrible shacks."[66] There were even a few stories of desperate war workers resorting to temporary stays in alley apartments. Representative Plumley insisted that since Congress held legal guardianship for the nation's capital, it would bear responsibility for any war-related epidemics stemming from the "absolutely shocking" situation.[67]

Leaders who steered the city through World War I were especially leery of conditions that could spread disease. In 1918 the Spanish Flu pandemic sickened over 33,000 people (close to fifteen percent of the total population) and killed almost 2,300 in Washington.[68] It swept through the crowded wartime city so quickly that Walter Reed Hospital stockpiled bodies for weeks in a temporary morgue because the city ran out of caskets. Desperate officials snatched two carloads of coffins headed for Pittsburgh from Potomac Yards railroad station in Virginia. Public schools, universities, theaters, bars, and stores closed or restricted hours; transit companies lost drivers and had to cut routes which forced federal agencies to stagger start times for employees; and all nonessential public meetings were banned. The disease raged throughout the fall and lingered in the area until the following spring.[69]

World War I Government Girls, similar to their replacements twenty years later, packed as many roommates as possible into as little space as possible, which exacerbated the spread of disease. Louis Brownlow, the District's Health Commissioner during the Spanish Flu crisis, recalled a tragic case involving war workers: "A girl had called to say that she and three other girls had a room together, that two of the girls were dead, another dying and she was the only one not stricken; would I please get some help there." By the time police arrived at their apartment, all four women were dead.[70] The flu not only spread quickly it killed quickly. Ellen Slayden, a Congressional wife from Texas, felt sympathy for Government Girls alone in the city without a support system or guidance. "The local death list has an added touch of pathos by so many of it being young girl war workers. Poor things! without [sic] home or friends, foolishly dressed, living on trash, inviting death from any illness," she wrote in her journal. "Eight, I hear, have been buried in the potters field because no one knew where they belonged."[71]

Authorities attempting to manage Washington's public health issues during World War II wanted to avoid such horrors still sharp in the city's collective memory. An outbreak of disease much less severe than the Spanish Flu could also cause an administrative shutdown of the government. Representatives from Congress, Social Hygiene Society, Public Utilities Commissions, Board of Public Welfare, and residential neighborhoods debated solutions for the "oceanful of ills" afflicting D.C. Congressman John Sparkman admitted that Washington, "the nerve center of the Allied nations," was a bad model for other wartime cities. Ideas on how to keep the capital healthy and functioning included building more government dorms, adding several thousand new hospital beds, and constructing an underground subway system. Most agreed that new growth outside the city's limits would be necessary.

The feared epidemic never occurred. While cases of bad planning, rushed construction, and contagious illnesses did create localized problems, city and federal officials addressed them before they initiated a systemic breakdown. These issues affected Government Girls, but they were generally less concerned about problems with the city's infrastructure as they were by challenges in their own personal living arrangements.

Government Girls exacerbated the city's housing shortage and taxed its transportation, public health system, community resources, and residents' good will. Where a woman lived depended upon the work she performed, rent she could afford, date she arrived in the city, and the color of her skin. The federal government took responsibility for accommodating military women, built dormitories for approximately twenty percent of civilian Government Girls, and ran a housing center to help the thousands of newcomers arriving in the city each week. However, the supply of rooms never kept pace with demand.

The apocryphal housing story tossed around Washington's wartime cocktail party circuit opens with one man discovering another man drowning in the Potomac. Before he agrees to help, the potential savior wants to know where the victim lives. As soon as he gets the address, he abandons the desperate man in the river and rushes to take his apartment. The landlady tells him it is already rented. "To whom?" he asks incredulously. "To the man who pushed him in," she replies.[72] Finding a place to call home, even temporarily, proved a daunting task in World War II Washington.

Notes

[1] Merlo Pusey, "Wartime Washington," *Washington Post*, February 24, 1942, 11.

[2] Mary Merrick Bliss Collection (AFC/2001/001/33087), VHP.

[3] Elizabeth McIntosh interview with author, March 25, 2003; Elizabeth McIntosh Collection (AFC/2001/001/30838), VHP.

[4] The Commissioners' Committee of Civilian Defense opened D.C.'s Housing Registry, the first in the nation, in March 1941. Representatives from the Board of Trade, Washington Real Estate Board, Alley Dwelling Authority, YWCA, and the Washington Housing Association served as the Registry's advisory committee. The staff consisted of volunteers who inspected rooming houses, a director paid by the Board of Trade, and a staff of Works Progress Administration office workers. The federal government took

over the registry in 1942 and appointed a new civil service director and staff. It was re-named the War Housing Center and became a model for programs nationwide. "State-ment of the Washington Housing Association to The Tolan Committee- January 13, 1942," 2-3, Washington Housing Association Records (WHA), Container 2, Folder 16, Historical Society of Washington (HSW).

[5] "Girl Tenants Not Desired," *Washington Post*, January 30, 1942, 1.

[6] Mary Tinder, "Memo to a 'D.C.'er," *Washington Post*, January 1, 1943, B1.

[7] John Maynard, "Tales of Our Time: Them Landlords," *Washington Times-Herald*, Octo-ber 18, 1942, E1.

[8] "Typical Questions Asked At Housing Registries About Supplying Rooms, Housing in Wartime Booth, War Fair, October 22 to 30, 1942," 3-5, WHA Records, Container 2, Folder 14, HSW.

[9] Carlisle Bargeron, "Washington Gets Soiled," *The American Mercury*, November 1943, 594.

[10] "Newcomers Discover Private Baths Went Out With Hitler," *Washington Post*, May 4, 1942, 16.

[11] Anna Florence Fogelman Collection (AFC/2001/001/33598), VHP.

[12] "Zoning Board Lifts Rooming House Bans," *Washington Post*, June 7, 1942, 21; Merlo Pusey, "Housing Divided Against Itself," *Washington Post*, February 24, 1942, 11; "84% Rooming Houses in D.C. Called Illegal," *Washington Post*, January 22, 1943, B10.

[13] Dixon Donnelly, "Boarding Houses 'God's Gift' to Government Girls," *Washington Daily News*, September 12, 1941, 27.

[14] Charlotte Carter Collection (AFC/2001/001/67868), VHP.

[15] "Just Because You Rent a Room, You're No Angel!" *Washington Post*, September 5, 1941, B2.

[16] Jean Ashby Sims Collection (AFC/2001/001/56965), VHP.

[17] David Brinkley, *Washington Goes to War* (New York: Alfred A. Knopf, 1988), 243.

[18] "Washington Housing Association Minutes," January 14, 1943, WHA Records, Con-tainer 2, Folder 14, HSW.

[19] "Washington Housing Association Minutes," November 17, 1943, 2, WHA Records, Container 2, Folder 16, HSW; Christine Sadler, "Plans Weighed to Steer Girls From Questionable D.C. Houses," *Washington Post*, December 3, 1941, 1.

[20] "Room Hunt," *Washington Daily News*, March 16, 1942, 34.

[21] John Maynard, "Tales of Our Time: Them Landlords," *Washington Times Herald*, Oc-tober 18, 1942, E3.

[22] "Girl Tenants Not Desired," *Washington Post*, January 30, 1942, 1.

[23] James B. Reston, "L'Enfant's Capital and Boomtown, Too," *New York Times Magazine*, June 1, 1941, SM6.

[24] Franke Burke Collection (AFC/2001/001/18447), VHP.

[25] U.S. Department of Labor, Women's Bureau, *Boarding Homes for Women War Workers* (Washington, D.C.: Government Printing Office, January 1943), 1.

[26] "Just Because You Rent a Room, You're No Angel!" 15.

[27] "Mary Haworth's Mail," *Washington Post*, January 27, 1942, 11.

[28] "Girl Tenants Not Desired," 5.

[29] The House of Representative's Select Committee Investigating National Defense Migration was informally known as the Tolan Committee for its chairman, California Representative John H. Tolan.

[30] "Statement of the Washington Housing Association to The Tolan Committee- January 13, 1942," 5-6, WHA, Container 2, Folder 13, HSW.

[31] "U.S. to Build Big Dormitory For Single Government Girls," *Washington Post*, March 19, 1941, 5; Frederick Law Olmsted, "Lessons from Housing Developments of the United States Housing Corporation," *Monthly Labor Review* 8 (May 1919): 27-38.

[32] Merlo J. Pusey, "Wartime Washington: War Housing Still Lags," *Washington Post*, September 1, 1942, 11.

[33] Helen Griffen Collection (AFC/2001/001/65829), VHP.

[34] Arlington Farms was designed and opened as a dorm for civilian women only. As greater numbers of servicewomen moved into the area, the Navy negotiated a takeover of several residence halls, usually reconfiguring them into barracks in order to accommodate more beds. This spurred vigorous debate among housing, war agencies, civil service and military officials who each had a stake in providing housing for Government Girls. The ratio of civilian to military women continually changed over the duration as the numbers of workers in each sector varied. "Dormitories Will Be Neat But Not Flossy," *Washington Post*, Aril 16, 1942, 10; Jerry Kluttz, "Navy Seeking More Arlington Farms Space," *Washington Post*, January 16, 1944, M12.

[35] Ellen Stiles interview with author, November 5, 2004.

[36] Eleanor Lake, "28 Acres of Girls; Arlington Farms," *Reader's Digest*, November 1944, 103.

[37] Ibid.

[38] Marjorie Barstow Greenbie, "Women Work With Uncle Sam," *Independent Woman*, March 1942, 74.

[39] Magdalene Maria Nuttall Collection (AFC/2001/001/11559), VHP.

[40] Eleanor Early, "Girls' Hotel Built for War Workers," *Washington Times-Herald*, March 25, 1942, 1; "Behind the Scenes in One of the Capital's Residence Clubs," *Washington Post*, November 30, 1941, L15; "Life Visit Scotts Hotel for Women," *Life*, August 10, 1942, 78-81; "Government Girls to Get Dream Home," *Washington Post*, December 4, 1941, 25; "New Girls' Dormitory Has Its 'Romeo and Juliet' Parlors," *Washington Evening Star*, May 11, 1942, Rooming & Boarding Houses 1940-1959 Folder, DCPL.

[41] Roselyn Dresbold Silverman, "World War II in Washington: Life at Dissin's," *The Record* 22 (1997), 42-44

[42] Elna Hilliard Grahn, *In the Company of Wacs* (Manhattan, Kansas: Sunflower University Press, 1993), 15.

[43] Anne Hagner, "Life With 'Uncle' Is 100% Army For 107 Wacs at Fort Myer," *Washington Post*, August 10, 1944, 4.

[44] Ibid., Grahn, *In the Company of Wacs,* 96; "WAACS Work Hard, Manage To Keep Hair in Order Too," *Washington Post*, March 20, 1943, 9.

[45] Cecilia Campbell interview with Wanda Driver and Fran Richardson, November 7, 2003, WIMSA.

[46] Margery Updegraff interview with Wanda Driver and Ardith Kramer, November 19, 2003, WIMSA.

[47] Elvera Feltes Collection (AFC/2001/001/66222), VHP.

[48] The ship's furniture was removed while in the process of being refitted as a troopship. The *Normandie* caught fire while docked in New York and never completed the transition.

[49] "5000 WAVES to Be Housed On American U. Property," *Washington Post*, February 24, 1943,1; Anne Hagner, "Rep. Smith Pleased With WAVE 'Homes,'" *Washington Post*, December 29, 1943, B1; Betty Wixcey, "They're Getting Ready to Go Home," *Washington Evening Star*, June 20, 1946, C3-5; Jean Ashby Sims Collection (AFC/2001/001/56965), VHP.

[50] Genevieve Reynolds, "A Tour of the WAVES' Quarters," *Washington Post*, August 21, 1943, B2.

[51] Feltes, interview.

[52] Elizabeth F. Splaine interview with Kate Scott, April 16, 2004, WIMSA.

[53] Marion Tompkins Collection (AFC/2001/001/18663), VHP.

[54] Crystal Theodore Collection (AFC/2001/001/16136), VHP.

[55] Margaret Mary Stone Reese Collection (AFC/2001/001/833), VHP.

[56] Joan Dunlap Collection (AFC/2001/001/63638), VHP.

[57] Demaris Schebig Collection (AFC/2001/001/66005), VHP.

[58] Alice Allison Dunnigan, *Black Woman's Experience: From the School House to the White House* (Philadelphia: Dorrance & Co., 1974), 187, 193.

[59] Dorothy Height, *Open Wide the Freedom Gates: A Memoir* (New York: PublicAffairs, 2003), 98-100.

[60] "Housing for Negro Defense Workers," *Monthly Labor Review* 53, no. 3 (September 1941): 647; Mary Herring Wright, *Far from Home: Memories of World War II and Afterward* (Washington, D.C.: Gallaudet University Press, 2005), 59, 99, 102.

[61] "Bissell Heads U.S. Residence Hall Project," *Washington Post*, October 20, 1942, 7.

[62] "Midway Hall, First Negro Government Dormitory, Opens," *Washington Post*, May 2, 1943, M10.

[63] Letter from Lydia M. Jettson to Mary McLeod Bethune, June 23, 1943, in the Records of the National Council of Negro Women, Series 5, Box 38, Folder 6, Mary Bethune Council House Archives; "2 Temporary Units Pose Problem on Sesqui Site," *Washington Post*, December 2, 1949, B1; Sandra Fitzpatrick and Maria R. Goodwin, *The Guide to Black Washington* (New York: Hippocrene Books, 1990), 124.

[64] "Housing Group Gets Report Showing Poor Sanitation, Epidemic Condition in D.C.," *Washington Post*, June 27, 1943, M14.

[65] Housing was a divisive political issue in Washington long before World War II. Tens of thousands of newcomers poured into the city in search of work and social opportunities during and immediately after the Civil War. The city's Jim Crow mindset and lack of available housing forced the rapidly expanding black population of Washington to live in hastily built and overcrowded alley dwellings. This temporary fix became a permanent solution for the city's poor. Congress established The Alley Dwelling Authority in 1934 to clear the alleys and relocate families living there. Roadblocks to resolving Washington's substandard housing issues mirrored the city's larger problems with race, zoning and development rights, and congressional oversight of the city. For a detailed study of Washington's alley dwellings, see James Borchet, *Alley Life in Washington: Family, Community, Religion, and Folklife in the City, 1850-1970* (Urbana, Illinois: University of Illinois Press, 1980) and Barbara Gale Howick Fant, "Slum Reclamation and Housing Reform in the Nation's Capital, 1890-1940," Ph.D. Dissertation (Washington, D.C.: The George Washington University, 1982).

[66] Tompkins, interview.

[67] "Insanitary Places Hold Danger of Epidemic, Plumely Warns," *Washington Post*, March 23, 1943, 1, 6.

[68] D.C. Health Department, *Annual Report of the Commissioners of Columbia Year Ended June 30, 1919. Vol. III: Report of the Health Officer* (Washington, D.C.: Board of Commissioners, 1919), 18.

[69] "Coffins Short in District; Aid Asked from Outside," Washington Post, October 10, 1918, 10; Louis Brownlow, *A Passion for Anonymity: The Autobiography of Louis Brownlow, Second Half* (Chicago: The University of Chicago Press, 1958), 69-73.

[70] Brownlow, *A Passion for Anonymity,* 72.

[71] Ellen Maury Slayden, *Washington Wife: Journal of Ellen Maury Slayden 1897-1919* (New York: Harper & Row, 1963), 343.

[72] Ray Mackland, "Washington Hospitality?????" *Life*, September 27, 1943, 12.

5

Sex in the City

Jesse Strieff's nude, battered body lay crumpled in the corner of a garage on Q Street. One leg, still sporting a soggy yellow sock and saddle shoe, draped incongruously over the rear bumper of a parked sedan. The smart, vivacious twenty-three-year-old War Department clerk from Iowa had run to nearby Duncan's delicatessen on a rainy Sunday afternoon in 1941 for a stick of butter. She needed it to finish making a lemon pie for her fiancé of three months. Stanley arrived for their dinner date as planned but learned from Jesse's roommate that she never returned from her errand. After pacing for an anxious hour, Stanley called the police. It wasn't like Jesse to keep him waiting. And she never got lost, even in a relatively new city. She was an accomplished pilot with a keen sense of direction. His worry deepened into despair the following morning. A maid stumbled over Jesse's remains as she hauled bags of trash into the back alley of a Dupont Circle row house. The coroner who examined the injuries concluded that she put up a "terrific struggle." Deep fingernail marks under Jesse's chin showed the extreme force her attacker needed to maintain the grip necessary to choke her. She was the second young woman in the area brutally raped and strangled within three months. A serial killer was on the loose in Washington.

This realization sent the city into a frenzy. The Metropolitan Police Department formed a "super-homicide" squad, the "most extraordinary group ever assigned to a murder in the National Capital," to catch the killer. Newspapers ran articles on "How to Defend Yourself against a Rapist" suggesting that women carry sturdy hatpins as possible weapons and learn jujitsu to fight off attackers. The First Lady warned women to "be very careful in choosing the men you go out with." Washington was in the throes of an aggressive defense build up in response to growing international tensions but the most immediate threat to the city that summer came from one of its own.[3]

Jesse's case helped set the tone for wartime attitudes about Government Girls. It initiated what would become an ongoing debate among federal, civic, and social leaders on how to protect the hundreds of thousands of women living and working in D.C. Who, if anybody, should assume responsibility for their safety? What role should the local and federal government take towards Government Girls—employer, guardian, landlord, disciplinarian, bodyguard, or all of the above? And, most importantly, how could they convince Government Girls to behave in ways that would keep them safe? The young women's desire for independence often butted up against official ideas for sensible and proper behavior pitting the two factions against each other.

Two months after Jesse's death, detectives arrested D.C. resident Jarvis Roosevelt Catoe for the murder of a waitress in New York City. The thirty-six-year-old confessed to over a dozen violent crimes dating back to 1935, including eight rape-murders in Washington. Jesse was his most recent victim in the capital. As she left the deli with her twelve cents worth of butter, Jesse got caught in a sudden, torrential downpour. Catoe happened to be parked nearby. Because Catoe wore the cap he used as a part-time taxi driver, Jesse mistook the car for a cab and flagged him down for a ride. She sought a safe refuge from a walk in the violent thunderstorm back to her apartment a few blocks away. Instead, Catoe drove her to a secluded alley where he raped, beat, and strangled her. Catoe then dragged Jesse's lifeless, bloody body about sixty yards to the garage where it lay until discovered by the maid.

Catoe's crime spree continued to make national headlines until his execution in January 1943.[4] Government Girls were understandably on edge. Most were in an unfamiliar city, living and working with strangers, and trying to keep pace with the changing political and social landscape churning around them. Such a newsworthy threat of sexual violence brought the dangers of being a single woman in a big city to public attention and personal concern. The majority of women were away from the protection and restraint of their families or communities for the first time. How were they going to navigate such alarmingly real threats, or even recognize them? The tragic end to Jesse's seemingly ordinary day cloaked even the most mundane activities in ominous overtones. Any woman in Washington was the next potential victim.

Doubts about effective police protection added to Government Girls' fears and feelings of vulnerability to possible attacks. Jesse's case was not solved by D.C.'s much-touted "super homicide squad." New York City detectives broke the case by tracking down the watch Catoe stole from a victim in that city. The situation prompted *Life* magazine to quip, "the District police force, long noted for its blunders and failures, suffered the supreme mortification" of being out-sleuthed. This bad publicity came on the heel of a recent congressional admonishment and reorganization of the Metropolitan Police due to the "disgraceful crime conditions in the Nation's Capital." The process gutted the upper ranks of detectives and administrators, replacing over twenty lieutenants and sergeants, installing new commanders in eight out of the thirteen precincts, and retiring the superintendent of police and chief of detectives, among others.[5]

The staffing shakeup did not necessarily fix the city's law enforcement problems. In 1947, the FBI investigated the Metropolitan Police Department for "whitewashing" several years of reported crime statistics, including rape. This makes it difficult to accurately calculate the number of rapes that occurred in Washington throughout the war. In 1941, D.C.'s vice squad reported 54 rape charges among 205 cases of sexual offenses. That number dropped to thirty-five rapes in 1942 and continued to significantly decline each year until only sixteen attacks were reported in 1945. On paper, this made the city seem relatively safe for women.[6]

Yet, the year after the FBI whitewashing investigation, police records list 128 reported rapes. Since there is no evidence that Washington's postwar criminal activity escalated enough to explain an eightfold increase in the number of rapes within two years, the low wartime numbers are questionable.[7]

Regardless of the exact statistics, the perception of sexual danger existed for Government Girls in their everyday activities and the sensational media coverage. One newspaper warned: "The war boom and the influx of a vast and heterogeneous population from all parts of the country have created in the District of Columbia a set of conditions similar in many respects to the nineteenth century frontier communities or the early twentieth century oil communities. Yet sexual crimes of the sort which have become almost commonplace in Washington were virtually unknown even in the most violent frontier communities."[8] Just like the ever-changing populations in frontier towns, the vast number of servicemen, war workers, government appointees, and international visitors passing through the city—over 365,000 servicemen frequented

Washington's United Service Organization (USO) clubs each month—made it difficult to know who to trust and who posed a threat.

Joan Dunlap knew how to handle the sailors she met working for the Navy. She was less sure of how to deal with those she encountered on the streets. One night, Joan and her friend Macy, another WAVE, left a crowded downtown movie theater and started walking home towards their hotel near Union Station. Joan recalled that "these two Marines came up and took our arms and said, 'You don't want to go back there. Let's go back to town.' We said, 'No, we have to get back to the barracks.' We tried to explain to them and they didn't understand, so they kept pulling us. We says [sic], 'No, we have to go!' There was a sailor we hadn't noticed across the street watching. Finally, all of a sudden he started across and said, 'Hi girls, we thought we'd missed you.' He grabbed [Macy's] hand and said, 'Come on, let's go.' So the Marines let go and they went their merry way and we could go back to the barracks. We thanked the sailor very much."[9]

The inevitable contact between tens of thousands of Government Girls and tens of thousands of servicemen in both professional and public situations did not necessarily make it easier to know which encounters could lead to violence. Frances Lynd Scott decided not to risk making the wrong judgment. Her friend and colleague was attacked while walking to the bus stop at the end of her night shift. After a long stay in the hospital, the young woman left Washington for good. Frances felt anxious every time she had to work late at the Naval Communications Annex. She assiduously avoided any man she encountered when she walked home alone at night.[10] Dorothy Wills took a different approach. Her fiancé suggested that she carry a rolled up magazine to use as a weapon during her midnight commute home. Dorothy would grip the periodical in her hand as she nervously took two buses and walked several blocks to get from her job breaking codes for the Navy to the house she shared on the outskirts of the city. "You get brave and you do it," she recalled.[11]

To offer reassurance and better security than the latest *Good House-keeping* to current and future Government Girls, the city hired auxiliary police to maintain around-the-clock patrols. Over 4,000 local men signed up to spend ten hours per week providing, as Police Chief Edward Kelly explained, "every possible protection to any women traveling on the street."[12] These patrols made a difference for Government Girls traveling along protected routes. Veda Ponikvar did not feel the same dread as Frances because her daily commute was lined with guards. Veda worked downtown at Naval Intelligence on Constitution Avenue but lived across town in Adams Morgan. Her shift started at 1 a.m. and the streetcars stopped running at midnight. Although Veda usually walked the three miles to the office, she "never worried about anything. I'd see policemen along the way. I felt very secure. I never thought of being afraid."[13]

The U.S. Attorney for D.C., Edward Curran—who had responsibility for all criminal matters in the city, Washington having no state court system or "District Attorney"—reinforced the increased police protection with additional legal measures. He instituted a "speedy justice" policy, which placed a priority on rape cases. Trials were typically held within three weeks of an arrest. "Washington must be made safe for women," Curran insisted, mirroring the sentiment of the police chief and demonstrating the united front of the criminal justice system.[14]

Under this new initiative, detectives managed to capture and process one noteworthy attacker within a week. A twenty-year-old War Production Board stenographer woke up as an intruder crawled into her bed and attempted to rape her. She fought him off by shoving an electric fan into his face. When he fled through a window, frantic and bleeding from wounds made by the fan's sharp metal blades (and the chair she subsequently threw at him), he forgot his jacket. Detectives seized on the pay stub left in his jacket pocket to fast track the search and arrest him two days later.[15]

The aggressive and public response of authorities shows how seriously they took the protection of Government Girls. No doubt part of the reason was an attempt to improve D.C.'s reputation for lackadaisical law enforcement. It was not only essential for the city to appear safe in order to attract American women for the war effort but also to showcase a well-ordered capital city to the thousands of international workers and visitors that came through Washington. European and Canadian political missions in the city often included civilian and/or military female staff members. British WRENS (Women's Royal Naval Service) had the largest presence in the city. In addition to working at the British Admiralty office, WRENS set up their own Washington bureau. So, the public safety issue for local authorities went beyond making the streets safe for locals, Government Girls, Red Cross trainees, and the U.S. Navy and Army nurses who "pop into town only momentarily." It included protecting an international contingency of women in a city contemporaries identified as "where the destiny of the world is being shaped."[16] Washingtonians were fully aware of the capital's administrative and symbolic importance to the war.

Congresswoman Mary Norton had a particular interest in Government Girls. She worked as a secretary and stenographer before starting a groundbreaking political career, which included chairing the House Committee on the District of Columbia. That committee, along with a corresponding Senate committee, maintained legislative control over Washington. Norton felt driven to help young women avoid potential danger in the city and knew what resources were available to do so.

Norton proposed expanding the number of specially trained officers in the Police Department's Women's Bureau to guide newcomers "away from the paths of danger and around the pitfalls of sin." She believed women could handle the problems connected with Government Girls better than men. "It is true that many girls who come to the District have left home for the first time," the Congresswoman acknowledged. "They are experiencing their first freedom from restraint. Unless properly balanced it is not difficult to see where this will lead but good advice from the proper kind of policewoman would be invaluable to them."[17]

The Women's Bureau opened in 1918 as an emergency measure to help handle these same types of issues brought about by the influx of Government Girls during the First World War. Ellen Slayden, wife of Texas Congressman James Slayden, included her candid opinions of those earlier Government Girls in the journals she kept to recount her twenty years in Washington society. She described the Government Girls running around the city spending their newly earned money like drunken sailors in an "orgy of extravagance" and "practicing their welcome on everything in trousers." This led many of them into "grave trouble." Ellen confided, "Village girls turned loose without guidance or responsibility are led into dangerous places and company every day."[18]

The perception of Government Girls as irresponsible and out of control carried through to the 1940s. William Bissell, who worked as a federal housing manager during both world wars, insisted the new crop of war workers were even worse than their predecessors. He insisted that the World War II Government Girls were "younger, more desirous of recreation; they drank more, smoked more, discussed their problems more freely." The drinking age in Washington was eighteen, so most Government Girls could legally frequent bars and buy liquor. "There are more alcoholic beverages consumed per capita right here in the Nation's Capital than in any other population center in the United States—and it isn't all accomplished by men," Bissell complained.[19]

The guiding principle behind the creation of the Women's Bureau as well as Congresswoman Norton's idea to expand its services during World War II was that such freewheeling behavior contributed to the danger—physical and moral—Government Girls faced in the city. While Captain Rhoda Milliken of the Women's Bureau publicly denied the rumors bandied about by Bissell and others that Government Girls as a group were overindulging in nightclubs, she insisted that the young workers did need guidance to navigate wartime Washington. "It's amazing how many nice girls seem to automatically find the wrong crowds," she revealed.[20]

Finding ways to protect the "nice girls" from sexual predators seemed straightforward for authorities compared to protecting them from their own youthful curiosity and exuberance. Government Girls sought out fun in Washington's rollicking social scene. And they found it.

Evelyn Stotler, a clerk with the Army Map Service, recognized that she and other Government Girls needed opportunities to let loose. "Everyone was working hard on various war activities," she said. "But also people were craving emotional release."[21] Enjoying the city's nightlife was a popular way to do that. Katharyn Rice Sockolov, who was twenty years old when she arrived in wartime Washington, admitted, "We did drink quite a bit in those days. That was what people did for entertainment, I guess. So when anybody came to town, that's what we did- went out for drinks."[22] This need to release the pressures and tensions brought on by the war and to forge personal connections in a city of transients drove Government Girls out on the town.

Compared to its pre-war reputation as a socially and culturally stilted backwater, World War II Washington was a city that truly never slept, with shifts of government employees working around the clock. One woman marveled at the transformation, "Now, to make a case in understatement, Washington isn't a slow town- not in any language."[23] The staid capital had become a party town. Society columnist Hope Ridings Miller enthused, "No doubt about it... Wartime Washington is the most thrilling city that ever was."[24]

An informal survey identified the Lotus, Mayfair, Neptune Room, and Casino Royal as some of the favorite hangouts for as many as 8,000 Government Girls and servicemen on any given night.[25] Associated Press reporter Beth Campbell Short found space at the clubs so tight that "you really needed pliers and a screwdriver" to get through the crowd.[26] Marine Jeanne Macgregor frequented the Matt Windsor Room, a popular, smoke-filled club. "It was not a 'pick-up joint,'" she contended. "It was just fun, so crowded that there was barely elbow room, loaded with service people. There was singing and you could talk to everybody. It was a great place to overcome the 'blues.'"[27]

Clubs and bars gave women a space to relax and encounter people outside of their work, boarding house, or barracks. Jean Simms joined a group of other Government Girls who frequented the Willard Hotel bar to try fancy—usually pink—cocktails and meet locals.[28] "Even with a war on," Jane Fowler, a Department of Labor clerk, recalled, "we had so much damn fun!"[29] Navy Cryptologist Ann Maderia agreed, "Washington was a lot of fun for a young single gal during the war. It sounds callus to say that but… there were always old friends or new friends coming through."[30]

Since much of the fun took place out in public, it reinforced officials' perception that Government Girls were out of control. But the drinking and smoking seemed like mild social missteps compared to the catastrophic concern over Government Girls having sex.

A 1944 *Washington Post* article titled "Girls on the Loose" detailed the "frightening degree of promiscuity" that existed among the city's war workers. The article suggested that, because of this increased sexual activity, the police department had a hard time determining which cases constituted true sexual offenses against women.[31] Dr. Winfred Overholser, superintendent of St. Elizabeths Hospital, D.C.'s federal psychiatric facility, also complained about what he perceived as increasing cases of female immorality. Overholser went so far as to claim, "Cynics say there is no reason to commit rape here in Washington."[32]

Overholser's assertion was as exaggerated as it was appalling. The allegations were based solely on anecdotal evidence. Venereal disease, prostitutes, and Victory Girls or Khaki-Wackies (amateurs, usually teens, who traded sex for dinner, Coca-Colas, or a feeling of patriotic fulfillment) vied for top concern of social hygiene specialists in American cities besieged by war workers and servicemen. Incidents of all three rose in direct proportion to an area's population. Officials worried this same type of "moral decay" would infect Government Girls.

At the start of the war, Washington did have the highest syphilis rate of any large city in the country. But this was due to lack of accessible, affordable health care for the city's low-income population (and penicillin did not become available as a treatment until 1943), not because of the growing number of Government Girls and their sex lives. The city's vice squad aggressively targeted prostitution and the public health office developed tactics to bring down the cases of venereal disease. These solutions did not necessarily alleviate authorities' fears.

Experts predicted that the wartime upheaval of social norms would unleash an unprecedented "era of sexual looseness." Famed psychoanalyst Sigmund Freud noted a connection between the excitement and danger of war with an increased recklessness toward sex during World War I. He termed it "war aphrodisia." Later studies argued that the live-for-the-moment mentality extended beyond the men and communities closest to the battlefields to entire populations mobilized for and disrupted by war.[33]

Government Girls' perceived susceptibility to war aphrodisia was due in part to the temptations of their environment and in part to the naiveté of their background. As John D'Emilio and Estelle Freedman explained in their study of American sexuality, "By accelerating the shift to city living, and by providing youth with more economic autonomy and freedom from adult supervision, World War II brought unprecedented opportunities for premarital experience. The war released millions of youth from the social environments that inhibited erotic expression."[34] A few extra policewomen would not be enough to hold back the tide of experimentation sweeping Government Girls up in this cultural phenomenon.

However, World War II did not initiate the trend towards more progressive sexual mores. It was part of a decades-long change in dating and sexual behavior ushered in by the Jazz Age and that, as Alfred Kinsey's reports famously indicated, would continue after the war ended. By the 1930s, young couples were forsaking formal courtship for "thrill-seeking behavior" like dancing, necking, and car rides.[35] U.S. manufacturers first created a mass market for contraceptives during this same period thanks in part to inroads made by the birth control movement and legislative and legal advances (or rather failure to pass more restrictive legislation). Condoms became a $300 million annual business. By 1940 the size of the female contraceptive market was three times greater than just five years earlier.[36]

A portion of these sales went to young adults. A 1938 nationwide survey of college juniors and seniors revealed that sixty-four percent of men and women already had or were expecting to have premarital sex. Moreover, in a reversal from their fathers' expectations, a large majority of men did not believe that it was essential to marry a virgin.[37] These students were the same age as many future Government Girls—and some of the women would even join their ranks.

Although officials in Washington were suspicious of Government Girls' morals, the women did not single-handedly break long-held social taboos. They did, however, challenge traditional ideas of acceptable behavior on a more public stage than most. As a residence manager, Marion Tompkins often helped tipsy Coast Guard SPARS coming back to the barracks after a night out. But her biggest problem was a lovesick ensign. "She went AWOL chasing after some sailor. They brought her back. Locked her up. This is terrible. They locked her up in a room and we carried the key to that room with us. Now that was bad in a temporary building like that but that's what we did. We'd have to escort her to meals and whatnot. She escaped from that, too," Marion reflected. "The next time they didn't bring her back from the barracks. They discharged her probably. I don't know what ever happened to that poor girl."[38] Whether it involved alcohol or sex, wading into unfamiliar territory could lead inexperienced women into the type of trouble officials wanted them to avoid.

Jean Ashby Sims was forced to find a new home because of her roommate's romantic entanglements. She rented an apartment with Fay, a fellow WAVE who shared Jean's watch at Naval Communications. Fay spent her weeknights going out for dinner and drinks with her boyfriend, a lieutenant in the Merchant Marine. But Fay soon revealed to Jean that she spent her leave time with the man she really loved, a married father of five who was twice her age. One weekend Fay returned to find a telegram from the man's wife asking, "Was Saturday night at the Kenmore [Hotel] all right?" Jean frantically worried the wife might come looking for Fay and confront her by mistake, possibly with a gun. "That reaction was fairly common in West Virginia," Jean recounted about her home state. "She might miss and shoot me!" Jean left Fay to her fate and moved out immediately.[39]

Elizabeth Delean also suffered because of someone else's complicated love life. She kept her romantic relationships to a strict "G" rating— "Hand holding and kissing at Haines Point for half an hour and that was it." So, it came as a shock when she was branded a mistress. Elizabeth parlayed her Government Girl experience with the federal court system and courses at George Washington University into a job at the Turkish Embassy. But the international opportunity came with an awkward complication. Every time a particular captain's wife came into the office, she made angry, rude remarks about Elizabeth in Turkish to the other employees. She mistakenly thought Elizabeth was the secretary having an affair with her husband. As Elizabeth sorted out the kerfuffle, she discovered that several secretaries were "carrying on" with their male bosses. The men viewed their assistants as a playing field of potential conquests. Many women, it seemed, were willing to join in the game.[40] These were the types of situations authorities like the Women's Bureau and Congresswoman Norton thought they could prevent through guidance and protection. But another high profile murder of a Government Girl pushed local officials to campaign for even greater safety measures.

Dorothy Berrum left her hometown of Chippewa Falls, Wisconsin almost immediately after graduating third in her class from McDonnell Catholic High in 1944. That fall her diminutive, 4'5" body was found beneath a weeping willow tree in the East Potomac Park golf course not far from the Jefferson Memorial. Dorothy was raped and then strangled with her dainty blue, white, and lavender snood, left knotted around her throat.[41] Her killer, a Marine with a long criminal history, lived on a nearby military base and was arrested less than two days later.

When Dorothy first arrived in Washington, the teenager lived in an overcrowded rooming house with two classmates from home. She then moved into a single room at Arlington Farms, the area's largest federal dorm, in order to be closer to her job at the Pentagon. The other Government Girls found a new boarding house instead of following their friend to the government dorm. Once Dorothy was on her own, the sheltered young woman who had never even been on a date threw herself fully into the wartime social scene.

Detectives discovered that Dorothy often went to dances and bars, stayed out late, and willingly went off with the stranger who killed her. She met Earl McFarland and another Marine while waiting on a downtown street corner for friends who never showed up. Dorothy accepted the arm McFarland flirtatiously offered and they walked off to be alone. She was dead within the hour. Her body was found the following morning. One reporter lamented, "there had been no one to report that the unsophisticated little girl just out of high school in a town of 9,500 population was missing; no one; indeed, to know that she had not returned home last night."[42]

Ray H. Everett, Executive Secretary of the Social Hygiene Society, insisted that Dorothy's behavior showed how young women were "too immature to be running loose in Washington." He recommended sending home all teenage Government Girls, as they were obviously not old enough to recognize social hazards.[43] James Nolan, director of the Washington Criminal Justice Association, agreed with Everett's logic but wanted to take it even further. He proposed firing any Government Girl under age twenty-one.

Everett and Nolan's suggestions stirred much public debate. First Lady Eleanor Roosevelt, generally a staunch advocate of women's wartime work, approved of the proposed age restrictions. She chastised parents for allowing daughters to arrive in the nation's capital "unprepared" to meet the temptations and dangers of the city. A Government Girl participating in a forum on the subject sponsored by the *Washington Evening Star* similarly urged parents to keep their daughters home, "unless they have taught her to take care of herself in all ways- and especially when it comes to men." This self-proclaimed older, wiser Government Girl believed naiveté and not age was the problem. She maintained, "It isn't uncommon to meet a girl who is ignorant in sex matters—who actually wouldn't know if, when or how she got into trouble."[44]

The First Lady additionally revealed that, "efforts to warn the families of prospective war workers or the girls themselves about conditions in Washington seem to have been discouraged by government agencies on the ground that it would interfere with the recruiting of women for Washington war jobs."[45] Local media joined the discourse by condemning both the women who behaved "badly" as well as the process that brought them to D.C. "It has been argued," one reporter declared, "it is mostly girls of naturally unstable personality who become sexually amoral or who get into serious trouble in Washington. However, since personality defects of this sort are said to be detectable by psychiatric examination, it is hard to see why girls, and especially minors, in this category were ever accepted in the first place by the civil service."[46]

The Civil Service Commission defended its hiring practices. The federal government accepted applications from women as young as sixteen. As demand for workers increased and the entrance requirements for employment diminished, teenage Government Girls became more common. A spokesman for the agency insisted that the women's participation was essential to national security. "We have to face the fact that this country is at war and therefore we have to call on young people for jobs we would not ask them to do in peacetime," he contended.

In addition to explaining the logistical and economic impracticality of sending thousands of Government Girls home, the Civil Service representative pointed out the gender bias in attempting to do so. He observed that no one dared demand "teenage boys overseas at fighting fronts be sent back home."[47] Despite the social and safety concerns, wartime needs of the administration—and therefore the country—trumped all other arguments. The government continued to hire teenage Government Girls and Dorothy Berrum was memorialized as "another victim of the war time crimes against women in this glittering capital."[48]

Perception more than reality may have driven the public outcry following Dorothy's murder. Although the teen's experimental behavior likely contributed to her tragic fate, the assumption that such behavior represented all young Government Girls held no merit. However, lack of decorum by individual women, as well as men, fueled such negative impressions held by local residents and authorities.

After several tours at sea without female companionship, Navy ensign Stephen Kanyusik thought his three-month post to the nation's capital was "loooovely... ten girls to every guy." He and other adventurous young men from Anacostia Naval Air Station went out five or six nights a week to take advantage of those supposed odds. "If you had a date and you were in one of the bars you could not go to the restroom without getting a fistful of phone numbers," Stephen recalled. "You had to be dead to not get a date."

Yet, Stephen confessed to being too inexperienced during the war to feel comfortable even wrapping his arms around a woman on the dance floor. He did not know what would have happened if he actually had the nerve to call one of those phone numbers. Others, he suggested, were not so hesitant, "In those days there was hanky panky going on. But if you went with a girl and she didn't want any hanky panky that was that and you went on to have a good time."

He recalled that many young sailors tried to impress the other guys with ribald stories of their conquests. One ensign in particular bragged about his frequent and impressive sexual feats until they discovered the guy actually spent his nights at the movies. Alone. Stephen laughingly figured, "Out of a hundred percent, maybe five percent were scorers. But there was a lot of wishers." Stephen wished for and then met the woman he would marry, Doris Surprenant, a clerk in the Navy Aeronautics Department. "Mine was a farm girl and a Government Girl and she wasn't easy. I had to marry her! And then things were okay," he fondly remembered.[49] For all the outward display of bravado, traditional sexual mores were often difficult to shed.

Determining how many Government Girls participated in various levels flirtation versus "hanky panky" can be tricky. The number of babies born in Washington soared over the course of the war. So much so that the Bureau of Vital Statistics outgrew the shelf space in its office and had to store new birth records in a cellar.[50] Yearly birth rates increased by over fifty percent between 1939 and 1945.

But D.C.'s illegitimacy rate fluctuated more erratically. From a pre-war high of 8.5 percent in 1939, it dropped to a low of 6.9 percent in 1943 and spiked back up to 8.5 percent two years later.[51] The number of babies born out of wedlock was at its lowest when the wartime population boom was at its peak. And only three percent of those infants belonged to Government Girls. According to D.C.'s Council of Social Agencies' Committee on Unmarried Parenthood, professional women (teachers, nurses, etc.) over age twenty-five and girls under age sixteen made up the two largest categories of unwed mothers.[52] Even if the rumors about Government Girls' sex lives were true, their frequent encounters did not result in a significant increase in pregnancies.

In fact, pregnancy rates for servicewomen ran about a fifth of those for American women overall and their dismissal for misconduct was significantly lower than that of servicemen. The numbers do not support the authorities' anxiety that Government Girls' sexual behavior was disproportionately out of control. Yet, these statistics did not change the general perception that Government Girls were immoral.

Women in uniform developed a particularly insidious reputation for being promiscuous. "I felt bad when I enlisted cause I found out a lot of people didn't think much of the WAVES," Ethel Standley lamented. She came from a small town in Michigan and was unaware of the bias against servicewomen. She also found it untrue during her time in Washington. "There was [sic] a few that were sort of rough and running around, but the majority of them were real nice people," Ethel recalled.

"They didn't seem to be going after the men or the men going after them. I didn't notice that. But that's the reputation they had I guess."[53]

Servicewomen challenged the traditional notion of the military as masculine domain. Stepping into this "unnatural" arena made the women automatically suspect to many people. In *Creating GI Jane*, Leisa Meyer concludes, "Public fears of the consequences of establishing a women's army were rooted in a cultural inability to reconcile the categories of 'woman' and 'solider.'"[54] Even though the women serving in Washington held office jobs, which did not threaten gender norms, they wore uniforms, which did.

They also felt the repercussions of a nationwide slander campaign aimed against the Women's Army Corps in 1943. Rumors, gossip, and jokes insinuated that WACs were either prostitutes in fancy uniforms "servicing" the troops or lesbians running amok. Regardless of reassurances to the contrary by military and political officials, doubts persisted about the moral character of all servicewomen.[55] Since Washington's federal agencies employed the most concentrated number of female military personnel (seventy-five percent of all WAVES worked in the city), Government Girls dealt with suppositions stemming from the rumors.

The innuendo hurt recruiting efforts. Magdalene Nutall felt a patriotic impulse to join the military. Her brother, his friends, and the boys she knew from high school and college in Omaha, Nebraska all left for the service and she wanted to go, too. But her friends were appalled. They warned her, "Oh, don't do that! That's not a good thing for a young girl to do." Magdalene was persuaded to protect her virtue and become a civilian Government Girl instead.[56]

Servicewomen in Washington knew they were being judged. Coast Guard SPAR Mary Lyne remembered, "We were all quite aware of the fact that civilians reasoned about us from the particular to the general. We were constantly under surveillance by the public eye. Should one of our numbers have too much beer, ergo—all SPARS are drunkards."[57] WAVE Helen Gunter wrote home to assure her parents that the rumors about degenerate servicewomen did not apply to her. "You asked me about smoking," she wrote. "You needn't worry about hearing 'all women in the armed forces smoke.' Instead of turning me on, that has turned me off."[58] Marine Patricia Anne Spohr remembered, "the general public sat in judgment of all women in uniform as being...uneducated, unemployable, unattractive 'ready teddys' who only joined the service to 'get a man.'"[59]

Cecilia Campbell felt the acute difference between her pre-war life as a respected, small-town schoolteacher and her wartime identity as a WAC while on a routine bus ride into downtown Washington. "I sat next to a well-dressed, matronly lady and wouldn't you know? She looked at me, 'humphed,' got up and moved... gave a big sniff and got up," Cecilia remembered. "I felt terrible."[60] Another WAC, Elna Grahn, recalled, "At some time or other all of us were cornered by at least one person who asked in a give-me-the-lowdown tone of voice, 'Why did you join the service?' Implying: 'I don't understand it. You seem like such a nice girl, too.'"[61]

The wariness was not confined to Washington's resident population. Some civilian Government Girls judged their military colleagues. Economic Warfare typist Margaret Crook viewed servicewomen within a hierarchy of acceptability. Becoming a Navy officer seemed "classier." Her cousin was a WAVE stationed in D.C., and she had the opportunity to meet and mingle with what she considered top-tier women. But Margaret was aghast when a socialite friend joined the Marines. "She had come out and everything," she mused. "Being a private was below expectations for her. It was seen as unfeminine. She was a society girl." But the bottom of the respectability order was reserved for WACs. "The Army was the low class choice," Margaret believed. "Maybe a little looser."[62]

Conversely, War Department clerk Lucille Davis considered WAVES to be the women "a little freer with their favors—that was what the feeling was... It wouldn't surprise me if some of the guys who were kind of operators might have gone over to [WAVES Quarters D] to see what they could find, what they could get."[63] And Shirley Weinberger, a lawyer with the federal government, was skeptical when servicewomen started working alongside her husband. "There were WAVES and WACs, that's when I put the wedding ring on Teddy," she recalled. "When he went into service, I said, 'I want the WAVES and WACs to know that you're married.'... I went to the PX. I paid four dollars and bought a wedding ring."[64]

Frances Lynd Scott lived with such judgment every day. She was excited to find a one-bedroom apartment to share with her good friend and fellow Navy cryptologist, Flossie. Their new neighbor was not so thrilled to have Government Girls in the building. "The lady next door in the next apartment thought we were some kind of low lives because my fiancé came down and would stay overnight." Flossie's fiancé visited often as well. It appeared to the neighbor that these newly independent young women were flaunting their sex lives. But Frances insisted, "There was no unmarried sex in those days. You just did not do that." Both men slept on the living room sofa. Frances and Flossie remained chaste and highly offended at the implications. "The lady next door thought we were having these men in our apartment," Frances sniffed. "*We* thought she was the one who had roaches in the kitchen."[65]

Like Francis, many other military and civilian Government Girls did not have the energy or desire to completely shatter the parameters within which they were raised. Joanne Lichty grew up in a very strict household and did not feel the need to rebel during her time as a Government Girl. The Treasury Department clerk witnessed other young women enjoying their newfound freedom, but, she qualified, "Compared to today it was so, even though it was war time, it was so tame compared to today that it's hard to really think of it as a time of loosening up. I'm sure that it was. After all, these guys went off to war and you never knew if you'd see them again. But compared to today it was still a very puritan time."[66]

Corinne McLure Moyers, a twenty-year-old from Montana who worked at the Bureau of Yards and Docks, also kept a practical approach to romance. "I didn't even try to get involved with anybody because they were going to be here today and gone tomorrow," she recalled. "They'd be in for maybe a week's training, two weeks, three weeks, maybe a month and then they'd be gone."[67]

Even Government Girls wanting to experiment with their freedom away from familial and community constraints still had space limitations in Washington. With most Government Girls living in boarding houses, military barracks, dorms, or crammed apartments, finding a place to have sex presented a challenge. Navy ensign Stephen Kanyusik remembered the problems sailors faced in making moves on women while stationed in D.C., "You couldn't go back to her place because there was probably four other girls living there... unless you were real sharp, a cool operator. Maybe you had money and went to a nice hotel room. It cost maybe four bucks."[68]

Finding a location for romance proved so difficult, an Allied spy used the situation as a ruse to gather intelligence. "Cynthia" (Amy Elizabeth Thorpe's code name) seduced Charles Brousse, a French attaché at the Vichy French Embassy. She then convinced her married lover to help steal secret naval codes from his own offices (yes, she was *that* persuasive). Charles gained access to the building by complaining to the security guard about his problem finding an available room for late night trysts with his mistress. The sympathetic guard allowed them to use an office for several weeks, over which time Cynthia gained access to the safe and copied the codes.[69]

Between self-imposed or situational limitations, many Government Girls social lives were relatively restrained. Some women worked six days a week and took night classes. Some sent every extra penny home to help with finances. Others volunteered their free time to community or war activities. But the numerous women seen frequenting bars and nightclubs still set the standard for the image of youthful abandon applied to all Government Girls. Another federal crusade targeting Government Girls used their public reputations against them. This time the women pushed back.

It's easy to picture Indiana Representative Earl Wilson as a sort of Harry MacAfee, the curmudgeon in the musical *Bye Bye Birdie,* sitting in his Capitol Hill office throwing up his hands in frustration and breaking out in a chorus of "Kids! I don't know what's wrong with these kids today!" before putting the final touches on his proposal to impose a bedtime curfew on Government Girls.

Although he had no evidence, the congressman suspected that Government Girls' unrestrained social lives made them less efficient at work. He claimed to be inundated by stories of women who showed up for work tired, loafed on the job by taking too many coffee and bathroom breaks, and requested an inordinate amount of sick leave.[70] Wilson decided these problems could only be caused by women's rambunctious nighttime activities. So he proposed a 10 p.m. curfew for all (and only) female federal workers. This, he claimed, would keep women "healthier, frisky and fine."[71] He hoped to obtain the cooperation of Washington's landladies to enforce the bedtime and federal supervisors to institute a "card system" in which workers would receive notices admonishing them for bad behavior.[72]

Wilson's idea generated support from several other congressmen. Michigan Representative Clare Hoffman recalled seeing "two young women—one smoking and the other fixing her nails" outside of a tempo office building. Hoffman could not determine "whether they were waiting for a bicycle or what," but believed the matter should be scrutinized.[73] Congressman Karl Stefan from Nebraska supported a thorough investigation of all personnel offices but admitted that carrying out such an inquiry would be difficult.[74] And Georgia Representative Robert Ramspeck agreed that "a general lack of understanding of the urgency of the war situation" existed among female war workers.[75] Wilson's advocates could not point to specific statistics on office productivity. However, they all agreed that Government Girls needed better guidance and control.

Outraged Government Girls quickly labeled Wilson an "ogre" and called the curfew "childish, ridiculous, and impossible." They discounted Wilson's argument regarding women's wild social lives and instead blamed terrible housing conditions, transportation delays, reduced lunch

breaks, inadequate work training, and long hours on the job for ineffi-
ciencies at government agencies as well as for worker exhaustion.[76] War
Department typist Patricia Watkins insisted, "These poor little Federal
slaves who are the victims of Wilson's silly curfew suggestion didn't create this condition and aren't responsible for the multiplying confusion in
Washington."[77] Hazel Henry, a stenographer with the Social Security
Board, related all of the after-work activities she performed every evening in order to prove that a 10 p.m. bedtime was impossible. After arriving home at 6:45 p.m., Hazel ate dinner, went over her budget, washed
and ironed her laundry, wrote home to her family, performed her night-
ly beauty regime, practiced her trumpet, and listened to the radio to keep
up with current events. She charged Representative Wilson with telling
her how she could "expedite herself into bed" in time for the curfew.[78]
Wilson dismissed the women's complaints and condemned their resistance as "thinking only of their own pleasure."[79]

Detractors of the proposal were not limited to Government Girls.
Senator Hattie Caraway from Arkansas—the only woman in the Senate—defended the women: "If the girls are old enough to be away from
home to work here, they ought to be able to take care of themselves."[80]
Representative Jennings Randolph from West Virginia cautioned
against imposing stringent regulations, because, "One cannot be too crit-
ical of girls working for the Federal Government. They are the back-
bone of the Government agencies."[81] Oklahoma Representative Victor
Wickersham argued that the women had "good reputations… and
should be allowed to go to bed when they get ready."[82] And some local
men also weighed in against the idea of women being forced to retire
early, because "a stag party is not attractive every evening that you go
out."[83]

As draconian as Wilson's plan seemed to Government Girls, other
cities considered or implemented wartime curfews. Military and civilian
authorities used them as a mechanism to control juvenile delinquency,
teenage venereal disease rates, enemy aliens, U.S. citizens of Italian,
German and Japanese descent, and off-duty GIs. Attempting to impose a

curfew on Government Girls, lumps them in with these groups considered possible dangers to society. A few weeks after his initial proposal, Wilson offered a compromise and suggested extending the curfew until 11 p.m. But he eventually backed down altogether from the impractical and unpopular idea.[84]

The numerous attempts to regulate the private lives of Government Girls illustrate the degree of discomfort that the social activities of these women caused. Self-appointed guardians of virtue, like Representative Wilson and Dr. Overholser, identified Government Girls' behavior as out of control. Yet, publicly labeling the women as promiscuous did not change their participation in the sexually charged wartime nightlife. Attacking the women's work, in essence their patriotism, was another attempt to maintain order in the changing wartime social climate. By calling the women selfish, lazy, and unprofessional, Wilson, a former high school principal, found an excuse to rein them in like misbehaving schoolgirls. Wilson's attempts to use landladies as glorified hall monitors and issue workplace report cards reveals the patronizing attitude he and his supporters held towards Government Girls.

A more effective, and mutually beneficial, method of controlling Government Girls' social lives was to offer alternatives to the behavior officials condemned. The Women's Bureau of the Department of Labor published a handbook recommending government-sponsored programs to help with the "special needs of women." The Bureau believed that "wholesome" recreation could help keep Government Girls out of trouble.[85]

In an effort to facilitate respectable, chaperoned male-female interaction, the newly created D.C. Recreation Department set up a Women's Battalion. This organization arranged for Government Girls to serve as dance partners, or "draftettes," to servicemen at nearby military posts like Fort Belvoir, Fort Meade, Quantico, and Bolling Field.[86] Other area clubs, charities, churches, and war relief organizations sponsored dances around Washington, but the Battalion was the only outfit that specifically and consistently targeted Government Girls.

These were low-key, low-budget events. Kathryn Kaufman Moffit, a dispersing clerk at the Naval Receiving Station, went to one dance at Fort Meade in Maryland. "It was very muddy and you walked on planks," she remembered. "We went on buses, danced for the evening, and went back to post."[87] While a military base was a decidedly unglamorous substitute for a nightclub, the non-alcoholic drinks were free and a dance partner was guaranteed.

In order to participate, women submitted their names in boxes mounted in government offices and dorms. Applicants then undertook a lengthy screening process to determine their suitability and eligibility. Each candidate filled out forms giving her name, hometown, employer, height, weight, age, and an estimation of her dancing ability. Once she passed this preliminary step, a potential dancer faced an interview with a Women's Battalion representative to rate her personality and appearance (attractive, good, or fair). The woman's employer filled out an additional form detailing her honesty, character, and loyalty to the United States. If chosen, the women received temporary guest cards for a thirty-day trial membership in the Battalion. Chartered buses, each carrying forty women, a chaperone, and two Red Cross nurses, left Washington around 7 p.m. for dances that went from 8 p.m. to 11:30 p.m. The Battalion also hosted its own dances for soldiers on leave at what is now the Mellon Auditorium.[88]

Government Girls enjoyed the mixers. Federal Communications Commission clerk Corrine Perry repeatedly volunteered for the dances because she thought the idea was "cute" and offered "a chance for girls coming here from other cities who have no social connections in Washington to meet some fine men."[89] Kay Wilson, a stenographer for the Civil Service Commission, admitted that she liked going to the military bases because she was "susceptible to uniforms." And Vanda Hermann, a typist for the Coast Guard, became a dance partner because, she explained, "The men in the service I know are all a very decent bunch of fellows. It's only fair to give them a chance to meet some nice girls."[90] Applications for membership outnumbered available slots throughout the war. Over 6,500 members regularly attended the dances offered at least four nights a week.[91]

The draftettes attracted national attention and sparked interest from women and promoters in creating similar programs around the country. A few negative responses came in as well. A Baptist preacher from Pennsylvania declared the plan "immoral and unsafe for young girls" and a local man insisted that, while he gladly gave his son to the war effort, he would never allow his daughter to be drafted as a dancer.[92] A widely reprinted story reporting that Washington-area servicemen used a "date machine" with levers marked for blondes, brunettes, redheads, tall, short, blue eyes, green eyes, etc. to order up the perfect partner may have given women momentary pause before applying for the Battalion.[93] However, area servicemen enthusiastically embraced the program. Joseph Jones, a twenty-year-old sailor stationed at the Navy Yard, remarked, "They're a nice bunch of girls. They all shape up pretty well. A little above average, I'd say."[94] Other appreciative GIs sent the volunteers fan mail and requests for dates. "Why not try a marine?" pleaded one admirer. "Uncle Sam needs you," another man wrote. "So do I." And one confident sailor suggested, "Have a date with a Navy man and see the world."[95]

The Battalion eventually expanded its repertoire. Free concerts became a warm weather favorite. Military bands often used the Sylvan Theater at the base of the Washington Monument for celebrations like the first anniversary of the WAVES, with 4,000 parading corps members; touring bands gave open-air performances in East Potomac Park; noon time concerts sounded out from the steps of the Treasury building, and the *Washington Post* sponsored musical acts like the Von Trapp Family singers (of *Sound of Music* fame) in Meridian Hill Park.[96] But the most memorable concerts for the co-ed outings took place at the Watergate, a floating barge anchored in the Potomac River off the west side of the Lincoln Memorial. Although the music began at sunset, audiences set up chairs and blankets along the river's edge by late afternoon. Government Girls sat with their friends or dates on the back of the Lincoln

Memorial or anchored lantern-bearing canoes and small boats in the water around the barge. Latecomers made do with an unclaimed patch of grass, which was equally detrimental to pastel summer dresses and Navy whites. Local musicians, the National Symphony Orchestra, big bands, and name draws like Frank Sinatra all played the unique venue.[97]

For additional activities to entertain Government Girls, personnel branches of government agencies like the Office of Price Administration (OPA) offered their employees athletic opportunities. An open strip of land behind the National Gallery of Art became known as the OPA campus. Government Girls could obtain special permits to play tennis, badminton, volleyball, croquet, and touch football.[98] The Census Bureau, Department of Agriculture, Veterans Bureau, and a dozen other agencies sponsored women's softball teams that played under the aegis of the U.S. Government Girl League. Games took place during weekends on a field in West Potomac Park complete with cheering sections of fellow workers. Although the Senators remained the epitome of baseball in Washington, Government Girls developed a competitive and popular league.[99]

The Women's Battalion, concerts, and sports leagues were available to all Government Girls, but African-American women were restricted as to which events they could attend because race remained a legal and practical impediment. Segregation in Washington extended into recreational facilities and entertainment venues.[100] However, because D.C. had facilities owned by both local and federal governments, policies varied according to which legislative body controlled a particular location. Secretary of the Interior Harold Ickes began the desegregation of federally owned properties in 1939. By 1941 most of the recreational facilities in Washington were integrated, but D.C. laws and local Jim Crow traditions remained intact. Even President Roosevelt's annual birthday balls, which he hosted as fundraisers for his March of Dimes charity, were held separately for white and black crowds at segregated venues.

A small number of African-American draftettes were bussed to dances at local military bases that included companies of black soldiers. Black

Government Girls could also attend segregated YMCA and YWCA activities and serve as hostesses at USO Clubs for African-American servicemen. One interracial canteen successfully operated in Washington. The Labor Canteen's Institute held in the Agriculture Department's auditorium welcomed servicemen and women of any "race, creed, or color" with hostesses representing the same. Although the idea of the canteen "horrified" many "important people," it ran without incident in the divided city. Other than the Battalion, however, none of these organizations specifically recruited Government Girls as volunteers or patrons.[101]

Outside of those service clubs, downtown nightlife remained off limits to African-American Government Girls. They could and did visit the U Street corridor in Northwest Washington, the busy commercial district for African Americans, which contained the core of the black community's business, retail, and entertainment venues. Navy clerk Mary Wright remembered that fellow African-American war workers at the Pentagon were "a group of young, single adults who liked to go to the clubs on U Street when they got off at night and party."[102]

These Government Girls could choose from cabarets, supper clubs, dance halls, and cafes that featured top contemporary black artists. The popular Club Bali, Club Bengasi, and Bohemian Caverns offered two shows daily with local and big name jazz and swing bands. The Casbah and a few other clubs stayed open every night until 1 or 2 a.m. These were rare after-hour hangouts even for a city that had broken from its prewar predilection for shutting down by 10 p.m.[103]

The nightclubs attracted near-capacity crowds every night, but the Lincoln and Howard Theaters drew the most patrons to the area. Government Girls flocked to hear greats like Nat King Cole, Jelly Roll Morton, and Frank Sinatra play at two of the largest black theaters in the country. The first-rate acts attracted audiences, oftentimes both black and white, from as far away as Philadelphia.

There were enough options along the U Street corridor to entertain the most sophisticated and hard-partying Government Girl. Yet, women who participated in the area's offerings did not necessarily exacerbate the public debate over increasing social delinquency. Because African-American Government Girls were smaller in number and relatively hidden from the frenetic nightlife frequented by white Government Girls, they were not subjected to the same moral handwringing by local officials. The racial divide in the city made their social lives invisible and culturally entrenched stereotypes about black women's sexuality made it less important for the white authorities who controlled Washington to protect their collective virtue.[104]

Jesse Strieff did not party in the U Street area. She did not get raped and killed because she was promiscuous or her social life was out of control. The possibility of Government Girls having sex by force or by choice created a schizophrenic frenzy to either protect the women from harm or blame them for misbehaving. This paradoxical response raised a complex set of questions over existing gender boundaries. Authorities' struggled to reinforce those boundaries and Government Girls pushed against them. Women enjoyed far greater social freedom than before, with more opportunities for encounters with members of the opposite sex, and a sense that normal rules did not apply in the face of so much imminent danger. World War II significantly changed relationships between the sexes both during the war and for generations to follow. Despite the attempts made by the local, military, and government authorities to control the behavior of young men and women, wartime Washington was the site of sexual experimentation and a general loosening of restrictive morality. As socialite Vera Bloom observed, "It seems to me that no one could have lived through these times, either at the Washington crossroad or in a remote-seeming village, without having his sense of values change deeply."[105]

Notes

[1] "Murder in the Capital," *Washington Post*, June 18, 1941, 10.

[2] Bonita Orr Bailey Collection (AFC/2001/001/19375), VHP.

[3] "On the Newsfronts of the World," *Life*, September 8, 1941, 30.

[4] The District Attorney decided to first try Catoe for raping and strangling Rose Abramowitz, a twenty-eight-year-old newlywed killed in March 1941, because he thought prosecutors had the strongest evidence in that particular case. Although Catoe initially confessed to his crimes, he later recanted. Regardless, Catoe was found guilty in the Abramowitz case and died in the District jail's electric chair on January 15, 1943.

[5] John Singerhoff, "Police Shake Up Shows Results," *Washington Post*, November 14, 1941, 26.

[6] District of Columbia Board of Commissioners, *Report of Commissioners of the District of Columbia* (Washington, D.C.: Board of Commissioners, 1942), 164; Ibid.,1945, 92.

[7] Rape is a historically underreported crime. A victim faced many deterrents to reporting rape, including having her full name and address printed in newspapers and having to prove not only use of physical force against her but that she resisted her attacker "to the utmost limit of her power." Brown v. State of Wisconsin (1906). Ibid., 1947, 107-8.

[8] "Anarchic Washington," *Washington Post*, June 26, 1941, 10.

[9] Joan B. Dunlap Collection (AFC/2001/001/63638), VHP.

[10] Frances Lynd Scott Collection (AFC/2001/001/48208), VHP

[11] Dorothy P. Wills Collection (AFC/2001/001/65739), VHP.

[12] "Nurse Fights Off Attacker on D.C. Streets," *Washington Post*, February 9, 1942, 17.

[13] Veda Ponikvar Collection (AFC/2001/001/29928), VHP.

[14] "Speedy Justice is Promoted in Sex Cases," *Washington Post*, August 8, 1941, 17.

[15] "Girl Mauls Attacker with Electric Fan," *Washington Post*, July 17, 1942, 36; "Suspect in Stenographer Attack Indicted," *Washington Post*, July 28, 1942, 7.

[16] Marie McNair "Washington Plays Host to Many Undiscovered Celebrities," *Washington Post*, September 6, 1943, B5.

[17] James Chin, "Rep. Norton Urges Increase in D.C. Policewomen's Force," *Washington Post*, October 26, 1944, 1.

[18] Ellen Maury Slayden, *Washington Wife: Journal of Ellen Maury Slayden from 1897-1919* (New York and Evanston: Harper & Row, 1963), 340.

[19] Ruth MacKay, "Girls Will be Girls," *Chicago Daily Tribune*, January 31, 1946, 17.

[20] Mabel Alston, "Washington Experts Deny Women Drink More Since Conflict Began," *Baltimore Afro-American*, December 11, 1943, 16.

[21] Evelyn W. Stotler, "Wartime in Washington, D.C." in Pauline E. Parker, ed., *Women of the Homefront* (Jefferson, North Carolina: McFarland & Company, Inc. 2002), 71.

[22] Katharyn Rice Sockolov Collection (AFC/2001/001/10028), VHP.

23 Emily Towe, "We're Making Up for Lost Time," *Washington Post*, October 3, 1943, L1.

24 Hope Ridings Miller, "Capital Whirl," *Washington Post*, February 8, 1942.

25 Towe, "We're Making Up for Lost Time," 5.

26 Beth Campbell Short interview #3 with Margo Knight, August 17, 1987, Washington Press Club Foundation Oral History Collection.

27 Peter Soderbergh, *Women Marines: The World War II Era* (Westport, CT: Praeger, 1992), 103.

28 Jean Ashby Sims Collection (AFC/2001/001/56965), VHP.

29 Jane Fowler interview with author, August 31, 2004.

30 Ann Ellicott Madeira Collection (AFC/2001/001/ 7563), VHP.

31 "Girls on the Loose," *Washington Post*, October 14, 1944, 4.

32 As quoted in Scott Hart, *Washington at War: 1941-1945* (Englewood Cliffs, New Jersey: Prentice-Hall, 1970), 90.

33 See John Costello, *Love, Sex, and War: Changing Values 1939-45 (London: William Collins Sons and Co., 1985)*, 30.

34 John D'Emilio and Estelle B. Freedman, *Intimate Matters: A History of Sexuality in America*, Second Edition (Chicago: The University of Chicago Press, 1997), 260.

35 William Waller, "The Rating and Dating Complex," *American Sociological Review* 2, no. 3 (October 1937): 727-34.

36 Andrea Tone, "Contraceptive Consumers: Gender and the Political Economy of Birth Control in the 1930s," *Journal of Social History* 29, no. 3 (Spring 1996): 485-506.

37 See Dorothy Bromley and Florence Britten, *Youth and Sex* (New York: Harper & Bros., 1938).

38 Marion Tompkins Collection (AFC/2001/001/18663), VHP.

39 Sims, interview.

40 Elizabeth Delean Cozad interview with author, June 14, 2004.

41 A snood is a fashionable hairnet, think more Andrew Sisters than lunch ladies.

42 William Moore, "A Country Girl Meets Death in U.S. Capital," *Chicago Daily Tribune*, October 7, 1944, 11.

43 "Welfare Head Advises Sending Young Government Girls Home," *Washington Post*, October 12, 1944, 1.

44 "Washington May Return Teen-Agers," *Atlanta Constitution*, October 12, 1944, 1.

45 "Girls on the Loose," 4.

46 Ibid.

47 "Government Girl Statistics Sought," October 18, 1944, 11.

48 Moore, "A Country Girl Meets Death in U.S. Capital," 1.

49 Stephen Kanyusik interview with author, August 3, 2004.

[50] "Big Increase in District Births Sends Old Records to Cellar," *Washington Evening Star*, August 28, 1946, Statistics, Vital Birth Regulation Folder, DCPL.

[51] "Births in District During 1943 Break All Records for One Year," *Washington Evening Star*, March 5, 1944, Statistics, Vital Birth Regulation Folder, DCPL; Richard Smith, "One Out of Every 12 Births In District Is Illegitimate," *Washington Times Herald*, October 25, 1945, Statistics, Vital Birth Regulation Folder, DCPL; "Illegitimate Birth Rate Shows Sharp Increase," *Washington Post*, May 15, 1946, Statistics, Vital Birth Regulation Folder, DCPL; U.S. Department of Commerce, Bureau of the Census, *Illegitimate Births by Race: United States and Each State, 1944* (Washington, D.C.: Government Printing Office, 1946), 255.

[52] "Illegitimate Birth Rate Shows Sharp Increase," *Washington Post*, May 15, 1946, 1, 14; Health Department, Bureau of Vital Statistics, "Live Births Reported in the District of Columbia—1940-150," August 22, 1951, Statistics, Vital Birth Regulation Folder, DCPL.

[53] Ethel Standley Collection (AFC/2001/001/38211), VHP.

[54] Leisa D. Meyer, *Creating GI Jane: Sexuality and Power in the Women's Army Corps During World War II* (New York: Columbia University Press, 2002), 3.

[55] John O'Donnell, a nationally syndicated columnist, gave the rumors credence by erroneously reporting that WACs received contraceptives in accordance with a "super-secret" agreement between the War Department and the Army. The story had some basis in reality. GIs were automatically issued condoms in their overseas kits and Army paperwork initially ordered the same kits for WACs assigned to foreign posts. However, this snafu was quickly fixed and different kits were prepared for the women. The reporter's story and his political motives were hotly debated in the press and quickly refuted by Congressmen, the White House and the Secretary of War. Jane Mersky Leder, *Thanks for the Memories: Love Sex, and World War II* (Washington, D.C.: Potomac Books, 2009), 44-46. For more on slander campaign see Mattie E. Treadwell, *The United States Army in World War II, Special Studies: The Women's Army Corps* (Washington, D.C.: Office of the Chief of Military History, Department of the Army, 1954), 191-218; Evelyn M. Monahan and Rosemary Neidel-Greenlee, *A Few Good Women: America's Military Women from World War I to the Wars in Iraq and Afghanistan* (New York: Alfred A. Knopf, 2010), 106-113.

[56] Magdalene Marie Nuttall Collection (AFC/2001/001/11559), VHP.

[57] Mary C. Lyne and Kay Arthur, "Three Years Behind the Mast: The Story of the United States Coast Guard SPARS," in Judy Barrett Litoff and David C. Smith, eds., *American Women in a World at War: Contemporary Accounts from World War II* (Wilmington, Delaware: SR Books, 2002), 60.

[58] Lieutenant Helen Clifford Gunter, *Navy Wave: Memories of World War II* (Fort Bragg, California: Cypress House Press, 1992), 61.

[59] Peter A. Soderburgh, *Women Marines: The World War II Era* (Westport, Connecticut: Praeger, 1992), 50.

[60] Cecilia H. Campbell interview with Wanda C. Driver and Fran Richardson, November 7, 2003, WIMSA.

[61] Elna Hilliard Grahn, *In the Company of Wacs* (Manhattan, Kansas: Sunflower University Press, 1993), 36.

[62] Margaret and Jim Crook interview with author, May 27, 2005

[63] Lucille Davis interview with author, March 23, 2003.

[64] Shirley Weinberger interview with author, March 13, 2003.

[65] Scott, interview.

[66] Joanne Lichty interview with author, July 29, 2004.

[67] Corinne McLure Moyers Collection (AFC/2001/001/19605), VHP.

[68] Kuyunak, interview.

[69] Elizabeth McIntosh, *Sisterhood of Spies: Women of the OSS* (Annapolis: Naval Institute Press, 1998), 21-32.

[70] "Girls in Capital Fight A Curfew," *Washington Post*; January 17, 1942, 4; "Curfew for Government Girls Proposed for Efficiency's Sake," *Washington Post*, January 7, 1942, 1, 3.

[71] Mary Hornady, "Sideglances in Washington: Wilson Puts 'Rest' Up to Boys," *Washington Post*, February 8, 1942, B6.

[72] Earl J. Wilson, "An Earl Wilson Gets in Hair of an Earl Wilson," *Washington Post*, February 2, 1942, 13.

[73] "Rep. Wilson Again a Teacher; Lectures on What Ails Us," *Washington Post*, February 4, 1942, 19.

[74] Ibid.

[75] "Rep. Wilson Charges Laxity in U.S. Offices," *Washington Post*, February 19, 1942, 12.

[76] "Trials of Government Girls," *Washington Post*, February 8, 1942, B6.

[77] "Why Blame Girls?" *Washington Post*, February 11, 1942, 6.

[78] Scott Hart, "Curfew Shouldn't Ring, Girl Proves," *Washington Post*, February 1, 1942, 12.

[79] "Check on Girls' Efficiency Sought," *Washington Post*, February 14, 1942, 1.

[80] "Curfew Sponsor Wants House to Check Girls on Efficiency," *Washington Post*, February 1, 1942, 1, 4.

[81] "Check on Girls' Efficiency Sought," 12.

[82] "Oklahoman Declares They Should Be Allowed To Retire When Ready," *Washington Post*, February 3, 1942, 15.

[83] Jack Westbrook, "A Man Protests Curfew," *Washington Post*, February 9, 1942, 10.

[84] "Curfew," *Washington Post*, February 3, 1942, 8; Charles Mercer, "11 p.m. Girl Curfew Proposed So They Won't Primp on Job," *Washington Post*, January 31, 1942, 1, 3.

[85] U.S. Department of Labor, Women's Bureau, *Recreation and Housing, Women War Workers: A Handbook on Standards* (Washington, D.C.: Government Printing Office, 1942), 2, 11, NARA.

[86] A group called Recreation Services, Inc. had been in charge of organizing dances for soldiers and women, but turned the job over to the new District of Columbia Recreation Department when it was approved by Congress in 1943. "Girl Workers' Recreation Plan Mapped," *Washington Post*, April 19, 1942, 14.

[87] Kathryn Jeanette Moffit Collection (AFC/2001/001/66978), VHP.

[88] "Army Dancees Will Register Every 2 Weeks," *Washington Post*, March 11, 1941, 3; Marjorie Barstow Greenbie, "Uncle Sam's Prettiest Battalion," *Christian Science Monitor*, April 11, 1942, 1, 14.

[89] "Cute, Say Girls Of Plan to Draft Dance Partners," *Washington Post*, February 6, 1942, 1,4.

[90] "Ready to Serve Their Country," *Washington Post*, April 8, 1943, B4.

[91] Women's Battalion To Provide 6500 Dance Partners," *Washington Post*, August 22, 1943, X13.

[92] "Girls Regard D.C. Draftettes With Envy, Letters Disclose," *Washington Post*, March 19, 1941, 2.

[93] Barstow Greenbie, "Uncle Sam's Prettiest Battalion," 14.

[94] "120 Girls Find Army Dancing 'Patriotic—and a Lot of Fun'," *Washington Post*, August 22, 1942, 5.

[95] "Marines, First in War, Try To Be First Dating D.C. Girls," *Washington Post*, November 15, 1942, 11.

[96] "Band Concert Loosens Rolls of Hepcats," *Washington Post*, April 1, 1942, 19; Peter A. Soderburgh, *Women Marines: The World War II Era* (Westport, Connecticut: Praeger, 1992), 103.

[97] Kanyusik, interview; Sibyl Smith interview with author, June 14, 2004; Paul K. Williams, *Washington, D.C.: The World War II Years* (Charleston, South Carolina: Arcadia, 2004), 59.

[98] Luther Huston, "Uncle Sam's Seminary for Girls," *New York Times Magazine*, December 6, 1942, 8, 31.

[99] In 1943, chewing gum magnate and Chicago Cubs owner Philip K. Wrigley sponsored the All-American Girls Professional Baseball League as alternative wartime entertainment for baseball fans. The league gained notoriety when it was portrayed in the 1992 film *A League of Their Own*. The four teams were set up in cities close to Chicago. The league lasted until 1954, soon after men's baseball became televised and attendance dropped off. Washington, D.C. did not have a comparable professional league for women. "Government Girls' League Will Open," *Washington Post*, May 8, 1938, X2; "Census Girls Top General Accounting," *Washington Post*, May 15, 1941, 26; Emily Yellin, *Our Mothers' War: American Women at Home and at the Front During World War II* (New York: Free Press, 2004), 300-1.

[100] For further discussion of segregation in Washington's entertainment outlets, see Marya Annette McQuirter, "Claiming the City: African Americans, Urbanization and

Leisure in Washington, D.C., 1902-1954," Ph.D. Dissertation, (Ann Arbor: University of Michigan, 2000).

[101] "D.C. Interracial Canteen is Victory for Democracy," *Baltimore Afro-American*, December 16, 1944, 11.

[102] Mary Herring Wright, *Far from Home: Memories of World War II and Afterward* (Washington, D.C.: Gallaudet University Press, 2005), 45.

[103] Paul K. Williams, *Greater U Street* (Charleston, South Carolina: Arcadia Publishing, 2002), 38, 54-55, 67, 79, 128; Sandra Fitzpatrick and Maria R. Goodwin, *The Guide to Black Washington* (New York: Hippocrene Books, 1990), 212.

[104] For discussion on the evolution of black female stereotypes, see Deborah Gray White, *Ar'n't I a Woman?* (New York: W.W. Norton and Company, 1999), 27-46.

[105] Vera Bloom, *There's No Place Like Washington* (New York: G.P. Putnam's Sons, 1944), 273.

Advertisement for RKO Radio Pictures' 1944 film.

Jesse Strieff's 1941 rape and murder set off a wave of concern over
Government Girls' safety.

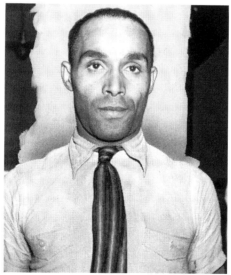

Serial killer Jarvis Catoe confessed to over a dozen violent crimes.

In 1918 D.C. trained its four policewomen to both protect and guide World War I Government Girls against the pitfalls of the city.

Eleanor Roosevelt gives advice to Government Girls taking classes at American University.

Dr. Winfred Overholser served as Superintendent of St. Elizabeths Hospital for twenty-five years.

Government Girls share some rare downtime in the lounge of their federal dorm.

Government Girls mingle with soldiers on a USO sponsored hayride.

Government Girls and servicemen both protested the idea of a Congressional curfew intended to limit the women's nightlife.

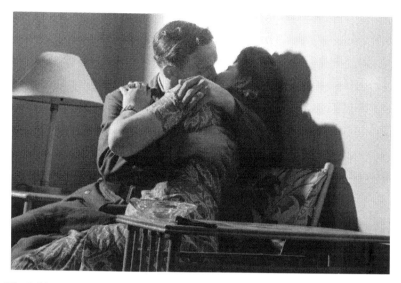

The lobbies of federal residence halls became popular spots for socializing in groups or couples. Men were not allowed to visit women's bedrooms.

The thousands of servicemen who came through Washington every week gave Government Girls ready-made, if temporary, dating opportunities.

Diana Prince/Wonder Woman epitomized the glamorous fictional
Government Girl.

In 1929 these Government Girls, like many female office workers, were
chosen for their looks as well as their skills.

Because of time and money constraints, most young women in Washington
maintained their beauty routines at home instead of at pricey salons.

"On the whole, they are a pretty unsophisticated lot," one reporter observed
about Government Girls.

Army-issued underwear generated more laughs than indecent proposals for
WACs.

Women living in federal dorms did not have access to electric dryers.
Clothes were drip dry only.

Government Girls' informal approach to their wardrobes and activities—like sunbathing on sidewalks—drew criticism from old guard Washingtonians.

Fashion shows using Government Girls as models were sponsored by federal agencies, department stores, and magazines.

VJ Day celebration on F Street in downtown Washington.

Stephen Kanyusik returned to Washington for the dedication of the World
War II Memorial in 2004. He proudly wore his old Navy dungarees.

Georgia Herron

Mary Brown

Pauline Menes

Postwar job opportunities in both the public and private sectors made staying in Washington a possibility for Government Girls.

WAVE Veda Ponikvar expressed a sentiment common to servicewomen stationed in D.C.: "All the money in the world could never come forward as far as the experiences I had."

6

Grit and Glamour

They walk four abreast in the streets. They chatter like magpies in the streetcars and buses. Most of them smoke cigarettes; lots of them like a cocktail. They like their jobs, but the bulk of them would rather be married.
~NEW YORK TIMES, DECEMBER 1942[1]

Can a Government Girl be happy without a girdle?
~WASHINGTON POST, MARCH 1943[2]

onder Woman muscled her way onto the comic book scene in December 1941, "As lovely as Aphrodite—as wise as Athena—with the speed of Mercury and the strength of Hercules."[3] The red, white, and blue clad Amazon princess used these innate talents along with her trademark magic bracelets, lasso of truth, and invisible plane to fight criminals and the Axis powers to protect the American way of life. As one of the first and most popular female superheroes, she became an enduring role model for young girls and adult women (as well as a cartoon pin-up for men). Yet, many forget that Princess Diana's alter ego, Diana Prince, also served as an ideal of female patriotism, strength, and capability. After saving the studly but accident-prone American military hero Steve Trevor (twice!) and nursing him back to health, Diana takes

179

a clerical job with Army Intelligence in World War II Washington. Wonder Woman was a Government Girl.

Wonder Woman embodied a progressive ideal. So progressive that thirty-one years after her debut, political activist Gloria Steinem chose Wonder Woman to grace the first regular issue of *Ms.* magazine as a symbol of contemporary feminism. The comic's creator, noted psychologist William Moulton Marston, purposely designed a superhero that challenged negative assumptions of female capabilities. But the character also reflected the standards of her time. Illustrator Henry George Peter (even though he was a self-identified feminist, Marston apparently gave little thought to hiring a female artist) developed a look for the heroine that incorporated feminine beauty ideals of the 1940s. Whether battling bad guys in a tiara or taking dictation in a dickey, she managed to remain perfectly groomed, coiffed, stylish, and in heels. She may have had the strength of twenty men, but she also had the glamour of twenty chorus girls.[4]

While Wonder Woman represented an extreme characterization of the average Government Girl, she became one of the many pop culture images that helped shape the public perception of the Lipstick Brigade—what they looked like, what they were capable of, and how they fit into the context of the war effort. Such mass-produced portrayals, along with those of servicewomen and industrial workers, provided Americans with an accessible way to absorb and understand women's newfound importance during the war.

Yet, these media inventions did not necessarily reflect reality. More often than not, the glossy, sanitized personae on the page and screen showed a narrowly defined, simplistic, unattainable version of Washington's young female workers. Government Girl was not simply a job description. It became the name of an idealized character developed by the press, government propaganda, and Hollywood. Actual Government Girls who could not or would not fit that mold had to decide whether to rebel against the manufactured role or create a new one for themselves.

While readers may not remember that Diana Prince worked as a wartime Government Girl, most can easily identify America's most endearing and enduring fictional defense worker: Rosie the Riveter. Redd Evans and John Jacob Loeb created the alliterative character with "Rosie the Riveter's Song," a modest success on the 1943 music charts. The upbeat tune extolled the virtues of a patriotic factory worker who was "making history, working for victory." Norman Rockwell's illustration for the May 1943 cover of the *Saturday Evening Post* gave Rosie her look. The powerful and witty portrait shows a strong, muscular woman sporting makeup and a compact mirror as a feminine contrast to her dirty work dungarees and rivet gun. The name scrawled on her lunchbox clearly identifies her as "Rosie." Westinghouse Electric Corporation's "We Can Do It!" poster gave Rosie lasting glamour. The graphic features a more delicate, typically beautiful woman in blue coveralls and red polka-dotted kerchief flexing her bicep. It was designed to encourage Westinghouse employees to remain focused on their work and develop company solidarity. Although neither a Rosie nor a riveter, the image was repurposed as an appealingly sleek and fashionable version of the World War II icon by later generations.[5]

Wonder Woman and Rosie the Riveter became part of a widespread attempt to shift public perception and beliefs of American women. A push to elevate the professional value of women was spurred by the need to entice them into the war effort. The media generated characters and stories focused on women's experiences and how they could contribute their labor, skills, and support to the national emergency. As historian Leila Rupp pointed out in her study on mobilizing women during World War II, "The war spawned a new genre, the women's wartime narrative."[6]

An organized effort to promote and convert these female centered through-lines into greater numbers of defense workers came from the Office of War Information (OWI). The federal government created the OWI to control and disseminate information to the general public. Its domestic branch worked through seven individual bureaus, including those covering publishing, news, radio, movies, and graphics. The OWI collaborated with producers, editors, writers, and artists to offer advisories, themes, story ideas, background material, and slogans. As the historian Maureen Honey has said, "Ties between propaganda groups and the media were extensive and the popular portrayal of women's role in the war was greatly influenced by the joint efforts of government agencies and media personnel to see that the economy functioned as smoothly as possible."[7]

Because of a sense of urgency over labor shortages, depictions of factory workers like Rosie dominated OWI's media blitz towards women.[8] Many of these campaigns aimed to convince women to join wartime defense industries, men to encourage them, employers to hire them, and society to accept them. A 1943 Gallup poll revealed that only thirty percent of husbands supported their wives taking industrial war jobs.[9] Creating a semi-fictional character like Rosie provided one way to reassure Americans that women could take over what was culturally labeled as "men's work" and still retain their traditional feminine appeal.

Government Girls did not blur the lines of gender distinctions in the same way Rosies did. Most Government Girls performed lower-level clerical duties, jobs ascribed to women for several decades. The need to reinforce the suitability of women in the office environment was less essential than emphasizing the appropriateness of their presence on the assembly line. Therefore, the Government Girl construct aimed more at convincing Americans that sending a young woman to Washington for war work would not corrupt her values or permanently change her character.

The national coverage of Washington as crowded, morally dubious, physically dangerous, where sex slayers ran loose and women ran looser did not reassure families on the fence about letting young workers accept a wartime appointment to the nation's capital. Articles broadcast warnings to potential Government Girls with titles like "Washington in Wartime: It is a Terrible Place to Live," "Washington Gets Soiled," and "'Nervous Girls' Are Advised Not to Come to Washington."[10] In 1942

Life magazine cautioned, "Washington, as this war gets going, is confused and chaotic beyond description." And a year later it reported that, "The U.S. capital is a wearing, worrying city with too many people and too many lines. It has too little time and space for the big job at hand."[11] Even the most enthusiastic potential Government Girls had to give pause when the superintendent of the city's psychiatric hospital proclaimed, "Many girls coming to Washington have become unstable, discontented and have gone off on a tangent."[12]

It is understandable that many young women had to battle familial doubt and disapproval to become Government Girls. Every time a friend stopped by to ask future Coast Guard SPAR Betty Splaine how her job application was coming along, Betty's brother would shake his head and mumble, "Goddamn fool, goddamn fool."[13] And while Mary Herring Wright had full backing from her mother to leave rural North Carolina to become a civilian typist for the federal government in Washington, when her father found out about her plans, he scoffed, "She's got no more business there than a pig has with a Bible."[14] The creation of a Government Girl archetype who was wholesome, patriotic, and fashionable served as incentive for women who hoped to be like them and ammunition to convince families like Betty and Mary's that they would be surrounded by positive role models while living and working in Washington. The same media outlets that were describing the horrors of living in the nation's capital were simultaneously portraying its female workers as somehow unscathed by the chaos.

A *Washington Post* photograph captured pretty, young Patricia Koerner smiling demurely into the camera. Patricia, a nineteen-year-old clerk/typist from small town Butler, Pennsylvania, represented the "typical Government Girl" for an article highlighting the women "talked about, written about and worried about from New York to California." Readers learned how Patricia set aside ten percent of her base government salary for war bonds; enjoyed listening to records after dinner with her boarding house roommates who were also close friends; swam and bowled for exercise; accepted dates to football games or the theater; and dressed with an eye for both practicality and style. Another photo showed Patricia diligently taking dictation during her workday, which could stretch upwards of nine or ten hours. Although employed at the Board of Economic Warfare, Patricia avoided making a personal budget because, as she laughingly admitted, "I never can keep my numbers straight!" Regardless of the stringent and tiring routine, Patricia insisted she was having a "marvelous time in Washington."[15]

Patricia's depiction exemplifies the Government Girl archetype. She is a young, single, naïve, fashionable white office worker temporarily relocating to Washington to aid the war effort. If Wonder Woman was an exceptional Government Girl, Patricia was a generic one. Washington's administrative corps came from diverse geographical regions, lifestyles, experience, and educational levels. However, the one-dimensional Government Girl construct offered a simple, reassuring ideal to use within the new wartime female narratives. The catchphrase that had been around since World War I became attached to a specific image and cemented by its use on a national level.

African-American women were excluded from the mainstream press's depiction of Government Girls. Magazines and newspapers referred only to white women as part of Washington's administrative corps. This was not unusual. The mainstream press of this era rarely included African Americans in feature stories. However, periodicals targeted towards African Americans also refrained from labeling black federal workers as "Government Girls."

The *Washington Afro-American*, the city's most widely distributed African-American newspaper, featured many stories about women in office work throughout the war. Articles included serious issues such as racism in federal agencies as well as lighter topics like the latest fashions. Instead of one catchall phrase, reporters used specific job titles to describe the women. For instance, the paper identifies Beatrice Black as a "junior astronomer at the Naval Observatory" and Gwendolyn Hemmingway as a "senior typist at the Department of the Interior."[16]

From 1942 to 1945 the paper profiled one female government employee each week, first under the headline "Career Women" and later "Uncle Sam's Nieces." The brief biographies included a photograph and detailed where the women came from, what government position they held, what education they possessed, and occasionally a bit of advice for other women seeking federal work. Neither reporters nor the workers used the term Government Girl to describe them.

The *Aframerican Women's Journal,* the National Council of Negro Women's magazine that focused on black women's issues, also did not include a single wartime article identifying federal employees as Government Girls. And the idiom never appears in 1942-1945 editions of *The Negro Handbook,* a reference tool for journalists. The books, written by Washington-based, African-American author Florence Murray, offered information on black culture and life across the nation and contained categories such as professions, war work, and government agencies.

Although the press did not use images of Washington's African-American women in association with Government Girls, such material did exist. Several federal agencies employed photographers to capture images of American life starting in the mid-1930s. During the war they were eventually brought under OWI's domain. The agency's News Bureau included the Negro Press Section dedicated to furnishing pictures and stories to black newspapers around the country in order to boost morale for the war effort.

However, as Barbara Orbach and Nicholas Natanson found in "The Mirror Image: Black Washington in World War II Era Photography," few black papers and even fewer white press outlets carried OWI product.[17] Major black newspapers such as the *Baltimore* and *Washington Afro-American* and *Pittsburgh Courier* had their own photographers and included OWI material only when unable to cover the same stories. Mainstream white press had access to OWI's photos and stories about African Americans but chose not to carry them.

Even though African-American women worked in all levels of the federal government, and material was available to illustrate their stories, neither the black nor white press included these women in their characterization of the iconic Government Girl. Historian Maureen Honey has observed that, during World War II, "racism proved to be an impenetrable barrier in creating expanded images of women."[18] This was true of press coverage in Washington. And it was true in Hollywood.

"Your weapon is film! Your bombs are ideas! Hollywood is a war plant!" proclaimed Frank Capra.[19] The popular movie director (and enlisted soldier) not only encouraged the Hollywood community to show its patriotism, but he created the award-winning documentary series *Why We Fight*, one of OWI's most successful and influential projects. The seven films aimed to explain the reasons behind America's involvement in the war—initially to the troops and later to the general public—and gain support for the cause on both battlefront and home front. As Americans purchased an average of eighty-five million movie tickets every week during World War II, the OWI believed feature films could have similar impact.[20]

Hollywood and the OWI developed an uneasy and often antagonistic relationship. The industry's studio system stood at the height of its power, but OWI had the ability to block a film's overseas distribution rights by claiming it harmed foreign relations. They formed a wary but successful wartime alliance that, for the most part, served their respective interests.[21] For instance, films depicting female defense workers satisfied both the studios' desire for profits and OWI's entreaty for positive material regarding the war effort. These "women's films" served as a practical way of handling the shortage of bankable leading men in Hollywood due to war enlistments and provided audiences with new material that mimicked their wartime experiences and struggles.[22]

Although they did not garner as much celluloid attention as female factory workers and servicewomen, Hollywood took notice of Government Girls. Four films feature the icon as a main character: *The More the Merrier, Government Girl, Pin-Up Girl,* and *Ladies of Washington.*[23] Because they reached such a large audience, these movies significantly influenced the appearance, style, and tone of the Government Girl public persona.

Washington's housing crisis serves as the impetus for the plot of Columbia Pictures' comedy *The More the Merrier* (1943).[24] Government Girl Connie Milligan (Jean Arthur) decides to share her apartment to help ease the city's wartime overcrowding and winds up toppling her orderly life. She hesitantly rents out half of her apartment to a man, grandfatherly Benjamin Dingle (Charles Coburn), in town for two weeks on defense business. Dingle, in turn, secretly rents out half of his space to Joe Carter (Joel McCrea), a "high type, clean cut, nice young fella," whom he identifies as a potential romantic match for Connie.

Connie works at a fictional war agency called "OPL." She is efficient, smart, and capable. After she presents Dingle with a morning schedule planned down to the minute, he observes, "You're a very systematic girl." "I used to work in the office of facts and figures," she answers proudly. Connie cannot, however, figure out her own love life. Her long-term engagement to her boss, a bombastic government official, leaves her bored and alone most of the time. Dingle's meddling ultimately costs Connie her fiancée and job, but gives her the chance to discover true love. She and Joe marry in order to save Connie's reputation (threatened because she lives with the two men), but realize their feelings for each other are genuine. The movie ends with a jovial Dingle celebrating his successful matchmaking.

Olivia de Havilland stars as RKO's *Government Girl* (1944), the second studio release featuring the eponymous character. The actress plays Smokey Allard, secretary to Ed Browne (Sonny Tufts), a dollar-a-year man,[25] who arrives in Washington to head up the government's Bomber Division. Smokey guides the inexperienced Ed through the city's political and bureaucratic red tape, but he undertakes unorthodox methods to get the airplanes completed on time (i.e., reallotting materials without permission and settling labor disputes with his fists). Smokey and Ed develop a mutual attraction, but, when he suggestively asks, "Do you always have to call me 'Mister?'" she dutifully answers, "Of course, Mr.

Browne. I'm your secretary. You wouldn't like it at all if your secretary became familiar." And then she proceeds to become very familiar with him.

A subplot involves Smokey and her roommate, May, in a scheme to oust a foreign secret agent. The FBI asks the women to "serve their country" by pretending to get drunk at the agent's apartment and feed him false government secrets. The plan goes awry and the women get drunk for real, but they still get their man. Smokey has a harder time getting the man she loves. She dates a scheming government lawyer who uses the "funny things" Smokey innocently tells him about Ed's business dealings to bring him in front of a senate investigating commit-tee. Smokey interrupts the hearing and saves Ed with an impassioned speech touting his patriotism and effectiveness in producing the much-needed bombers. Ed declares his love for Smokey and asks her to marry him. "Might as well be around to get me out of trouble," he tells her be-fore grabbing her up in a kiss.

Twentieth Century-Fox produced the third movie about a Govern-ment Girl as a showcase for the country's most famous wartime pin up model, Betty Grable.[26] *The Pin-Up Girl* (1944) follows flirty, capricious Lorry Jones (Grable), a popular small-town singer and pin-up girl (capi-talizing on the actress' famous wartime photo), as she and her mousy friend Kay (Dorothea Kent) relocate to Washington to work as Navy Department stenographers. Lorry, who harbors ambitions to sing pro-fessionally, convinces Kay to stop in New York for an adventure before she ends up "pushing a typewriter and eating drugstore lunches and be-ing a fixture in an office." When the pair meet war hero Tommy Dooley (John Harvey), sparks fly between Tommy and Lorry. In order to appear more glamorous, Lorry pretends to be a famous nightclub songstress. The women leave on the late train for D.C. before Lorry can reveal the truth.

After two uneventful weeks at work, Lorry gets assigned to record the naval air exploits of none other than Tommy Dooley. She borrows Kay's glasses and conservative outfit and, à la Diana Prince/Wonder

Woman, creates an alter ego that fools her new love. She works as Tommy's dowdy secretary during the day and dates him as the alluring performer at night. The ruse lasts until the arrival of one of the five hundred men Lorry offhandedly promised to marry while volunteering at the USO back home. Lorry clears up the misunderstanding and unveils her true identity when she takes to the stage in her stenographer "costume" and sings. Tommy welcomes the chance to love both sides of Lorry, the sincere stenographer and the dazzling nightclub star.

Another Twentieth Century Fox production, *Ladies of Washington* (1944), gives audiences a military Government Girl, Coast Guard SPAR Carol Northrop (Trudy Marshall). She works as a recruiter but she's never seen on the job and it plays no significant part in the story. The plot focuses on the romantic lives of friendly, smart, kind, honest Carol and her greedy, adulterous, murderous acquaintance Gerry Daily (Sheila Ryan). The women share a room with a group of boarders, mostly civilian Government Girls, in a large private home run by a kindly, elderly male owner nicknamed "Mother Henry." The film uses romance to weave a morality tale warning young women about the perils of pursuing money and flashy men instead of selflessly serving others and the war effort. Carol finds a wonderful man and Gerry winds up in an asylum. The main subtext of the storyline is summed up in an exchange between a boarder and Mother Henry as they watch Carol and her new fiancé kiss. "Wonder what those two are thinking about? Getting married?" the boarder asks. "Does anybody in this house think about anything else?" Mother Henry replies.

Each of the four films helped create a singular cinematic vision of Government Girls—one that visually and thematically reinforced the media archetype. The casting of popular leading ladies known for playing pragmatic and sympathetic characters gave the icon a patina of respectability. Arthur created populist romantic heroines in a series of Frank Capra films, de Havilland was best known for her Academy Award-nominated performance as self-sacrificing Melanie Wilkes in *Gone with the Wind,* and even Grable's immensely popular pin-up photo was considered more girl-next-door than sultry siren.[27] The least famous actress of the group, Trudy Marshall, was a former fashion model who was promoted as "the typical American girl." These stars carried the imprint of being upstanding and relatable into their Government Girl characters.

The female protagonists of the films have a similar if unremarkable look. The characters' clothes have more in common with the Hollywood society debutante from the 1930s than with the contemporary on-screen defense workers. Unlike Rosie's visual association with her work—overalls and kerchief—the Government Girl cannot be immediately identified by the way she dresses. She would fit in equally well in an office or at the country club. Connie, Smokey, and Lorry wear stylish, tailored suits, hats, and gloves to work and form-fitted lace or beaded gowns for nighttime dinners, dancing, and dating. Carol deviates only in the substitution of a perfectly fitted uniform instead of a work suit. An informal study of actual Government Girls revealed that, "the World War II girl is a shirtwaist girl," meaning they preferred simple, affordable button-down blouses that could be interchanged with many outfits.[28] However, putting their idealized counterparts in chic clothing fits historian Leila Rupp's findings that most of the wartime publicity concerning women workers emphasized glamour over realism in order to make defense jobs appealing.[29]

The fictional women's surroundings match their refined, feminine image. Real life Government Girl Jean Kearney remembered, "We all laughed at the movies portraying a romanticized version of living and working in Washington... [the characters] lived in a whole apartment (while we were lucky to have one room to ourselves)."[30] Even though *The More the Merrier* and *Government Girl* include scenes making fun of Washington's severe housing crisis, the women's living quarters appear comfortably furnished, well decorated, and uncommonly spacious. Placing women in lush, frilly homes with flower boxes, fancy curtains, and lace-trimmed pillowcases, not only reinforced Government Girls' glamorous image but offered a visual contrast to the spare, drab office furniture and decor in the films—a symbolic reminder that home is a feminine space where these young women ultimately fit best.

While the movies highlight Government Girls' strengths and capabilities, they fall short of accurately depicting their professional work and environment. The details of the characters' professional lives are vague, often erroneous, and take second place to personal considerations, especially romance. Audiences noticed the job-related inaccuracies. Stenographer Ruth Miller complained, "Have just seen Olivia de Havilland in *Government Girl* and the way she handles a notebook! I'd like to see any white collar girl take fast dictation with a book held up in the air like that."[31] The onscreen Government Girls are not well-trained career women. They are temporary workers dedicated to serving their country, sometimes even saving it from corruption or espionage.

Hollywood validated Government Girls' participation in defense work by creating stories about them. However, it also reinforces the media ideal that emphasized style over substance and marriage over career. As one capital observer declared, "Washington was quite as crowded as the movies portrayed it, but without the tinsel the movies had shown. Government girls who lived four in a room didn't find dashing soldiers to marry, and they didn't dress In Hollywood fashion."[32]

White Government Girls could watch a fictionalized version of themselves onscreen, but African-American federal workers could not. None of the main characters in the Government Girl films work alongside, speak to, mention, or come in contact with black women. Wartime movies generally failed to portray black women in defense jobs. A 1942-43 OWI analysis concluded that, in terms of the war effort, Hollywood portrayed African Americans "as offering nothing, contributing nothing, expecting nothing."[33] Black actresses did appear in mainstream films, but usually in the same domestic servant roles as they had before the war. One major studio release, MGM's *Since You Went Away* (1944), does depict a black woman participating in defense work. This occurs in a scene about white female factory workers, and the African-American employee—also the main character's maid—appears for a moment in the background.[34] The black Government Girl did not exist in movies.

Helen Holden—Government Girl gave the nation its only radio portrayal of Washington's clerical army.[35] The serial followed the adventures of an intrepid young woman from the Midwest who moved to D.C. and was "sworn to protect the homeland against enemy infiltration and aggression" for fifteen minutes, Monday through Saturday. In the 1940s nine out of ten people owned at least one radio and tuned in to three to four hours of broadcasting each day.[36] During the war, soap operas featuring female central characters dominated daytime programming. Audiences could listen to one of the popular dramas on at least one station continuously between 10 a.m. and 5:30 p.m. every weekday.[37]

As with the Hollywood heroines, *Helen Holden* focused more on the title character's private life than her work as a Government Girl. Storylines mostly revolved around Helen's romance with her boyfriend David and her relationship with her single, lovesick Aunt Mary, who had the misfortune to also be in love with David. "All I can tell you about the show is that it was about a stupid young girl," Nancy Ordway later said about her leading role as Helen. "It was not a spectacular show. I don't think it had much personality." Others must have felt the same way as it only ran for a year. Even though Ordway recorded the character's lines in a closed studio using only her voice, the producer decided she was not glamorous enough to represent the heroine in publicity photos. "They asked me would I pluck my eyebrows," Ordway remembered. "And I said: 'hell no.'" The actress was eventually replaced.[38] The woman chosen to literally act like the ideal Government Girl could not live up to the image the media wanted her to project. Even for the radio, the archetypal Government Girl was one of narrowly defined beauty and style.

Helen Holden had literary contemporaries in Faith Baldwin's *Washington, USA*, a collection of six interconnected stories about young Government Girls and their quixotic escapades. The author, an enormously popular novelist who wrote specifically for women, introduced the book saying, "These pages that follow contain merely a number of stories, love stories for the most part. For wartime sharpens the arrow... [in] the city of transients, rumors, heartbreaks, success, disillusionment, wisdom and folly."[39] Government Girls made convenient, ready-made romantic leads. There was widespread curiosity about their lives, young women could aspire to be one, and they served as a vehicle for readers to transport themselves to what many reporters described as the most exciting wartime city in the world.

Yet, the perky, pretty, stylish, romantic Government Girl depicted in the media did not accurately reflect the average young woman working in Washington. "The beauty parade at the doors of the war agencies at quitting time has become a thing of wistful memory. Where once minced only the choicest blondes, brunettes and redheads, picked with care to make visiting 'defense' contractors visually happy, now stamped-ed a herd rounded up with an eye solely for quantity," quipped an editorial in the *Washington Post*.[40] In addition to pointing out the beauty discrepancy between actual Government Girls and her fictionalized namesake (and the reporter's offensive comparison of women to cattle), this description shows the expectations for women seeking to get or keep jobs in Washington. Government Girls were judged against both the iconic media image and ideal office worker.

The "proper fit between face and job," as historian Kathy Peiss phrased it, became increasingly important as women entered clerical work in greater numbers throughout the 1920s and 1930s. Beauty was considered an essential business tool for women. Office interviews routinely judged an applicant's appearance, leaving space on evaluations for comments about her makeup and hairstyle. Some companies even included instruction on beauty techniques in their training programs alongside dictation and office protocol.[41]

"Men want a girl to look nice. You know what I mean," a federal stenographer advised potential job seekers in 1934. She reassured women that male bosses in Washington were not overly hard to please. "They like to have us dress up. Not flashy, but just to look well," she confided. "They appreciate it and are proud of the office girls when outsiders come in."[42] Being attractive to men inside the office and those visiting it was unquestionably part of a woman's job description.

By World War II it became more important to find enough workers to fill Washington's expanding bureaucracy than to fulfill employer's requests for women "able to meet the public."[43] This resulted in Government Girls who looked less polished than those who had gone through testing and/or instruction. Buckner Blackerby, a training specialist for stenographers at the Office of Price Administration, gave newcomers advice on how to dress and behave professionally. Blackerby remarked on the women's earnest but often inadequate habits, "They want to do and say the right thing, but the city ways are quite different from their lives back in the small towns whence they came."[44]

Newcomers received a lot of fashion advice, regardless of whether they wanted it or not. An article entreatingly titled "Look Pleasant, Please" pleaded with Government Girls to banish the "Zebra-Leg Scourge," brown and white streaks resulting from badly applied leg make-up.[45] Young women used the drugstore products on their bare legs to give them the illusion of wearing stockings. Skirts or dresses worn with hosiery were still the business norm for women. Since silk, nylon, and rayon stockings were rationed and alternatives could be itchy, droopy or discolored, bare legs became the trend in the Washington workplace. Skillfully applied makeup could offer the "silk stocking glamour" as promised in the ads. Unfortunately, many Government Girls were not particularly skilled at using the difficult, messy liquids and creams. These are the ones who sported the offensive brown and white "zebra" stripes.

Slacks worn in the downtown shopping district also made the list of fashion faux pas committed by Government Girls. "Would you think of walking down F Street in a bathing suit?" a reporter admonished. "It would be just as appropriate."[46] Coincidentally, Wonder Woman did exactly that in one of her first storylines. She strutted through Washington's crowded streets in her star-spangled, strapless costume. A shocked doyenne of high society remarks, "The hussy! She has no clothes on!"

Venturing downtown for business or pleasure was considered a formal occasion worthy of looking a woman's best. Pants were unacceptable at any hour day or night. Diana Prince quickly caught on. Many young Government Girls did not.

The most disturbing style trend in the eyes of Washington's traditional culture guardians was the unsightly appearance of Government Girls' "bouncing derrieres."[47] The absence of girdles, the restrictive undergarments considered proper for respectable women (even pregnant women, who routinely bought maternity girdles) and essential to the slim lines of 1940s couture, branded young war workers as inappropriate and radical. "It is an aesthetic must even if you have a Klieg-light figure," a style setter reminded her readers.[48] Although the rubber used in the garments was rationed and new girdles could be uncomfortable, ineffective, and hard to find, women of all ages were expected to control their "protruding" backsides in the name of good taste and decency. After all, "War or no war, women's figures have not changed," insisted one Washington journalist.[49]

This perceived fashion blunder beat out a litany of other complaints over "rolled socks, the bare legs, the too short skirts, the 'kiddish' styles," white shoes worn at the office, and startling tableaux of "tropic abandon" on sunny days when Government Girls spent their lunch breaks sprawled over the lawns of the Pentagon and Capitol wearing shorts and drinking Coca-Colas.[50] These breaches of etiquette offended Washingtonians proud of their classically rigid customs. "Normally, Washington was a formal city in its appearance and in its living habits," a wartime observer noted. "But the girls from Thompkins Corners [meaning Small Town USA] have changed all this... All the old rules for formal street clothes are off."[51]

Margaret Bundick grew up in Washington and dressed according to its traditionally strict and staid code. Margaret's mother trained her under the dictate that a woman, "didn't dare go downtown Washington to a business office without wearing hat and white gloves even in summer. You had to be dressed *appropriately* for a business office." When she became a clerk at the General Accounting Office, she was shocked that other Government Girls did not seem to live by the same fashion guidelines. "They started hiring people from all over the country," she recalled of the war years. "We had different types of people from different backgrounds who came to work there. They came more lax in their code of dress. I couldn't get rid of my bringing up and training of being a more properly dressed person, but there were a lot of people who came to work wearing little babushkas and it even got to the bobby socks for women. I couldn't believe that. That was a no-no!"[52]

The disconnect between how Washington fashion arbiters and the media expected Government Girls to look and how they actually appeared on a daily basis had more to do with the women's youthful sense of informality and fun than a campaign to upend conservative Washington. *Vogue* editor-in-chief Anna Wintour has said that fashion reflects the times we live in. For wartime Washington, that meant Government Girls' clothing mirrored the ongoing conflict between the free-spiritedness of youth and the seriousness of the war effort. Women often had a hard time balancing the two extremes.

The difference also had to do with money. One sympathetic reporter explained that women often looked "frowsy" because laundry facilities were scarce and expensive. They wore bobby socks and moccasins in contrast to the "sheer hosiery of the movie government girls" because glamour required money and time that the real-life workers did not have.[53] After rent, clothing was the biggest financial concern for Government Girls. Staring salaries of $1440 per year before taxes (a little over $19,000 in today's currency) did not stretch far in the expensive wartime capital. This was especially true for women working in offices for the first time who had to invest in new business wardrobes.

If a woman shopped downtown at one of the most popular department stores—Garfinckel's, Hecht's, Woodward & Lothrop, Lansburgh's—she could expect to pay $40-$50 for a wool suit, $5 for a decent blouse ($10-$15 for a more fashionable one), $20-$30 for a dress, $9 for patent leather pumps, $14 for a mid-size purse, and $2 for a slip. Government agencies issued booklets to women with suggested budgets to help them manage their money. The recommended (and optimistic) $6 a month clothing allowance meant that a young woman would have to save money for five months in order to afford a new dress. Government Girls could scout out budget stores for cheaper prices or, if they were lucky enough to find a boarding house or YWCA with an available sewing machine, make their own dresses using a $.50 McCall or Simplicity pattern. But these alternatives rarely reflected the styles and quality of outfits worn by the iconic glamorous Government Girl.

In addition to clothes, the highly sculpted hair rolls, pompadours, and waves popularized in movies and magazines were difficult at best to achieve at home. Most government dorms incorporated beauty parlors into their amenities—Arlington Farms, the largest residential complex in the area, had fifty stylists operating on double shifts to coif its 8,000 residents. But the cost and access to salons needed to maintain complicated updos left many Government Girls dependent on setting their own hair. A visitor from Chicago complained, "The shortage of beauty operators to keep in curl the heads of Washington white collar girls has been the source of deep dissatisfaction. The beauty shop in my hotel turned out to be tiny and so crowded that it was difficult to avoid casualties."[54]

A manicure, haircut, and set could run $5.50 at a time when an egg salad sandwich and cup of coffee cost $.75. Individual hand-held hair dryers would not become light and effective enough to warrant popular use for another two decades. So it took women many hours to wash and cold set their hair into a semblance of film star chic. The clichéd social excuse "I can't tonight, I have to wash my hair" had a basis in beauty reality. But this was the option most Government Girls chose because every penny counted.

WAVES telegrapher Mary Bliss and her friends attempted to keep their hairstyles looking crisp without constant visits to the salon. "We would wear our rain hats to go into work at seven in the morning," Mary recalled about her time at Naval Communication Headquarters. "Get there early, go into the locker room take off the rain hats, and take

the curlers out of our hair."[55] Women walking around in curlers probably did nothing to alleviate that local reporter's wistful longing for
Washington's by-gone beauty parade.

The city's notoriously humid summers challenged Government Girls'
attempts to maintain both hairstyles and outfits. Ann Maderia's commute to her job as a cryptologist at the Navy Department on Constitution Avenue was, "hot as hell. We wore cotton dresses and by the time
we were even on the bus to get there were dripping."[56] Soaring tempera-
tures in the summer of 1943 set record highs during the city's most congested year of the war. Although some of the area's newer office
buildings, hotels, and movie theaters offered the welcome relief of air
conditioning, such luxury was too costly for most private homes and
non-existent on public transportation and in temporary office buildings.
Even if Ann could afford to buy stylish outfits, conditions in wartime
Washington limited her chances of maintaining a perfectly groomed
appearance.

So, was there any way for young women to transform from frowsy
to fabulous? Similar to the comedic sequence in the 1992 film *A League of
their Own* showing a prim and overly articulate woman instructing play-
ers from the first female professional baseball league in poise, charm,
and appearance, Government Girls could rely on professional lifestyle
gurus to help bridge the gap between the image in the mirror and the
icon in the media.

The real-life ballplayers had cosmetic maven Helena Rubenstein to
ensure any rough beauty edges were polished smooth. Rubenstein drove
the women hard. After all, she once famously declared, "There are no
ugly women, only lazy ones." Government Girls could get similarly helpful (or unhelpful) advice by attending clinics that served as makeshift
charm schools for women willing to put in the time and effort to transform themselves.

Federal agencies ran free seminars designed to teach Government
Girls "how to be happy though haggard, or beautiful though bumpy, and
all on $1440 a year."[57] Personnel counselors initiated the tutorials. They

were concerned that some women's "haggard" appearances prevented them from fitting in socially and also from getting promotions at work; both of which contributed to high employee turnover. An initial afternoon talk called "how to dress on a budget in Washington" was deemed a success. It included a fashion show using Government Girls from the Ordnance Bureau as models. This led to an ongoing series of lectures and catwalks focused on improving the women's beauty and behavior.

One four day, jam-packed symposium was co-sponsored by *Mademoiselle*, nationally known as the "magazine for smart young women." Designers, modeling agencies, charm schools, and magazines agreed to participate likely because they saw potential current and future customers in the concentration of young women living in the capital. Government Girls learned tips like how to stash extra clothes, accessories, and beauty supplies in spare drawers at the office in order to look good throughout the day and be prepared to go out at night. "Beauty is your duty," insisted Ann Delafield, director of the DuBarry Success Course, a weight loss and makeover system, in one of the assemblies.[58]

The Government Girl School for Self Improvement at American University's downtown campus also sponsored lectures from experts such as fashion legend Elsa Schiaparelli. The flamboyant designer known as "Schiap" was noted for her eccentric styles (she wore an turban, overlapping strings of pearls, and an armful of gold bangles to address the young women in Washington), however she recommended the exact opposite for Government Girls. Schiap cautioned them to "exercise the utmost discretion" in choosing their clothes. She suggested that women "strike a golden mean with a simple but tasteful costume that will not offend their bosses." A question about proper footwear for Government Girls made Schiaparelli cry out, "high-heeled shoes are impossible, absolutely impossible."[59] While Schiap understood the desire to look like a Hollywood icon, she knew that practical but polished would better serve D.C.'s working women.

More individualized advice was offered through living facilities and local women's groups. The Beauty Clinic for Government Girls at Meridian Hill Hotel analyzed each enrollee for problems with hair, skin, makeup, manicure, posture, and clothing. Arlington Farms held a course in which its residents could learn grooming habits determined by their specific personality traits. They took away free sample cosmetics to apply their instructions at home. And members of D.C.'s Democratic Women's National Council offered Government Girls one-on-one advice and accompanied them on shopping trips.[60]

Bea Meloon knew one woman who could have benefitted from a clinic or two. Meloon and her husband rented the living room of their one-bedroom apartment to a Government Girl from Texas. Meloon recalled, "Every payday she'd go downtown and get a whole new outfit—whole new outfit!—from skin out and she'd have a date. Well, she had a date with this one fellow who had beautiful red hair. And he told her, 'Never wash your hair, put cornmeal through it. Brush it, brush it, brush it.' So, she got in the bathroom at the end of the hall brushing that corn meal all over the bathroom and who had to clean it up but me!"[61]

Whether a Government Girl wanted to enhance her appearance to fit into city life or look like her namesake icon, she was inundated with advice and products in order to do so. Some women did follow the experts and managed to create an appealing approximation of the Government Girl media persona. For instance, a magazine profile of twenty-four-year-old Milly Flados, a "typical Government gal from North Dakota," described her transformation from small town hick to big city slick. "Nine months of Washington have changed Milly's former pageboy bob to a long bob of the debutante type, put in moth balls the run-of-the-mill dresses with which she arrived, in favor of a collection that shows off her slim waist," boasted the copy accompanying her smiling photos. Maintaining Milly's new look cost the stenographer a whopping thirty-five percent of her monthly salary, the same as her food and rent budget combined.[62]

Not every woman could afford to spend that much money sculpting and maintaining the sophisticated ideal. This inability often exacerbated insecurities for women who compared themselves to the thousands of other Government Girls jostling around Washington every day. Kathryn Moffit was twenty-one years old when she came to D.C. from Iowa and felt her simple, practical style was out of place among her peers. "To me they were all such polished, professional college girls," Kathryn recalled. "I was possibly older than some of them. I just felt as though they knew everything and I didn't."[63] Constant pressure to look good, such as style warnings that, "a girl has to look glamorous even in the rain," kept women aware of their appearance even if they felt they could never measure up.[64]

Since Government Girls in uniform were required to look and dress according to code, they did not have the same style issues as civilian workers during the duration. Recruits received a one-time allowance and were sent to a department store to buy regulation clothes from top-coat to handbag. Women purchased their own shoes (pumps for officers and oxfords, "klunky shoes with serviceable heels," for enlistees), gloves and underwear, including the obligatory girdle.[65] Women, just like men serving in the military, could not wear civilian clothes off duty.

Women tended to approve of and appreciate their uniforms. Lieutenant Junior Grade Marian Bonds was one of the 24,000 servicewomen assigned to Washington. She gushed over memories of wearing her Navy Blues. She said parading them around the city gave her "a feeling of great confidence. I am somebody. I was so proud of my uniform and felt so confident. I could do anything I put my mind to."[66]

The Navy even used the uniform as a recruiting tool. Brochures enticingly proclaimed: "The trim uniform was especially designed by the famous stylist Mainbocher to flatter every figure and to make you look—and feel—your best!" The distinctive outfit with its rounded shirt collar layered over the pointed lapels of a fitted jacket showcased the refined elegance for which the designer was known. Sally Kirkland, the influential fashion editor of *Life* magazine for more than two decades, described Mainbocher's style: "He not only made a woman look like a lady, but as if her mother had been a lady too."

The exclusive couturier was more accustomed to serving socialites and celebrities than government institutions out of his New York studio, but his designs for the Navy garnered the most attention and excitement during World War II. When WAVE recruits arrived for training, the first thing they received- before uniforms, instructions, or lunch—was the much coveted Mainbocher hat. It was a designer symbol of their entry into a new life.

And yet some young women still felt the urge to stand out and set their own style. Katharyn Rice Sockolov, a twenty-year-old photography specialist working at the Anacostia Naval Air Station, admitted, "I'm the one that had the heels too high and the skirt too short and the hair too long." She did, however, keep plain, regulation lace-up shoes in her file drawer in case of a surprise inspection. One day the WAVES director on base requested to see her. "This was scary stuff," Katharyn recalled. "I had no idea what I had done. I took off my high heels and put on the oxfords; unzipped my skirt a little ways so I could pull it down and make it look longer; and rolled my hair up to get it off my collar." She ran every possible uniform infraction and corresponding punishment through her mind on the walk over to the director's office. "I finally got to see this woman and she said, 'You left your locker unlocked.'" Katharyn flooded with relief and started readjusting her outfit before she even made it back to her desk.[67]

While the media and beauty industries tried to shape the Government Girl ideal from the outside in, the women worked to develop and individualize themselves from the inside out. Government Girls did not reject the look and style of their public namesake. They willingly and enthusiastically attended improvement clinics, competed in local beauty contests such as Miss Government Girl, and vied with hundreds of other women to strut onstage in government-sponsored fashion shows. But they also expanded the definition of Government Girl beyond the one-dimensional romantic ingénue.

After the rousing success of the Government Girl warplane drive that raised over $159,000 to purchase two fighter planes, one each for the Army and Navy, women did not want to let go of the sense of purpose and achievement they felt throughout the campaign. Women instigated, organized, and worked together to surpass their fundraising goals and public expectations. What else might they be capable of achieving?

Members of the Honor Guard—those chosen to represent Government Girls from their respective federal agencies—and other key organizers of the drive decided to form a permanent Government Girl Club. Lead by Lenora Haag, a White House secretary, club members decided that if they could help the war effort they could also help each other. A collection of committees planned breakfasts, fashion shows, concerts, dances, and lectures. They also created partnerships with existing organizations in Washington to address both social and professional ambitions of the group.

The women approached their new venture with the same enthusiasm as they showed in the fundraising campaign. They wrote a charter for the club to define its mission and the organizational structure. The elected officers had clearly outlined duties, responsibilities, and term limits (with elections symbolically held each year on the anniversary of the warplane dedication ceremony). Members emphasized and advertised the group's inclusionary nature: to attract all Government Girls and not just the Honor Guard. The women met regularly and aimed for at least one activity per month. These women invested time and energy in networking, cultivating their abilities, and broadening their reach into the community. They viewed themselves as more than temporary war workers. The club existed for over two decades.

The Government Girl Club was not the only structured program run by and for young women in Washington. For instance, each federal dorm had a council of elected representatives to deal with the issues and needs of its residents. The councils held regular, formal meetings governed in part by Roberts Rules of Order. They were responsible for generating ideas to continually improve living conditions, dealing with violators of dorm regulations, and creating a harmonious and supportive environment. One way they hoped to achieve this last goal was to develop programs similar to the self-improvement schools.

But instead of makeup application and slim down secrets, Government Girls requested and participated in a more varied set of courses including economics, foreign languages, sculpture, dance, acting, sewing, and religion. Performing arts were especially popular. Esther Janto, an Army Signal Corps employee, wrote and staged several shows at Arlington Farms. Her production, "Government Issue," received standing ovations, which encouraged her to keep writing during and after the war. Other Government Girls organized choirs, dance productions, and comedic skits to present for each other as well as the larger D.C. community.[68] By taking control of their education, the women defied the caricature of the appealingly ditsy Government Girl unable to handle a personal budget.

Social committees also created weekly group activities for residents of the dorms. These events ranged from theater and concerts to observing sessions of the Supreme Court and Congress. One favorite outing involved dressing up and heading to the elegant Tea Room at the Woodward & Lothrop department store, where the English-style high tea included Wellesley fudge cake, the house specialty.[69] Navy WAVE Margaret Liddle, another resident of Arlington Farms, recalled the scope of possibilities, "We played softball, basketball, we went on tours and trips, we went to New York City... we'd even catch a flight to Florida and go to the beach and come back—all in one weekend!"[70] Regardless of which classes and activities Government Girls chose, being exposed to new ideas, places, and people brought a new sophistication to many women's small town naivety.

The shared pursuit of fun also allowed them to become part of an extended community of women. Over the course of the war, this sense of camaraderie deepened which helped to forge a distinct group identity. The media attention gave Government Girls their group name, their newness to the city and wartime mission set them apart from established Washingtonians, and the immediacy of living, working, and socializing with each other created a shared sense of belonging. Being a Government Girl became a source of pride and empowerment for many women. For some, this led to political activism on the group's behalf.

Amelia Beck and Mary Gaines, Alabama and Louisiana natives respectively, began a public campaign on behalf of 600 other Government Girls. The women notified the press that they were all filing their income tax returns in Virginia under protest. Amelia and Mary argued that because the women lived at the federally owned and operated Arlington Farms property, they did not officially reside in Virginia. Federal agencies and not the state provided all necessary services—road, utilities, medical—to the dorms. Additionally, because a large majority of Government Girls retained legal residence in their home states, many were being forced to pay taxes twice. After Harry Green, the Arlington County Revenue Commissioner, dismissed the women's complaints as a bid for cheap publicity, Amelia and Mary lead a vigorous crusade to convince U.S. senators to pass the House-generated O'Hara Bill (which would eliminate multiple taxation of government workers), and notified the local and national media of their plight.[71] The bill became law in 1946 and Government Girls once again proved that their collective abilities reached beyond achieving a cinematic sheen.

While unfair taxes rallied hundreds of Government Girls, threat of eviction mobilized thousands. As the wartime need for Government Girls shrank after 1945, federal dorms began shutting down. The last remaining temporary residences were mandated to close no later than 1950. As the deadline approached, over 3,600 women still lived at Arlington Farms and several hundred more rented rooms at Midway and Slowe Halls, built for African American workers. These Government Girls did not leave quietly.

They raised "war chests" to pay for campaign expenses. They circulated petitions, put pressure on congressmen and senators, generated press coverage, and offered alternative solutions, including consolidating residents into fewer halls and building permanent low-rent dorms. Newspapers referred to them as lobbyists and credited the "Government-Girl attack" with forcing housing authorities to extend the dead-lines. All the dorms were either closed or sold by mid-1950, but the women's political force kept them open over a year longer than sched-uled.[72] The collaborative campaign reveals that the identification with being a Government Girl extended beyond the original group dynamic cemented by wartime necessity. These women used their youthful en-thusiasm for more than bucking conservative fashion trends.

The iconic Government Girl developed by the media detailed how the women *should* look and act. However, that invention did not neces-sarily reflect the identity women created for themselves. Appearance is an important form of self-expression and clothes, hair, and makeup were tools many Government Girls used to redefine themselves during the war. However, many others sought a chance to transform their in-tellectual, creative, political, and leadership skills as well. Being a Gov-ernment Girl gave them a sense of belonging within a community of active, accomplished women.

The media created the Government Girl ideal and women expanded it, but time ultimately diminished it. Wonder Woman and Rosie the Riveter became enduring symbols of potential female power. Their T-shirts, lunchboxes, laptop cases, cell phone covers, and even tattoos sell well to cross-generational buyers over seventy years after they first ap-peared. But Government Girls, "the most discussed working girl in the nation," were largely forgotten.[73] What happened? Why didn't they last?

While Rosie the Riveter is frozen in time, inextricably linked to the romantic nostalgia of World War II, Government Girls still exist. Their jobs and image were adopted by female office workers, both public and private, who remained in or came to Washington after the war. Gov-ernment Girls did not go away. They evolved. But like the Wonder Woman character—who became a boutique owner, fashion assistant, lost her powers, and was then resurrected by the Women's Movement—many Government Girls continued their personal search for identity in postwar society.

Notes

[1] Luther Houston, "Uncle Sam's Seminary for Girls," *New York Time Magazine*, December 6, 1942, 8.

[2] "Beauty Clinic to Put Zip in War Work," *Washington Post*, March 3, 1943, 1.

[3] Charles Moulton [William Moulton Marston], *All Star Comics 8* (New York: DC Comics, December 1941).

[4] William Moulton Marston wrote *Wonder Woman* under the pen name Charles Moulton. For back story on the creation of the character, see Jill Lepore's *The Secret History of Wonder Woman* (New York: Knopf, 2014).

[5] See James J. Kimble and Lester C. Olson, "Visual Rhetoric Representing Rosie the Riveter: Myth and Misconception in J. Howard Miller's 'We Can Do It!' Poster," *Rhetoric & Public Affairs* (Winter 2006): 533-570; Maureen Honey, *Creating Rosie the Riveter: Class, Gender, and Propaganda during World War II* (Amherst: University of Massachusetts Press, 1984); and Sherna Berger Gluck, *Rosie the Riveter Revisited: Women, the War, and Social Change* (Boston: Twayne Publishers, 1987).

[6] Leila Rupp, *Mobilizing Women for War: German and American Propaganda, 1939-1945* (Princeton: Princeton University Press, 1978), 144.

[7] Honey, *Creating Rosie the Riveter*, 28.

[8] See Honey's *Creating Rosie the Riveter* for a discussion on recruitment campaigns and government's perceptions and misconceptions of women workers.

[9] Emily Yellin, *Our Mothers' War: American Women at Home and at the Front During World War II* (New York: Free Press, 2004), 45.

[10] "Washington in Wartime: It is Terrible Place to Live," *Life*, January 4,1943, 47-50; Carlisle Bargeron, "Washington Gets Soiled," *The American Mercury*, November 1943, 593-598; and "'Nervous Girls' Are Advised Not to Come to Washington," *The Washington Post*, May 9, 1942, 1.

[11] Milton Mayer, "Washington Goes to War," *Life*, January 5, 1942, 64; "Washington in Wartime," 48-49.

[12] "'Nervous Girls' Are Advised Not to Come to Washington," 1.

[13] Elizabeth F. Splaine interview with Kate Scott, April 16, 2004, WIMSA.

[14] Mary Herring Wright, *Far from Home: Memories of World War II and Afterward* (Washington, D.C.: Gallaudet University Press, 2005), 18.

[15] Anne Hagner, "Government Girl," *Washington Post*, October 15, 1942, B3.

[16] "Girl Gets Naval Astronomer Post," *Washington Afro-American*, February 7, 1942,1; "Career Women," *Washington Afro-American*, March 7, 1942, 9.

[17] Barbara Orbach and Nicholas Natanson, "The Mirror Image: Black Washington in World War II Era Federal Photography" *Washington History* 4, no. 1 (Spring/Summer 1992): 4-25.

[18] Maureen Honey, "Remembering Rosie: Advertising Images of Women in World War II," in Kenneth Paul O'Brien and Lynn Hudson Parsons, eds. *The Home-Front War: World War II and American Society* (Westport, Connecticut: Greenwood Press, 1995), 101.

[19] Gene Brown, *Movie Time: A Chronology of Hollywood and the Movie Industry from Its Beginnings to the Present* (New York: Macmillan, 1995), 166.

[20] Brown, *Movie Time,* 163, 169, 173, 177.

[21] For further discussion of the relationship between Hollywood and OWI, see Clayton R. Koppes and Gregory D. Black, "What to Show the World: The Office of War Information and Hollywood, 1942-1945," *Journal of American History* 64, no. 1 (June 1977): 87-105.

[22] Edwin Schallert, "Drama and Film," *Los Angeles Times,* July 27, 1943, 15; Molly Haskel, *From Reverence to Rape: The Treatment of Women in the Movies* (Chicago: University of Chicago Press, 1987), 182.

[23] Several other movies take place in wartime Washington but do not revolve around Government Girls, most notably *The Doughgirls* (1944), *Standing Room Only* (1944), and *Without Love* (1945).

[24] Writer/Director Garson Kanin co-wrote *The More the Merrier* based on his and his wife's (Ruth Gordon) own experiences living in wartime Washington while he served in the Army. Because the government forbade GIs from partaking in outside work, Kanin remained uncredited. Garson Kanin, *Tracy and Hepburn: An Intimate Memoir* (New York: Viking Press, 1971), 76-7; Ruth Gordon, *My Side: The Autobiography of Ruth Gordon* (New York: Harper & Row, 1976), 253-5.

[25] Dollar-a-year-men were successful business executives recruited for civilian government service. They had no civil service status and therefore could be let go without notice or appeal. The administrators continued to receive their regular salaries from their companies, but the government gave them a token wage to make them official employees.

[26] For discussion on the cultural and political role played by wartime pin-ups see Robert Westbrook, "I Want a Girl Just Like the Girl That Married Harry James: American Women and the Problem of Political Obligation in World War II," *American Quarterly* 42 (December 1990): 587-614.

[27] See Elizabeth Kendall, *The Runaway Bride: Hollywood Romantic Comedy of the 1930s* (New York: Alfred A. Knopf, 1990), 117-133 and Westbrook, "I Want a Girl, Just Like the Girl that Married Harry James," 596-605.

[28] Sally Dee, "Meet Miss 1943," *Los Angeles Times,* January 17, 1943, g18.

[29] Rupp, *Mobilizing Women for War,* 146-151.

[30] Jean Kearney, "My Life as Kitty Foyle," in James E. Thierry, ed., *Looking Back at War: Archives Volunteers Remember World War II* (Washington, D.C.: National Archives and Records Administration, 1993), 40, HSW.

[31] Ruth Mac Kay, "White Collar Girl," *Chicago Daily Tribune,* April 6, 1944, 22.

32 William Moore, "A Country Girl Meets Death in U.S. Capital," *Chicago Daily Tribune*, October 7, 1944, 11.

33 As quoted in Clayton R. Koppes and Gregory D. Black, "Blacks, Loyalty, and Motion-Picture Propaganda," *Journal of American History* 73, no. 2 (September 1986): 399.

34 Producer David Selznick removed another scene from *Since You Went Away* that contained black defense workers after several African-American Army WACs complained at a preview screening. The sequence showed a group of silly, giggling black WACs as extras at a train station, and the women felt it undermined their seriousness and dedication to the war. Thomas Cripps, *Making Movies Black: The Hollywood Message Movie from World War II to the Civil Rights Era* (New York: Oxford University Press, 1993), 86-88.

35 The government sponsored a few radio programs such as *G.I. Jane Presents* and *Everything for the Girls* to promote women's roles in the military. Women read inspirational stories based on their service experience, bands performed patriotic music, and actors presented dramatic vignettes of battlefront scenes. However, these shows concentrated on women serving overseas. Clerical workers did not appear in the programs.

36 Gerd Horten, *Radio Goes to War: The Cultural Politics of Propaganda during World War II* (Berkley: University of California Press, 2002), 2.

37 Susan M. Hartmann, *The Home Front and Beyond: American Women in the 1940s* (Boston: Twayne Publishers, 1982), 196.

38 As quoted in Jim Cox, *Historical Dictionary of American Soap Operas* (Lanham, MD: Scarecrow Press, 2005), 98; John Kelly, "Answer Man: Beholding Helen Holden," *Washington Post*, October 4, 2004.

39 Faith Baldwin, *Washington, USA* (New York: Farrar & Rinehart, Inc., 1942), VII.

40 The Post Impressionist column, *Washington Post*, October 2, 1942.

41 Kathy Peiss, *Hope in a Jar: The Making of America's Beauty Culture* (New York: Metropolitan Books, 1998), 193.

42 Irene Hasbrook, "Better Dress Conservatively for Women Bosses, Says Stenographer Who'd Rather Work for Men," *Washington Post*, May 10, 1934, 13.

43 Ibid.

44 Genevieve Reynolds, "Women's Council Hears OPA Specialist," *Washington Post*, November 17, 1942, B4.

45 Jeanne Contini, "Look Pleasant, Please," *Washington Post*, June 15, 1943, B2.

46 Ibid.

47 Malvina Lindsey, "Washington Summer Girl," *Washington Post*, July 24, 1943, B2.

48 Jeanne Contini, "Foundations," *Washington Post*, February 3, 1943, B2.

49 Drew Pearson, "The Washington Merry-Go-Round," *Washington Post*, December 17, 1943, B13.

50 Contini, "Look Pleasant, Please," B2; Lindsey, "Washington Summer Girl," B2.

51 Sally Reston, "Girls' Town- Washington," *New York Times*, November 23, 1941, SM8.

[52] Margaret Rector Bundick Collection (AFC/2001/001/5891), VHP.

[53] Moore, "A Country Girl Meets Death in U.S. Capital," 11.

[54] Ruth MacKay, "White Collar Girl," *Chicago Daily Tribune*, July 7, 1944, 15.

[55] Mary Merrick Bliss Collection (AFC/2001/001/33087), VHP.

[56] Ann Madeira Collection (AFC/2001/001/7563), VHP.

[57] "Beauty, Happiness on $1440 a Year Will Be Clinic Theme," *Washington Post*, March 8, 1943, 1; Anne Hagner, "Government Girls Pack Charm Clinic," *Washington Post*, March 9, 1943, 1.

[58] "Beauty Clinic to Put Zip in War Work," *Washington Post*, March 3, 1943, 1.

[59] Chandler B. Brosard, "Girls Here Told to Shun High Fashion," *Washington Post*, March 13, 1943, B1.

[60] Martha Ellyn, "Upswept Hairdo Must Be Neat To Be Pretty," *Washington Post*, April 30, 1943, B3; Jerry Kluttz, "7500 of Fair Sex Populate Girl Town," *Washington Post*, October 29, 1943, B1; Reynolds, "Women's Council Hears OPA Specialist," B4.

[61] Beatrice Cole Meloon interview by Patricia Meloon Brown July 8, 2004, Courtesy of Patricia and Bill Brown.

[62] "Girl in a Mob," *American Magazine*, October 1942, 35.

[63] Kathryn Jeanette Moffit Collection (AFC/2001/001/66978), VHP.

[64] Jane Driscoll, "Clothes for Fall," *Washington Post*, August 6, 1942, S7.

[65] Doris McLean Hays in Margaret Hewitt George, ed., *We Knew We Were at War: Women Remember World War II* (Margaret Hewitt George, 2006), 108.

[66] Marian Oliver Bonds Collection (AFC/2001/001/69654), VHP.

[67] Katharyn Elizabeth Sockolov Collection (AFC/2001/001/10028), VHP.

[68] "Government Girl Writes Show for Women in Service," *Washington Post*, October 10, 1945, 15.

[69] Joanne Lichty interview with author, July 29, 2004; Sybil Smith interview with author, July 8, 2004; Roselyn Dresbold Silverman, "World War II in Washington: Life at Dissin's," *The Record* 22 [Jewish Historical Society of Greater Washington] (1997), 44.

[70] Margaret Cope Liddle Collection (AFC/2001/001/13722), VHP.

[71] "Arlington Girls Protest Filing Va. Tax Return," *Washington Post*, April 17, 1945, 2.

[72] "U.S. Defers Closing of Girls' Dorm in Arlington," *Washington Post*, May 18, 1949, B1; Thomas Winship, "'Girls' Town' Gets Respite From Closing," *Washington Post*, May 20, 1949, B2; "Government Girls Petition to Keep Lucy Diggs Slowe Home," *Baltimore Afro-American*, March 20, 1948, 11.

[73] "Government Girls to Learn Right Dress," *Washington Post*, January 21, 1944, 13.

7

New Beginnings

Let [your man] know you are tired of living alone... You want him to take charge. You want now to have your nails done.
~U.S. GOVERNMENT "READJUSTMENT" GUIDE, 1945[1]

This one night, the war was over and I was on Constitution Avenue near the Capitol building and all of a sudden the lights, everything came on. I parked the car and looked and watched to see the dome and everything lighted up. It was really a thrill. You can't imagine what it was like. Can't imagine. I'll never forget that.
~WILDA BEEBY, WAVES TRANSPORTATION DIVISION[2]

ven though Marion Tompkins was exhausted, she could not get comfortable enough to fall asleep on the crowded train to D.C. The young woman from Albany, New York had joined the Coast Guard SPARS after seeing a magazine spread about crisply uniformed recruits drilling seaside under the Florida sun. Ironically, she now returned from specialized training at a station in, of all places, New York. These mentally and physically demanding weeks of education to qualify as a coxswain would be the last of her military career. Marion was hardly the same person she had been in that dentist's office flipping through *Holiday* magazine almost two years ago. She had traveled, been exposed to people and situations she had previously only read about, and pushed herself beyond her own preconceived boundaries in terms of learning, leadership abilities, and management skills as head of a bustling SPARS barracks in the nation's capital. Marion had never felt happier or more fulfilled.

However, the war in Europe had ended three months earlier and Marion spent some of her sleepless train ride considering what she would do once her service in the SPARS ended and she was automatically decommissioned. Would her next trip to New York be a permanent one-way ticket? Could she go back home to the same routine she left? Would she even fit back into her former life? All worries over her personal future subsided once she arrived at Union Station that hot, humid August night and heard the news. After days of false reports and rumors, it was official. World War II was over.

"When I got to Washington I couldn't get back to the barracks," Marion remembered. "The streets were so crowded the buses couldn't run on time. The taxis were so full they couldn't take people. I think I waited an hour before I could get any transportation back to the barracks. It was a madhouse. Screaming and yelling and hollering. Buses and trucks full of servicemen going down the street, everybody hollering and yelling."[3] According to the *Times Herald*, Marion returned to "the wildest, noisiest, most joyous and most colorful night this capital has ever known."[4]

City offices, restaurants, and stores closed so workers could join the celebration. Church bells pealed. Musicians spilled out of theaters to lead an impromptu victory parade. Streetcars stuck in the impenetrable gridlock became makeshift viewing stands. A sailor somehow got ahold of a white horse and rode it down Pennsylvania Avenue to enthusiastic cheers of approval. A screaming throng pressed against the wrought iron fence outside of the White House chanting "Harry, Harry" until President Harry Truman's spoke live over a public address system.

Freda Segal, a stenographer at the Veterans Administration, recalled the intimacy that developed from being part of such an emotional high: "Everyone was manic. There was so much grabbing, kissing. It was like you were passed around."[5] According to at least one report, several couples in Lafayette Square used the chaos as an excuse to go well beyond kissing. The public displays prompted a concerned journalist to remark, "If I were a mother, I'd certainly have my daughter locked up tonight."[6]

When the revelry waned in the early hours of the morning, Government Girls made their way home through ankle-deep ticker tape, confetti, toilet paper, broken bottles, and trash littering the streets. Marion Tompkins was already back on duty at the SPARS barrack awaiting their return. The countdown to her new civilian life had begun.

Combustible joy marked the capital's public recognition and relief that the war was over. Federal and city governments declared a two-day holiday. But after the initial celebration, the work of war continued. Government agencies maintained overseas operations, arranged to bring troops home, set up foreign and domestic peacetime programs, and managed newly expanded departments. Bureaucratic Washington still needed administrative help from the Lipstick Brigade. Government Girls' continued presence in the region—whether they stayed in the government, moved into private practice, or retired and became part of the local community—helped transform many longstanding Washington traditions.

By August 1945 Washington was already recovering from its boomtown frenzy. The frantic growth of the city's workforce, housing, and utilities leveled off after its population hit a wartime peak of 891,000 in 1943, up from 663,000 just three years earlier. The number of people in D.C. seesawed over the next decade as war workers went back home, servicemen returned to the area, and new developments lured young families out to the suburbs. However, the city would never return to the size, demographics, or urban geography it had before the war.[7] As David Brinkley noted in his first-hand account of World War II Washington, "The city had come out of the war as the capital of the only major country in the world on the winning side, or any side, to survive without a scratch. But those looking for a return to the quiet, easy Washington life they had known in peacetime would not find it."[8]

City officials anticipated postwar change and started planning for possible scenarios and problems early in the defense buildup. Part of the public discourse in D.C., as well as boomtowns around the country, focused on what to do with the tens of thousands of women working for the war effort. Towards the end of the conflict, there were almost 160,000 female federal employees in Washington, nearly sixty percent of its workforce.[9] One reporter wondered about the future for Government Girls, "Will these war workers return to their homes when the war is over, or will they remain here to run a government that is increasing its control over the whole nation every month?"[10] If given that choice, the women wanted to run the government. In a survey conducted by the Washington Board of Trade, an overwhelming seventy-five percent of the city's war workers hoped to stay.[11]

While the government's need for lower-level clerks dropped from its all-time high, many bureaus initially retained or even added Government Girls to help bridge the transition during the postwar reorganization. The Civil Service Commission reported that a year after the war, the ratio of Government Girls in D.C. fell from six out of every ten federal employees to four out of ten. This was in part due to the increasing numbers of men hired back into the government and in part because of downsizing.[12] But civilians who worked for the war effort could often transfer to permanent agencies instead of leaving public service. Women were added to the full-time employment rolls at the rate of 2,500 to 4,000 a month. Pauline Menes was one of the Government Girls who made the switch. She was initially recruited from Hunter College in New York City to become an economist in the Office of the Quartermaster General. Once the war ended, Pauline moved on to the Army Map Services where she spent a year and a half updating charts using classified information provided by returning servicemen.[13] In a similar transition, Dorothy Finley Wilbur, a typist with the Army, used her skills and military knowledge to land work as an editorial assistant for Army publications related to veterans' assistance programs.[14] And Betty McIntosh, whose housing complications left her literally hanging out of windows, parlayed her work in Morale Operations with the Office of Strategic Services into a thirty-year career with its peacetime successor, the Central Intelligence Agency (CIA).

Another hiring uptick in 1951 meant that women with work experience continued to have options within the federal system. As a local newspaper article titled "Government Girls Find New Horizons" noted, "A government that operates via paperwork needs a lot of women behind the typewriters and shorthand notebooks, and every week increases the need."[15] Ninety-five percent of federal stenographers and typists were women, which gave women lateral mobility within the civil service as well as an entry point for those looking to generate a career path.[16] Vila Hunter, for instance, joined the war effort as a junior clerk typist with the War Production Board. She found a similar position after the war in the Veteran's Administration. But, once there, Vila steadily advanced until she earned the position of senior management analyst. She stayed with the agency until 2006.[17]

Enlisted Government Girls also maintained a postwar presence in federal offices. The military did not decrease its female forces in Washington until mid-1946. Like their male counterparts, women enlisted for the duration of the war plus six months and were sent home according to a point system based on how long they had served. Although the Coast Guard SPARS and Marines disappeared entirely by that fall, local Army and Navy offices retained several thousand women each.[18] One of the women who stayed was Army WAC Antoinette Loezere. She served as an intelligence officer during the war and continued in that capacity at the Department of Defense afterwards. Antoinette ended up staying at the Pentagon for almost thirty years.[19] Penelope Smith also extended her service in the capital. Her wartime work as a WAVE cryptologist made her desirable as a postwar analyst. After several more years in the Navy, Penelope worked at the CIA for nearly two decades.[20] The continued willingness of those branches to utilize servicewomen stemmed from the recognition of their reliability. Navy Secretary Frank Knox publicly acknowledged that, as a group, the WAVES "proved more efficient than the males they had replaced."[21]

Women with specialized skills like Penelope and Antoinette had a relatively easy time retaining their positions. Others took a more circuitous route back to public service after being forced out during demobilization. When SPAR Betty Splaine, whose first boss in Washington rearranged the furniture so he would not have to look at a woman working in his office, was decommissioned in 1946, she reluctantly returned to a civil service job in Boston. Betty wanted to get back into the Coast Guard when Congress passed the Women's Armed Services Integration Act in 1948. Although the legislation permanently incorporated women into the military, the Coast Guard only accepted women as reservists. Betty worked in Washington for a law firm headed by a former Coast Guard supervisor during the day and drilled twice a week with her SPARS unit at night. She was finally able to return to full-time active duty in 1953. Betty went on to become the Coast Guard's first female warrant officer, which recognized her as a leader and expert in her field.[22]

Betty's perseverance demonstrates her dedication to the career goals born out of her time as a Government Girl. She could follow that path because she, along with the other 24,000 servicewomen, proved her merit and talent during the war. Women like Betty paved the way for the enduring presence of servicewomen in Washington offices. But her experience also shows how difficult it could be to pursue postwar dreams. Even when the United States entered the Korean War in 1950, women made up less than one percent of the military's total strength.[23] Neither the country nor the government mobilized to the same degree as it had during World War II. Opportunities for Government Girls to fully utilize their capabilities within the military during the 1950s and 1960s remained limited.

So, many Government Girls attempted to capitalize on their experience instead. Over one and a half million women entered college between 1945 and 1950. Army WACs, Navy WAVES, Coast Guard

SPARS, and female Marines were eligible for education benefits as part of the Servicemen's Readjustment Act of 1944. Under this "G.I. Bill," the government covered tuition, books, and fees up to $500 per school year (tuition averaged $75 per semester) and paid a monthly allowance for each veteran who served at least ninety days and received an honorable discharge.[24]

Although the military did not keep precise records, one report estimates that 65,000 female veterans utilized their educational benefits between 1946 and 1956. This was equal to almost twenty percent of eligible servicewomen.[25] Government Girl Margery Updegraff, who once slogged through the mud to reach her job at the Pentagon, jumped at the chance to go back to school. After leaving the WAVES, she used the G.I. Bill to earn a master's degree in Fine Arts from the University of Iowa. She returned to Washington and worked for the Department of the Interior and Library of Congress for a combined total of thirty-one years.[26] Dorothy Gondos Beers also used her wartime service in the Navy to help finish her education. Dorothy earned her Ph.D. at the University of Pennsylvania immediately after the war and then came back to D.C. and spent over three decades on the faculty at American University. She served as chair of the history department and Dean of Women before she retired.[27] These two women benefitted so greatly from their service in Washington, they chose to return to the city to forge their life-long careers.

Veteran's educational benefits technically applied equally to men and women. But they were not always administered equally in practice. Elizabeth Stewart, a cryptologist for the WAVES, also hoped to take advantage of the G.I. Bill for graduate school, but never got the chance. "I wanted to be an architect, really," she lamented. "When I got out of the Navy, I applied at Yale, Penn, and MIT. I was turned down by all three because they were saving all the spots for men who had been in service. I said, 'I've been in the service.' They said, 'Too bad.'" Elizabeth found a job drafting for an architect instead of becoming one. She soon married and permanently left Washington as well as the workforce.[28]

Women represented a smaller percentage of the overall student population than men. One contemporary study revealed that women in the postwar era were twice as likely to enter college as their mothers, but much less likely to graduate because they interrupted their education for marriage.[29] Because of women's lower graduation and overall participation rate (over 7.6 million veterans received some training under the program), the G.I. Bill did not necessarily provide Government Girls with the same widespread boost as men in academic and professional advancements.[30]

But opportunities for former Government Girls with or without additional education were available in Washington's burgeoning private sector. The city continued its rapid economic growth after the war. The total number of employees in private businesses nearly doubled between 1945 and 1950.[31] This upswing mirrored the trend around the country (with the exception of a mild recession in 1949). Financial columnist Joseph Livingston described the boom, "Economically, these postwar years have been like a lottery—a happy lottery: boys and girls getting out of college have had no difficulty finding jobs. And chances are that anybody who ventured into a business made good. It was a rarity not to."[32]

In the Washington area those businesses included restaurants, construction companies, department stores, barber and beauty shops, appliances and home goods (for the two million housing units built between 1950 and 1952 alone), electronics, and country clubs. This "strange world of plenty" was a contrast to wartime consumer restrictions and the region's aggregate buying power produced enough jobs for Government Girls who wanted to transfer their professional skills outside of public service.[33] Since clerical work paid more than sales jobs—two of the most prominent employment categories for women, as they were still sex-typed into what is called the "pink collar" professions—most Government Girls chose to remain in administrative positions.

Women could, for example, usually find an opportunity within the Research and Development industry. It emerged as one of the fastest growing fields in the Washington area. A wide range of scientific companies worked in collaboration with expanding public institutions like the Bureau of Aeronautics, National Institutes of Health, and the Naval Research Institute. Defense contractors in particular sprang up in Northern Virginia near the recently created Department of Defense (formed by the 1947 National Security Act) headquartered at the Pentagon. Within two decades after the war, local research and development firms employed one out of every thirty Washington area workers.[34] Government Girls had expertise to fit this growing need. Businesses sought out women with experience in government agencies or military offices as they had familiarity with the procedures and jargon of the field.

African-American Government Girls had little choice but to find postwar employment within the private sector. Initially, federal wartime work helped many local black women move out of domestic service positions and gain greater financial and personal freedom. Female African-American government employees increased from 8.4 percent to 19 percent of the federal workforce between 1938 and 1944.[35] However, once the national emergency ended, many of these women lost their positions in the first cycle of layoffs.

Grace Ridgely Drew held several positions within the National Labor Relations Board for the duration, but received a pink slip immediately after hostilities ended. "I was promoted, first to higher clerical jobs, then to professional jobs, so that by the end of the war my salary was $2,500," Grace recalled. "But that was also the end of my job. When the permanent workers came back from military service or jobs in wartime agencies, temporary workers were let go." She had impressed her bosses, and they recommended her for secretarial work to several private employers they knew in Washington. According to Grace, "They put me in touch with a man who was in the process of setting up a research office for a labor union. I met him and he hired me. I worked for that union for many years." Grace retired decades later without ever again working for the government.[36]

Grace's experience was not unique, but it was unusual. Although female clerical and sales jobs grew in both public and private quarters, black women faced increased competition from displaced white war workers. This resulted in many black women remaining segregated into service-oriented positions like food servers and housekeeping staff.[37] As late as 1960, only seventeen percent of all African-American women employed outside the home worked in white-collar jobs, compared to fifty-nine percent of their white female counterparts.[38]

Washington's postwar employment situation for black women closely mirrored this trend. Whether in government or private industry, the majority of the area's African-American women worked as unskilled labor. Historian Karen Tucker Anderson argues, "For black women, especially, what is significant about the war experience is the extent to which barriers remained intact."[39] Most African-American former Government Girls and servicewomen remained stymied by those barriers and the lack of professional opportunities. A 1946 Presidential Advisory Committee on Civil Rights report concluded that, because of racial discrimination, Washington's black workers often took jobs far below their ability levels. The Committee found that African Americans, "are confined to the lowest paid and least skilled jobs," because of their race rather than their aptitude.[40] Even African Americans who earned degrees or acquired skills were excluded from white-only trade unions and professional associations.

Clerical positions were similarly elusive. Alice Allison Dunnigan, who had to fudge local character references in order to secure housing when she initially arrived in D.C., worked her way up from being a typist to a professional grade employment classification during her stint at the Office of Price Administration. Yet, each time she arrived for a postwar government interview set up by the placement center, the supervisor insisted that no vacancy existed. Both Alice and her placement clerk became frustrated at the agencies' unwillingness to hire African Americans for office work. Alice found greater opportunity in the private sphere. She leveraged some previous newspaper experience into a reporter's position with the Associated Negro Press. She became chief of the organization's Washington Bureau and the first African-American woman to receive press credentials to cover the White House, State Department, and the Supreme Court. Alice's groundbreaking career proved the Presidential Advisory Committee correct in concluding that racism, and not ability, prevented employers from hiring African Americans.[41]

In 1940 only about twelve percent of all black workers in Washington held white-collar jobs. Two years after the war ended black workers still held fewer than fifteen percent of those positions.[42] Christine McCreary was in that small percentage. Her wartime secretarial work with Chairman Stuart Symington at the Surplus Property Board carried over to his tenure at the Reconstruction Finance Corporation, Air Force, and, finally, to his terms in the U.S. Senate. Christine's administrative role at that level of government generated disbelief, alienation, snide remarks, and resentment—even among other African Americans working on the custodial, cafeteria, and mail staffs. "It was just a lonesome time," she recalled about her first few years on Capitol Hill. Professional color barriers in D.C. took many forms.[43] The wartime exigencies that produced employment changes in federal and local policies and practices involving employment of African-American women disappeared as the labor scarcity subsided.

Whether former Government Girls undertook work in Washington's public or private sector, they all had to deal with a continued postwar housing crunch. Overcrowding remained a problem through the late 1950s, when vacancy rates still hovered between three and four percent. Competition for living space increased as the federal government began closing or selling area dormitories immediately after the war. American University, for example, bought the enormous WAVES Quarters D in Northwest for use as offices, dorms, and recreational facilities.[44] Howard University acquired dormitories built for African-American workers and utilized them for residential students.[45] The Army took over a portion of Arlington Farms and converted residences into housing for servicemen and their families at Fort Myer.[46] Arlington

National Cemetery absorbed the complex's remaining acreage for burials as well as a visitor's center and administration bureau. Temporary buildings on the National Mall became offices for expanding government agencies.[47] By the end of 1950 the government had divested all of its civilian dorms. Government Girls joined returning veterans and the rest of the area population in seeking affordable housing.

The shortage of available apartments and houses in the District hastened the migration of current and former Government Girls to the suburbs. Nearby counties like Arlington and Fairfax in Virginia and Montgomery and Prince George's in Maryland attracted thousands of workers and their families. Federal Housing Administration and Veteran's Administration loans often made buying a newly constructed home in the suburbs a better financial investment than renting an apartment in the city.[48] Planned improvements in transportation promised easier access to outlying areas, though it would be decades before the additions (new bridges across the Potomac and Anacostia Rivers, a beltway connecting Washington to close-in suburbs in both Maryland and Virginia, and a Metrorail system) were completed.[49] And modern shopping centers with plentiful parking and convenient evening hours offered shoppers goods and services previously available only in the city. At least five of downtown's largest department stores opened satellite branches to capitalize on this growing market. These developments contributed to Metropolitan Washington's suburban population doubling between 1940 and 1950.[50]

The majority of Government Girls who moved to the suburbs did so after getting married. Unlike some companies and state governments during the 1940s and 1950s, the federal government did not require women to resign once they became married. But Government Girls could still feel societal pressure to leave the workforce for the home. "It's a historical fact that after every war a campaign is made openly to drive women out of the offices and back to the kitchens," observed a local reporter.[51] The propaganda that helped battle social expectations in order to get women into wartime jobs now campaigned to get them out in hopes of restoring the prewar social order.

At the height of the conflict, Mary Anderson, Director of the Women's Bureau at the Department of Labor, identified employers and family members' concerns about changing gender roles as one of the obstacles women faced in finding work: "Some among us are worrying for fear [women] will not be willing to call it a good day's work and go home when the war is over and Johnny comes marching back for his job. That fear, which is so large a part of the prejudice against employment of women, is being used in subtle ways to keep us from making full use of that great reserve of labor."[52] Media campaigns launched by the Office of War Information (OWI) addressed these anxieties by emphasizing the temporary nature of women's, including Government Girls', war work.

Less than a year later, Frank Hines, the man in charge of orchestrating veterans' return to civilian jobs, spoke at a Washington conference about women's proper place in postwar society. "Let the women do the light and artistic things, the things requiring finesse," he argued. "Or perhaps better than any of these, the mothers of children and the makers of homes, for these are jobs too."[53] The Daughters of the American Revolution could not have agreed more. In 1947 they issued a statement reminding women, "The social order must now reassert itself. That is our job. That is our purpose." Women who did marry or have children, they argued, were simply selfish.[54] Whether officials were trying to get women into or out of wartime jobs, the message they promoted was that a woman's place in 1940s America was ideally in the home.

Government Girls did not necessarily need such formal pronouncements to feel public pressure to leave their jobs. Many received personal reminders on a near daily basis. WAVE Phyllis Paxton decoded messages at the Naval Communications Annex during the war and authorized special order discharges for Navy Personnel during demobilization. "I was at the bus one time and we still had to wear our uniforms to work," she recalled. "We didn't have to wear them otherwise, but we had to wear them at work. But I was at the bus and this woman said, 'Why

don't you go home. The war's over.'" Phyllis encountered open disapproval until she left the Navy to have her first child three years later.[55]

The popular press also promoted a return to the male-dominated
workplace by running articles with titles such as "Getting Rid of the
Women" and "Give Back the Jobs."[56] One magazine piece cautioned
Government Girls about the consequences of keeping their wartime
jobs: "Most social observers are of the opinion that just as there were
thousands of unmarried women in the capital after the last war, so too,
after this one there will be left a new generation of spinsters, living one
day on their hard-earned pensions."[57] Another warned women that government work would not guarantee long-term physical or emotional
stability. The reporter cautioned women to "picture yourself growing
older, a dependent in the home of relatives" before choosing a career
over marriage.[58]

Joanne Lichty met women from that previous "generation of spinsters" who chose careers. She worked as a typist in the Treasury Department with Government Girls dating back to World War I. "They
were mostly older single women that had no family of their own. That
was their life. That was their career—working as a clerk or typist or
something like that. It was all clerical work. Nothing real exciting," Joanne recalled of her possibly bored but seemingly stable co-workers. She
found nothing about these women's lives to warrant such alarm in the
media. "There was a feeling of camaraderie. I don't think it was just a
job. At least the way I remember it," Joanne observed about the veteran
female clerks and supervisors in the department. She was aware of the
intentional messages aimed at workers like her that, as Joanne put it, "It
was ok to do your part for the war effort, but once it was over you've got
to get back and act like a woman. Like a lady, excuse me, like a lady."[59]

Whether it was because of the social pressure, fear of becoming a
spinster employee, or the fact that most Government Girls were single
and fit the average age range for marriage, many of the capital's clerical
corps chose to leave the office and become housewives and mothers.
They seemed to agree with former Government Girl Claire Shrivener's

assessment that, "The main goal in those days was to get married and have a family."[60] The number of American marriages reached a twentieth-century peak between 1945 and 1950.[61] The 1950 marriage rate in D.C. ranked as the second highest among major U.S. cities. As one local reporter phrased it, Washington earned "a score of 120.8 brides for every 1000 spinsters."[62]

The accompanying baby boom kept thousands of former Government Girls concerned with childrearing responsibilities. Between 1946 and 1951, a record twenty-two million babies were born in the U.S. The birthrate in Washington during those years peaked at 28,926 in 1950. This was over 5,000 more babies than were born at the height of the war, and over 13,000 more than were born a decade earlier.[63] Former federal court clerk and embassy employee Elizabeth Delean became part of this trend. Elizabeth quit working to have the first of her seven children and remained home to care for the family as they relocated around the country with each of her husband's career promotions.[64] Likewise, Leonora Haag, a wartime secretary at the White House and president of the Government Girls Club, left her prestigious position to move to Delaware with her husband and raise their two daughters.[65]

These women became part of the widespread focus on traditional home life that historian Stephanie Coontz analyzed in her research of marriage trends. Coontz concludes that this emphasis was partly a reaction to the physical and emotional deprivations of war and partly derived from government and social incentives such as military benefits to married veterans, federal income tax regulations favoring male-headed married households, and a cultural emphasis on achieving personal happiness through marriage.[66] An attempt to fit into established social roles and create marital harmony was the reason Ellen Stiles quit her job at the Air Force Foreign Assignments Branch. She left to please her husband. "It wasn't that he was against women working," Ellen recalled. "He wanted me home for all the family's sake."[67] Navy illustrator Guinn Cooper concurred, "I didn't even think about not leaving work after I got married. It was just expected. Just something you did."[68] Although women sometimes returned to work once their children got older or started school, many felt economic or cultural pressure to stay at home immediately after their babies were born. Numerous Government Girls followed suit and left the workforce for several years or for good.

The return to prewar marriage traditions was by no means absolute. Living without male supervision and developing individual skills and confidence made it possible for Government Girls to imagine social and economic possibilities less feasible before the war. Calista Wehrli enjoyed the sense of independence and acceptance that she experienced in Washington during her military service as a Marine. Although she dated and maintained close friendships with several men over the years, Calista made the conscious decision to remain single and develop her career. She used her wartime training as a recreational instructor to work as a physical education teacher at high schools and universities throughout California.[69] Likewise, Virginia Edwards chose to fulfill her professional ambitions over domestic considerations. When Virginia's boyfriend drove her in his old black Buick to become a Government Girl, he jokingly told her, "If you're not a success, I don't want to see you again." She did earn success, but she never did return to her rural Virginia hometown. Virginia parlayed her experience at the Federal Trade Commission into postwar work at the Agency for International Development. This often took her overseas to Turkey, Nepal, Brazil, and Israel—places she never dreamed she would see. She also took periodic night classes at George Washington University. Virginia started college in 1947 and graduated thirty years later. Along the way, she decided not to marry or have children. "I think it was that breaking away from home when we were so young," Virginia speculated. "We were just cut off from the idea of family."[70]

Some men who worked alongside Government Girls in wartime Washington also carried new insight into expectations for marriage. Stephen Kanyusik, who worked at the Naval Air Station photo lab with over four hundred WAVES, readily admitted that this changed his mindset. Stephen remembered: "That was my first experience of working with women, and they were better and more diligent, more orientated towards duty and working than the men were. They were good.... That's why I firmly started in marriage knowing the woman could do many more things than men could do."[71] Whether they maintained a more traditional or progressive home life, by 1956 over half of Washington's families relocated beyond the city limits.[72]

The impact of this shift out to the suburbs went beyond mere population numbers. Suburban growth extended the area of urban influence, bringing the habits, values, and ideological beliefs of the World War II workforce to previously rural and conservative areas. These changes affected the political climate of the metropolitan region. As early as 1946, women's voices in area politics rang louder than in any previous election year. *Washington Post* reporter Malvina Lindsay, who wrote a column called "The Gentler Sex," followed the trend of women who were "dirtying their skirts in politics as a public duty."[73] She identified contemporary female candidates and campaigners as individuals who had long used indirect approaches for societal change through letter writing to elected officials, joining social and philanthropic clubs, attending forums and study classes, but who, because of their wartime experiences, felt the time had come for direct action.[74]

That action reflected beliefs not always in tune with existing local practices. By 1946, Dorothy Dennison, a resident of the northern Virginia suburb of Vienna, observed changes in racial segregation beginning to occur. Most notably the separate schools for black and white children merged into one larger facility. She credited the change with the advocacy of wartime women who moved into the area from all over the country and brought their more progressive views on race with them. "Coming from Massachusetts it was shocking to see segregation," Dennison remembered. "I knew about it, but being in it was much different."[75] Although local women failed to make immediate political inroads, their presence in suburban affairs remained steady. By the 1960s they were regularly winning elections to local offices and changing the shape of suburban politics.[76]

The experience of former Government Girl Pauline Menes, one of the political newcomers, epitomizes how suburban ideological transformations took place. Pauline left the government after giving birth to her first child. She and her husband (whom she met while training him as her replacement at the Quartermaster General's office), both liberal Democrats, moved into a new development in what had traditionally been a conservative rural farming area of Prince George's County. Pauline got involved with local affairs because she and another young transplant sought information on voter registration. During their investigation, the two women were recruited to help administer local elections. Pauline met other newcomers with similar beliefs, and soon worked on campaigns attempting to elect progressive candidates who dealt with issues important to the new, younger residents (such as school additions, commuter taxes, and civil rights). She became a state delegate herself in 1966, an election year with more female candidates than ever before in the county, including several other former war workers. Pauline remained in elected office for the next forty years.[77]

Women's increasing political and community influence reached beyond the D.C. area and liberal causes. The GOP labeled 1966 the "Year of the Woman," because of the high percentage of women running for office.[78] However, the types of changes made by permanently transplanted Government Girls and their families leaned towards the progressive, creating a more liberal political base in the Maryland and Virginia settlements closest to the Washington border. Maryland State Senator William Hodges, a self-described "old school politico," recognized this transformation, as it was reflected in the make-up of the state's legislature. In 1966 Hodges complained, "I don't know whether that's going to carry—all that liberal thinking in here... It's a strange set-up."[79]

Five years later Helen Levine Koss, another former Government Girl and liberal community organizer, won a seat in the Maryland General Assembly representing Montgomery County. She spent sixteen years fighting for legislation such as eliminating sex and age discrimination in financial transactions and approvals, passing the Maryland Equal Rights Amendment, and establishing the first center to counsel and train homemakers for economic independence. Although 1966 served as a benchmark, Government Girls' influence carried on for decades.

In addition to instigating changes in the political climate of the Washington area, Government Girls helped pave the way for social changes. Most notably, the cultural acceptance of Washington's postwar "bachelor girl."[80] The sensational attention paid to Government Girls by the media virtually stopped once the war ended. By 1945 the OWI no longer ran propaganda campaigns aimed at recruiting women into the workforce, and the federal government had started to reduce its forces in Washington. The iconic Government Girl featured in movies, magazines and on radio went from national ideal to local interest. The press still covered Government Girls as part of the Washington scene, but the glorification and glamorization of her appearance, attitude, and activities subsided. The term began to once again identify the occupation of a young woman rather than refer to a constructed persona. Even when federal agencies recruited additional administrative forces during the Korean War, media attention paid to Government Girls remained nominal. The moniker gradually disappeared in the 1960s.

The term bachelor girl co-existed and eventually usurped Government Girl as shorthand to describe the single, independent women who "work for the love of working and take pride in playing a part in the pulsating life of their nation's capital."[81] This latest incarnation was not solely defined by her work with the federal government. Bachelor girl referred to any unmarried young woman working on her own in the city. However, she was characterized and treated very similarly to World War II Government Girls.

"That Washington bachelors are badly spoiled is a well-known fact. A big reason is the number of pretty girls in town who are bachelor girls... She is unique to this generation. It is only in her time that jobs for girls have been the rule rather than the exception," explained one local reporter.[82] The press highlighted her appearance, whimsical lifestyle and adventures, and offered advice on how to decorate, dress, and entertain. The emphasis was again on the personal rather than the professional. But media coverage also showed tolerance for both.

"Today, living alone is as acceptable for women as smoking and drinking publicly. Not an eyebrow is raised at the bachelor girl who maintains her own apartment as long as it's clean and well run," insisted a supporter of this new generation of working women.[83] Even the well-respected advice columnist Mary Haworth argued that, "many nice girls today choose to 'shove off' into bachelor-girl living as an alternative to getting married."[84] In 1961, *Potomac*, the forerunner to the *Washington Post Magazine*, featured four attractive, professional young women striding confidently toward the camera on the cover of its debut issue. "They Don't Want To Go Home" ran the headline. A three-page photographic spread inside showed how "Four Career Girls Enjoy Bright, Busy Lives." The article reveals organized, efficient, focused, and happy women both at home and in the office.[85] Similar to the World War II propaganda on Government Girls, assurances that young single women living in Washington could remain "nice" and "bright" could help alleviate familial questions or fears about their physical and moral safety.

In the postwar period, officials stopped publicly obsessing about bachelor girls' sex lives and started worrying about men's. The spotlight shifted from young women having premarital sex to grown men engaging in sex with each other. In 1950 a representative from the State Department generated national interest when he testified before a senate committee that ninety-one employees had been fired within the previous three years for being gay. This ignited anxieties over "sexual deviants" infiltrating the government and led to widespread investigations. Furthermore, President Eisenhower issued Executive Order 10450 in 1953, which mandated the firing of any federal worker found guilty of what was nebulously termed "sexual perversion." Gays and lesbians in the civil service were labeled security risks on par with Communists because their secret lifestyle supposedly made them vulnerable to blackmail. This witch-hunt, dubbed "panic on the Potomac" by *New York Post* columnist Max Lerner, continued throughout the 1950s and 1960s. Washington's gay community organized and fought back through legal means and direct protests during these same decades.[86] Such activities directed the attention of authorities and the media away from pervasive concerns over bachelor girls' intimate behavior.

The young women did still receive occasional editorial reminders that "premature sexual experimentation" could lead to disappointment and endanger their "capacity for permanent human relationships and therefore [their] interest in marriage and lasting friendships."[87] But the public preoccupation about women's safety and virginity relaxed after the war, since government and city officials no longer felt overwhelmingly responsible for them. Bachelor girls worked in the city through personal choice and not because they were putting themselves at risk for the war effort.

Social acceptance of bachelor girls did not indicate unconditional approval of career women. One argument in favor of the bachelor girl was that she gained valuable experience for becoming a wife and mother. A woman who lived on her own before marriage developed household skills and avoided the "bride's traditional helplessness to boil an egg."[88] Even presidential daughter and operatic hopeful Margaret Truman, the city's "No. 1 bachelor girl," could expect accolades for her independence only "from the time she graduates until the time she marries" according to an etiquette expert.[89]

Bachelor girls had greater opportunities and freedom than ever before. But pressure to eventually relinquish work and follow traditional roles remained. An article titled "Marriage or Career? They Count on Both!" did not encourage bachelor girls to pursue work and marriage at the same time, but rather as successive steps along life's journey.[90] After all, as Pulitzer Prize-winning journalist Meg Greenfield recalled, "The Washington I came to in 1961 was known as 'a man's town,' and that's exactly what it was."[91] Marian Norby agreed. She worked for the Foreign Economic Administration during World War II and then built a successful postwar career at the White House and the Air Force before retiring in 1980. "I saw how women were treated," she recounted. "Secretaries were like furniture. They went with the office." Marian chose to challenge the restrictions and dismissals she witnessed in Washington. She became one of the founding members of the local chapter of the National Organization for Women and lobbied for the passage of the Equal Rights Amendment.[92] Government Girls helped stretch the boundaries of acceptable behavior for Washington's postwar workforce, but bachelor girls still lived under society's conventional expectations for women.

While Government Girls upset several longstanding customs, their influence did nothing to alleviate systemic racial tensions within the city. Although black and white women interacted in professional and recreational arenas during the war, postwar cultural barriers remained intact. Because black women generally disappeared from government service and white women's migration out to the suburbs created a geographic boundary between races, social relations between the two groups stayed limited—sometimes by design.

Washington native Georgia Herron and her growing family moved to the Takoma Park neighborhood just outside of the District line in 1948. She looked forward to living on the beautiful street of single-family Victorians and starting her new job as an elementary school science teacher. But immediately after the Herrons became the first African Americans to buy a house on their block, several white families put their homes up for sale.[93] Washington's black community continued its campaign for equality and made several groundbreaking strides to end segregation through postwar protests, boycotts, and legal action. But longstanding contentions kept residential Washington mainly functioning as two separate communities.[94]

The economic and population growth during World War II would have changed Washington with or without the Lipstick Brigade. But the fact that Government Girls made up so much of the city's wartime population determined what the lasting postwar changes in Washington would be. They forged a continued presence in federal agencies; greater opportunities and appreciation of women's skills and abilities in the area's private workforce; breaking of racial and political barriers; and the acceptance of bachelor girls into what had been largely traditional professional and social systems. SPAR residence hall manager Marion Tompkins did not know where or if she would fit into this new, dynamic Washington once the war ended. "I really didn't even look forward to going home again. Life was so much more interesting. I didn't know what I wanted to do. My job was there, but I didn't want to go back to it," Marion recalled. She finally decided to build on the skills she developed in the service and used the G.I. Bill to earn a degree in hotel hospitality. She enrolled in Paul Smith's College near her hometown in upstate New York. She met a man at school, got married, had children, and worked in management for over twenty years. While Marion chose not to remain in the nation's capital, she felt as transformed by the city as it was by the Government Girls. "I'll always be grateful," Marion firmly asserts. "It changed my whole life."[95]

On the cusp of World War II, the *New York Times* declared, "The capital has been captured and subdued by an army of young women workers, 80,000 strong."[96] By the end of the war, that number of Government Girls would almost double, and rather than subdue Washington, they lit it on fire.

Notes

[1] As quoted in Betsy Israel, *Bachelor Girl: The Secret History of Single Women in the Twentieth Century* (New York: William Morrow, 2002), 149.

[2] Wilda Beeby Collection (AFC/2001/001/9304), VHP.

[3] Marion S. Tompkins Collection (AFC/2001/001/18663), VHP.

[4] Roland Nicholson, "Screaming Crowds Welcome Peace In Hilarious Spree," *Washington Times-Herald*, August 15, 1945, 1.

[5] Freda Segal Collection (AFC/2001/001/30833), VHP.

[6] Scott Hart, *Washington at War: 1941-1945* (New Jersey: Prentice-Hall, Inc., 1970), 275.

[7] U.S. Department of Commerce, Bureau of the Census, Statistical Abstract of the United States, "Provisional Estimates of Population by States," (Washington, D.C.: Government Printing Office, 1940 to 1960 editions); Washington Board of Trade, Postwar

Planning Committee, "A Survey of Washington and Its Environs," June 20, 1945, 1, GWU.

[8] David Brinkley, *Washington Goes to War* (New York: Alfred A. Knopf, 1988), 281-2.

[9] Margaret C. Rung, "Paternalism and Pink Collars: Gender and Federal Employee Relations, 1941-50," *Business History Review* 71 (Autumn 1997): 383.

[10] James B. Reston, "L'Enfant's Capital and Boomtown, Too," *New York Times*, June 1, 1941, SM23.

[11] "A Survey of Washington and Its Environs," 3.

[12] "Government Girls' Ranks Are Thinning," *Washington Post*, December 7, 1946, 12.

[13] Pauline Menes interview with author, May 11, 2006.

[14] "Dorothy Finley Wilbur Obituary," *Washington Post*, August 13, 2005, B6.

[15] Melvin Altshuler, "Government Girls Find New Horizons," *Washington Post*, March 8, 1951, S1.

[16] Jerry Kluttz, "Many Letters Protest Women in Federal Jobs," *Washington Post*, January 10, 1947, 9.

[17] Vila L. Hunter Obituary, *Washington Post*, January 28, 2006, C6.

[18] Jerry Kluttz, "Uniformed Girls in D.C. To Disappear Shortly," *Washington Post*, November 2, 1945, 12.

[19] Antoinette Loezere interview with Kate Scott, January 5, 2004, WIMSA.

[20] "Penelope P.P. Smith Obituary," *Washington Post*, June 4, 2006, C8.

[21] Jerry Kluttz, "Knox Finds WAVES More Efficient," *Washington Post*, March 4, 1943, B1.

[22] Elizabeth F. Splaine interview with Kate Scott, April 16, 2004, WIMSA; "The Coast Guard/NOAA Retirees' Newsletter," January-March 2010, 14.

[23] Vicki L. Friedl, *Women in the United States Military, 1901-1995* (Westport, Connecticut: Greenwood Press, 1996), 12-13.

[24] WAACs (the Women's Army Auxiliary Corps before it became the Women's Army Corps, a part of the regular Army in 1943) and WASPS (Women Air Force Service Pilots) were not eligible for the G.I. Bill because they were not officially part of the military. In the late 1970s and early 1980s, after a nearly thirty-year campaign for recognition and inclusion, the two groups were awarded the benefits. For most women, it was too late to take advantage of its provisions.

[25] Peter A. Soderburgh, *Women Marines: The World War II Era* (Westport, Connecticut: Praeger, 1992), 159.

[26] Margery Updegraff interview with Wanda Driver and Ardith Kramer, November 19, 2003, WIMSA.

[27] Biographical Notes, Box 1, Dorothy Gondos Beers Papers, American University Library Special Collection.

[28] Elizabeth Bigelow Stewart Collection (AFC/2001/001/68970), VHP.

[29] Elaine Tyler May, *Homeward Bound: American Families in the Cold War Era* (New York: Basic Books, 1988), 78-80.

[30] For in-depth discussions on the effect of the G.I. Bill, see Suzanne Mettler, *Soldiers to Citizens: The G.I. Bill and the Making of the Greatest Generation* (New York: Oxford University Press, 2005) and Keith W. Olson, *The G.I. Bill, the Veterans, and the Colleges* (Lexington: University Press of Kentucky, 1974).

[31] Washington Board of Trade, Postwar Planning Committee, "Postwar Plans of Metropolitan Washington Employers: A Survey for the Postwar Planning Committee" (Princeton, New Jersey: Opinion Research Corporation, 1945), 1, GWU; Keith Melder, *City of Magnificent Intentions: A History of Washington, District of Columbia* (D.C. and Silver Spring, Maryland: Intac, Inc., 1997), 501.

[32] "Postwar Housing Boom on Wane, Says Loan Board," *Washington Post*, August 10, 1952, R6; J.A. Livington, "Postwar Boom Brings Upturn of 22% in 'Own Boss' Ventures," *Washington Post*, September 12, 1952, 22.

[33] J.A. Livington, "Postwar Youngsters Taste Living in Non-Boom World," *Washington Post*, March 31, 1954, 25.

[34] William Graves, "Washington: The City Freedom Built," *National Geographic* (December, 1964): 774.

[35] Doris Kearns Goodwin, *No Ordinary Time: Franklin and Eleanor Roosevelt: The Home Front in World War II* (New York: Simon & Schuster, 1994), 540.

[36] Grace Ridgeley Drew, "Everything was Segregated" in Pauline E. Parker, ed., *Women of the Homefront: World War II Recollections of 55 Americans* (North Carolina: McFarland & Co. Inc., 2002), 75-77.

[37] Darlene Clark Hine, ed., *Black Women in America: An Historical Encyclopedia* (Brooklyn, New York: Carlson Publishing, Inc., 1993), 1292.

[38] Jesse Carney Smith and Carrell Peterson Horton, eds., *Historical Statistics of Black America: Agriculture to Labor and Employment* (Detroit, Michigan: Gale Research, Inc.: 1995), 1089.

[39] Karen Tucker Anderson, "Last Hired, First Fired: Black Women Workers During World War II," *Journal of American History* 69, no. 1 (June 1982): 91, 97.

[40] Committee on Civil Rights, "Racial Discrimination in Washington, D.C.," in Mortimer J. Adler, ed., *The Negro in American History I. Black Americans 1928-1971* (Encyclopedia Britannica Educational Corporation, 1971), 369, 373; James A. Pawley, "Jobs Held Limited For Area Negroes," *Washington Post*, June 5, 1949, F11.

[41] Alice Allison Dunnigan, Black Woman's Experience: From the School House to the White House (Philadelphia: Dorrance & Co., 1974), 203-4.

[42] "Board of Trade Newsletter," Volume 6, Number 6 (August 22, 1960): 2, Record Group IX: Publications, Box 185-2, Board of Trade Newsletters, 1960-1961 Folder, GWU.

[43] "Christine S. McCreary, Staff of Senator Stuart Symington, 1953-1977 and Senator John Glenn, 1977-1998," Oral History Interviews, Senate Historical Office, Washington, D.C., May 19, 1998, 17.

[44] Betty Wixcey, "They're Getting Ready to Go Home," *Washington Evening Star*, June 20, 1946, C3-5.

[45] "U.S. to Close Three Resident Halls for Girls," *Washington Post*, September 27, 1947, B1.

[46] Dorothea Andrews, "Arlington Farm Soon To Be a Memory to G-Girls," *Washington Post*, July 23, 1950, M10.

[47] "Dormitories To Be Used For Office," *Washington Post*, August 6, 1949, B1.

[48] Before World War II, mortgage lenders often required fifty percent of the purchase price of a home as down payment and typically issued five to ten year loans. The Federal Housing Administration required only five to ten percent down and guaranteed mortgages for up to thirty years at low interest rates. The Veteran's Administration asked for a single dollar as down payment from prospective homeowners. Stephanie Coontz, *The Way We Never Were: American Families and the Nostalgia Trap* (New York: Basic Books, 1992), 77.

[49] See Zachary Moses Schrag, *The Great Society Subway: A History of the Washington Metro* (Baltimore: Johns Hopkins University Press, 2006) for further discussion of Washington's postwar mass transit systems.

[50] "Board of Trade Newsletter," Vol. 6, No. 4, June 23, 1960, 1, Record Group IX: Publications, Box 185-2, Board of Trade Newsletters, 1958-1959 Folder, GWU.

[51] Jerry Kluttz, "Men Again Taking Girls' Federal Jobs," *Washington Post*, February 1, 1946, 16.

[52] Mary Anderson, "16,000,000 Women at Work," *New York Times*, July 18, 1943, SM18.

[53] "Address of Brigadier General Frank T. Hines, Administrator, Retraining and Reemployment, Office of War Mobilization, Before the Conference on War and Postwar Employment, Washington, D.C., May 5, 1944," 1, 1944, War Manpower Commission Records, RG 211, Box 32, NARA.

[54] Israel, Bachelor Girl, 175.

[55] Phyllis Paxton Collection (AFC/2001/001/64009), VHP.

[56] "Getting Rid of the Women," Atlantic (June 1945): 79-82; "Give Back the Jobs," Woman's Home Companion (February 1943): 56.

[57] Sally Reston, "Girls' Town – Washington," *New York Times*, November 23, 1941, SM22.

[58] Tom Dryer, "Foretaste of Fear," *Washington Post*, June 14, 1945, 8.

[59] Joanne Lichty interview with author, July 29, 2004.

[60] Claire Shrivener interview with author, June 4, 2004.

[61] This was despite an immediate postwar increase in the national divorce rate. U.S. divorces reached a record high of 610,000 in 1946. Washingtonians and local media

attributed the divorce rate to impetuous wartime marriages, incompatibility, money problems, and postwar return to routine life. Women's wartime employment did not appear as a probable reason. "Causes of Divorce as Seen By Six District Residences, *Washington Post*, April 21, 1947, 2; "U.S. Divorce Rate Declines 7 Percent," *Washington Post*, December 2, 1950, B14; "Divorce Rate Trend Still Downward," *Washington Post*, October 18, 1948, 7; May, *Homeward Bound*, 5-7.

62 Glendy Culligan, "Your Chances of Marriage are Darned Good Here," *Washington Post*, September 23, 1951, S1.

63 Bureau of Vital Statistics, Health Department, "Live Births Reported in the District of Columbia—1940-150," August 22, 1951, Statistics, Vital Birth Regislation Folder, DCPL.

64 Elizabeth Delean Cozad interview with author, June 14, 2004.

65 "Leonora Haag Obituary," *Washington Post*, August 10, 2006, B5.

66 Stephanie Coontz, *Marriage, A History: From Obedience to Intimacy or How Love Conquered Marriage* (New York: Viking, 2005), 220-225.

67 Ellen Stiles interview with author, November 5, 2004.

68 Guinn Cooper interview with author, August 2, 2004.

69 Calista Wehrli interview with author, July 7, 2003.

70 "The War Girls," *Washington Post*, January 28, 1997, 22.

71 Stephen Kanyusik interview with author, August 3, 2004.

72 S. Oliver Goodman, "Are Business Upsurge Brings Fresh Records," *Washington Post and Times Herald*, January 4, 1956, 33.

73 Malvina Lindsay, "Women on the Stump," *Washington Post*, May 28, 1946, 16.

74 Malvina Lindsay, "Women Take the Plunge," *Washington Post*, April 26, 1946, 14; Malvina Lindsay, "Can Women Lead," *Washington Post*, July 2, 1946, 14.

75 Dorothy Dennison interview with author, July 19, 2004.

76 Richard Homan, "Learning About Lawmaking," Washington Times-Herald, November 23, 1966, B1; Walter B. Douglas, "Women Eye School Vote Plan," *Washington Times-Herald*, February 20, 1966, B2.

77 Menes, interview.

78 Marie Smith, "It's 'Year of the Woman' in GOP Politics," *Washington Times-Herald*, October 21, 1966, C4.

79 Richard Homan, "Learning About Lawmaking," *Washington Times-Herald*, November 23, 1966, B1.

80 For evolution of the term see Israel, *Bachelor Girl*, 98-100, 110-2, 174-5.

81 Marjorie Binford Woods, "Marriage or Career? They Count on Both!" *Washington Post*, March 3, 1946, S1.

82 Elizabeth Maguire, "A Washington Miss Must Be a Hit As a Hostess, Careerist and Playgirl," *Washington Post*, July 10, 1949, S1.

[83] Cora Carlyle, "Living Alone Can Have Its Benefits, Too," *Washington Post*, August 1, 1950, B11.

[84] Mary Haworth, "Bachelor Girl Asks 'Moving Question," *Washington Post*, April 23, 1959, C14.

[85] Al Horne, "When Women Were 'Girls,'" *Washington Post*, February 2, 1986, SM28-31.

[86] See David K. Johnson, "'Homosexual Citizens': Washington's Gay Community Confronts the Civil Service," *Washington History* 6, no. 2 (Fall/Winter 1994-95): 45-63.

[87] Agnes E. Meyer, "'Sex Freedom' Is the Path of Delusion," *Washington Post*, August 17, 1950, B13.

[88] Carlyle, "Living Alone Can Have Its Benefits, Too," B11.

[89] Elizabeth Maguire, "A Washington Miss Must Be a Hit As a Hostess, Careerist and Playgirl," *Washington Post*, July 10, 1949, S1.

[90] Woods, "Marriage or Career? They Count on Both!" S1.

[91] Meg Greenfield, *Washington* (New York: Public Affairs, 2001), 114.

[92] "The War Girls," 22.

[93] Georgia Herron interview with author, March 31, 2011.

[94] In 1949 the Catholic Archdiocese of Washington desegregated its educational institutions. In 1953 the U.S. Supreme Court ruled that segregation in Washington was unconstitutional in District of Columbia v. John R. Thompson Co. and in 1954 the locally based Bolling v. Sharpe became part of the landmark Brown v. Board of Education Supreme Court decision declaring separate education unconstitutional. For discussion on local postwar civil rights gains see David A. Nichols, "'The Showpiece of Our Nation': Dwight D. Eisenhower and the Desegregation of the District of Columbia," *Washington History* 16, no.2 (Fall/Winter 2004-2005): 44-65.

[95] Tompkins, interview.

[96] Reston, "Girls' Town," SM8.

Conclusion

How did it affect my life? It was pervasive in ways I would have to stop and think about to even tell you. But it was something you can't forget. Something that says in a way you are part of a much larger community than you think you are. And what you do counts.

~PEARL SCHER, MARINE CORPS[1]

overnment Girls saw opportunity and seized it. They were not fictional, one-dimensional patriotic pin ups. They were not romantic Hollywood archetypes. And they were not wild, sex-crazed coeds on an extended wartime version of spring break. The young women who made up the so-called Lipstick Brigade wanted to change their lives and saw coming to wartime Washington as the chance to do so. "All of this was like someone opened a door, opened a light and the light was shining saying here is something that you can do. And I agreed," Anna Fogelman reminisced. "It really was the first time that I had the chance to learn that I could make a choice as to what I was going to do with my life. And what would happen to me later."[2] By consciously walking through that door and becoming a Government Girl, Anna altered the course of her life. After the war Anna went to college on the GI Bill and then got her master's degree, traveled, and had a professional career—

239

none of which would have been possible had she stayed home during the war.

Although Government Girls hoped to determine their own futures, they were not necessarily out to change the world. They were trying to get through the war like everyone else- day by day. Each woman had a unique experience in Washington and in the war. Some hated it, some loved it, some felt changed by it, others saw it as a benchmark in their lives, and many viewed it as one brief sojourn on the journey of their lives that, on reflection, seemed heightened in memory for good or for bad. As Army WAC Demeris Black Schebig recalled of her time in D.C., "It was an experience of a lifetime. It was what I thought it would be. It was adventurous, believe me. Lots of stories that you remember. Rough times but they were fun because you had other people in the same boat with you doing the same things. I was just proud to have been there. It was a fun time in my life."[3]

Despite pervasive, and often dangerous, living and working difficulties, Government Girls' experiences in Washington gave women professional and personal skills they would use for the rest of their lives. Not only did they work in new and different jobs and earn needed money, but as they persevered and succeeded, they gained self confidence and personal affirmation of their strength, skills, and endurance. Women found the knowledge that they could financially support themselves empowering. Charlotte Millan who had borrowed $300 from a local bank to relocate to Washington from South Dakota, felt the investment in herself more than paid off. Charlotte became a housewife after the war, but needed to work during a brief separation from her husband. Because of her previous experience, Charlotte found a job that provided enough money to care for herself and her young son. Knowing that she could survive on her own allowed Charlotte to approach her marriage and her life differently. She relied on that knowledge a few years later when her husband died and she needed to support her two children.[4] The majority of women in Washington did not experience the war as some kind of cultural atomic bomb that shattered their prewar existence. But it changed them on many levels, often in ways revealed only as time and circumstances challenged them.

In 1942 journalist Marquis Childs tried to explain the challenge of covering wartime Washington, "So much is happening that it is possible to know only fragments. Tremendous changes take place and are hardly reflected on the churned up surface. We are all caught up in it, high and low."[5] World War II was the defining event in the lives of millions of men and women. And yet, as Childs wrote at the time, it is still difficult to piece together the full picture of its impact. This may be why, after almost seventy years, Americans continue to celebrate, memorialize, and analyze the war in articles, books, films, television programs, museums, monuments, and yearly tributes.

It's popular to herald the American men and women who experienced and fought in World War II—newsman and author Tom Brokaw famously labeled them "The Greatest Generation"[6]—as somehow different and better than the rest of us. It seemed they had to be in order to meet the challenges of the extraordinary circumstances they faced. But the hundreds of interviews I conducted or examined for this book prove that claim wrong. Government Girls were exactly like us. They confronted the war with hope, fear, doubt, disappointment, frustration, determination, and resignation. Most of them simply did what they felt they had to do in order to make it through the war and provide themselves with a future. No one knew how things would turn out. And that's what makes these women so much more impressive. They show us what we're all capable of. Greatness doesn't always come in the form of grand gestures and famous deeds. It's often the seemingly ordinary incidents that lead to great feats.

Government Girls did not necessarily aim for recognition either. They chose to participate in the war effort in accordance with their own needs, abilities, courage, and sense of duty. But by doing so they gained more than just a job for the duration. As Lilly Hogan simply put it, "I grew up during the Depression. I think I was looking as a way to better myself. I grew up in a poor family. I wanted to go to college but we couldn't afford it. I was just looking for something better. It was the best thing I ever did for myself... It fulfilled my dreams."[7]

Notes

[1] Pearl Crystal Scher Collection (AFC/2001/001/25482), VHP.

[2] Anna Florence Fogelman Collection (AFC/2001/001/33598), VHP.

[3] Demaris L. Schebig Collection (AFC/2001/001/66005), VHP.

[4] Wayne Millan interview with author, September 22, 2006.

[5] Marquis Childs, "I Write from Washington" in Katharine Graham, ed., *Katharine Graham's Washington* (New York: Alfred A. Knopf, 2002), 289.

[6] Tom Brokaw, *The Greatest Generation* (New York: Random House, 1998).

[7] Lilly Loise Hogan Collection (AFC/2001/001/30446), VHP.

Acknowledgements

For welcoming me into their homes and their memories, I wish to express my gratitude to the women and men who agreed to share their personal stories with me.

I am variously and often profoundly indebted to the following kind people:

Peter Kuznick, Donald Ritchie, Valerie French, and Laura Kamoie for their valuable comments and suggestions on portions of the manuscript.

I thank the legendary John Taylor at the National Archives, Britta Granrud at the Women In Military Service For America Memorial Foundation, and Alexa Potter at Library of Congress for their invaluable research assistance.

I am grateful to the Association of Oldest Inhabitants of D.C., most notably Bill and Pat Brown, Robert Barbuto, Georgia Herron, Mary Brown, and Austin Kiplinger, for generously offering insights and extraordinary access to the living history of the nation's capital.

My family has played an important part as first readers and listeners on this project as it moved forward through each phase of its development. I thank Lisa Regnante for her astute, insightful, and incomparable guidance. Tom, Charles, Thomas and Calvin Regnante gave their enthusiasm and support from conception to completion.

I am eternally grateful to Charles and Alberta Gueli for being fierce, ceaseless, exhaustive, and irreplaceable editors, advisors, and champions of this project, as they are with every project I undertake. I am also indebted to them for hours spent on the National Mall handing out flyers and soliciting interviews during the World War II Memorial dedication weekend.

I owe a great debt to Alec Farr for the constructive ideas, exceptional and tireless feedback, editorial counsel, and steadfast encouragement. How fortunate I am to have his support and friendship.

And I am grateful to my ever-present dog Watson for being a truly exceptional writing companion.

Photo Credits

INTRODUCTION
Courtesy of the *Washington Post*

SECTION 1
Library of Congress: 49 (top), 50, 53, 54, 55, 56, 57, 58 (top), 59 (top), 63, 64, 65, 66
Women in Military Service For America Foundation, Inc.: 52, 58, 60, 61, 62, 67
National Archives: 48, 49
District of Columbia Public Library, Washingtoniana Division: 51
Acme News Photos: 50 (top), 51 (top)
Courtesy of University Archives and Special Collections, American University Library: 59
Courtesy of Joanne Lichty: 54 (top)
Courtesy of Elizabeth Delean: 56 (top)
Author's Private Collection: 57 (top)

SECTION 2
Library of Congress: 168 (top), 169, 170, 171, 172, 173, 174, 175, 177, 178 (top)
Women in Military Service For America Foundation, Inc.: 174 (top), 178
District of Columbia Public Library, Washingtoniana Division: 167, 176 (top)
Acme News Photos: 167 (top), 170 (top), 173 (top)
National Archives: 169 (top)
Courtesy of University Archives and Special Collections, American University Library: 168
DC Comics: 172 (top)
Courtesy of Maryland State Archives: 177
Courtesy of Stephen Kanyusik: 176
Author's Private Collection: 166, 177 (top, middle)

Bibliography

AUTHOR'S INTERVIEWS

Anne Treske Bahny
Mary E. Brown
Mary Connolly
Guinn Cooper
Elizabeth Delean Cozad
Margaret and Jim Crook
Lucille Davis
Barbara deFranceaux
Dorothy Dennison
Jane Fowler
Georgia Herron
Stephen E. Kanyusik
Austin H. Kiplinger
Joanne Lichty

Pauline Menes
Elizabeth McIntosh
Anne McLaughlin
Wayne Millan
Hope Ribbeck Nussbaum
Loretta Pattison
Virginia Scagliarini
Claire Shrivener
Sibyl Smith
Ellen Stiles
Bill Tamminga
John Taylor
Shirley Weinberger
Calista Wehrli

ORAL HISTORY COLLECTIONS

Veterans History Project, Library of Congress

Betty E. Allan
Bonita Orr Bailey
Ellenora Spratt Barker
Ruth Alberta Batic
Frances Green Loehr Beales
Wilda Beeby
Janice M. Benario
Lisa Bennett
Mary Merrick Bliss
Marian Oliver Forbes Bonds
Patricia Shumway Bradley
Barbara Jean Brown
Margaret Rector Bundick
Franke C. Cooper Burke

Charlotte L. Getterny Carter
Norma L. Louseth Clark
Lucille Lydia Tessmer Clements
Julia Montgomery Coleman
Lillian Mae Colombo
Mary Evans Comstock
Norma Faricy Condee
Shirely Cook
Helen C. Melesinsky Coyte
Elizabeth K. Cullen
Erlene Paulk Denson
Alyce L. Dixon
Joan B. Baxter Dunlap
Suzanne Harpole Embree

Pearl E. Faurie
Elvera M. Schwartz Feltes
Anna Florence Fogelman
Inez Dyer Dyer Foley
Betty J. Gibbs
Anita Wernz Galofaro
Lillian Green
Marjorie Sue Bleakley Green
Helen Janet Dalton Griffin
Mary Jane Halak
William Hart
Jeannetta F. Hermans
Henrietta Hibbs
Lilly Loise Culp Hogan
Marilyn Shirley Hogle
Marilyn McGehearty Hrncir
Audrey Hutchinson
Margaret Huff
Bette Jochinsen
Eethel H. Johnson
Lahoma Isen Johnson
Betty Jane Kaske
Doris Kirkwood
June Kleber
John Kluge
Virginia L. LeBouef
Margaret Cope Liddle
Ann Ludwig
Ann Ellicott Madeira
Virginia Pauline Maitland
Elizabeth Marsh
Jo Ann Martin
Mary Francis Martin
Dorothe McCowen
Rose Sacks Merron
Ocie L. Louseth Miller
Kathryn Jeanette Kauffman Moffit
Marcia Moore
Marie D. Townsend Morrison
Corinne M. Moyers
Ruth Murray

Magdalene Marie Keller Nuttall
Helen Edith Osmun Parker
Phyllis Paxton
Veda Frances Ponikvar
Susanna Laing McWhorter Reckard
Margaret Mary Stone Reese
Margaret Mary Byrne Riordan
Ruth Salmi
Roberto P. Sanchez
Demaris Schebig
Pearl Crystal Scher
Priscilia Shinkle
Frances Lynd Scott
Beatrice Sheld
Mary Shipley
Jean Ashby Johnson Sims
Katherine Gilbert Sluka
Katharyn Elizabeth Rice Sockolov
Ethel Standley
Madalyn Steffy
Elizabeth Bigelow Stewart
Donald Holt Stewart
Dorothe Stream
Cora Mae Jones Summers
Bill Swope
Elizabeth S. Swope
Crystal Theodore
Joy Mercedes Ismond Tod
Margaret Frances Kaim Tofalo
Marion S. Tompkins
Virginia Tomlinson
Gretchen Grace Kiel Turner
Marie Voltzke
Elizabeth Votaw
Edith Walker
Elizabeth Law Watkins
Audrey Weissert
Miriam Wheeler
Joe L. White
Lois Widmark
Dorothy Wills

Wilma Leota Martin Wilson
Vonda Lee Bronson Wise

Norene Yohn
Bernice Mary Zimmerman

World War II Oral History Collection,
Women in Military Service of America

Dorris Adams Brogan
Cecilia Campbell
Margaret Engelberg
Marilyn Forslund
Lorraine Foulds
Antoinette Loezere

Martha Settle Putney
Elizabeth F. Splaine
Margery Updegraff
Louise K. Wilde
Eunice Wilson

American Red Cross Oral History Collection

Helen Thompson Colony
Margaret Gooch Duffy
Lois I. Laster

Eve Lewis
Barbara Pathe

The Washington Press Club Foundation Women in Journalism
Oral History Project

Jane Eads Bancroft
Ruth Cowan Nash
Beth Campbell Short

The Rutgers Oral History Archives of World War II

Clifford Elling
Kurt Leuser
Robert MacDougall
Theodore Stier

U.S. Senate Historical Office Oral History Project

Christine McCreary

MANUSCRIPT COLLECTIONS

The Archives of American University

The Eagle Collection
Drew Pearson Papers
Dorothy Ditters Papers

Gelman Library Special Collections, George Washington University
Washington Board of Trade Papers

Historical Society of Washington
D.C. Social Hygiene Society Papers
National Capital Housing Authority Records
Records of the Alley Dwelling Authority for the District of Columbia
Records of the D.C. Courts, Landlord and Tenant Division
Washington Housing Association Records

Jewish Historical Society of Greater Washington
The Record Collection

National Archives for Black Women's History
National Women's Advisory Committee on Social Protection Papers
Records of the National Council of Negro Women

National Archives and Records Administration
Committee on Women's Defense Work Records
Office of Civilian Defense, Public Housing Administration Records
Records of the Washington Metropolitan Area Region- Rent Control
Records of the Women's Bureau
War Department Records
War Manpower Commission Records
Washington, D.C. Government Records
Washington, D.C. War Price and Rationing Board Records
World War II Military Service Records
Women's Army Corps Recruiting and Training Records

Washingtoniana Collection, D.C. Public Library
Annual Reports of the Commissioners of the District of Columbia, 1938-1955
Vertical Files
Washington Afro-American Collection
Washington Star Collection

GOVERNMENT PUBLICATIONS

Committee on Washington Metropolitan Problems, *Transportation Plan For The National Capital Region*. Washington, D.C.: Government Printing Office, November 1959.

D.C. Health Department, *Annual Report of the Commissioners of Columbia Year Ended June 30, 1919. Vol. III: Report of the Health Officer*. Washington, D.C.: Board of Commissioners, 1919.

National Bureau of Economic Research. *The Role of World War II and the Rise of Women's Work*. By Claudia Goldin. Cambridge, Massachusetts: NBER Working Paper Series, December, 1989.

National Security Agency. *Sharing the Burden: Women in Cryptology during World War II*. By Jennifer Wilcox. Ft. Meade, Maryland: Center for Cryptologic History, 1998.

U.S. Army Intelligence and Security Command. *Breaking Codes, Breaking Barriers: The Wacs of the Signal Security Agency, World War II*. By Karen Kovach. Fort Belvoir, Virginia: Office of the Chief of Staff, History Office, 2001.

U.S. Department of Commerce, Bureau of the Census. *Historical Census Statistics on Population Totals By Race, 1790 to 1990, and By Hispanic Origin, 1970 to 1990, For The United States, Regions, Divisions, and States*. By Campbell Gibson and Kay Jung. Washington, D.C.: Government Printing Office, September 2002. (Working Paper Series No. 56).

_____. *Illegitimate Births by Race: United States and Each State, 1944*. Washington, D.C.: Government Printing Office, October 31, 1946. (Vital Statistics—Special Report).

_____. *Statistical Abstract of the United States—1940*. Washington, D.C.:Government Printing Office, 1940.

_____. *Statistical Abstract of the United States—1948*. Washington, D.C.: Government Printing Office, 1948.

_____. *Statistical Abstract of the United States—1950*. Washington, D.C.: Government Printing Office, 1950.

U.S. Department of Labor, Women's Bureau. *Boarding Homes for Women War Workers*. Washington, D.C.: Government Printing Office, 1943. (Women's Bureau Bulletin No. 11).

_____. *Changes in Women's Occupations 1940-1950*. Washington, D.C.: Government Printing Office, 1954. (Women's Bureau Bulletin No. 253).

_____. *Handbook of Facts on Women Workers*. Washington, D.C.: Government Printing Office, 1948. (Women's Bureau Bulletin No. 225).

_____. *Negro Women War Workers*. Washington, D.C.: Government Printing Office, 1945. (Women's Bureau Bulletin No. 205).

_____. *Progress Report on Women War Workers' Housing*. Washington, D.C.: Government Printing Office, April 1943. (Women's Bureau Special Bulletin No. 17).

_____. *Recreation and Housing, Women War Workers: A Handbook on Standards*. Washington, D.C.: Government Printing Office, 1943. (Women's Bureau Bulletin No. 190).

_____. *Women Workers in Ten War Production Areas and Their Postwar Employment Plans.* Washington, D.C.: Government Printing Office, 1946. (Women's Bureau Bulletin No. 209).

U.S. Special Police Investigation Subcommittee of the Committee on the District of Columbia House of Representatives. *Investigation of the Metropolitan Police Department of the District of Columbia.* Washington, D.C.: U.S. Government Printing Office, 1941.

DISSERTATIONS

Fant, Barbara Gale Howick. "Slum Reclamation and Housing Reform in the Nation's Capital, 1890-1940." Ph.D. Dissertation. Washington, D.C.: The George Washington University, 1982.

Head, Julia Elizabeth. "Visit Status for Mental Patients." M.A. Dissertation. Washington, D.C.: Catholic University, June 1946.

McQuirter, Marya Annette. "Claiming the City: African Americans, Urbanization and Leisure in Washington, D.C., 1902-1954," Ph.D. Dissertation. Ann Arbor: University of Michigan, 2000.

Rackow, Lawrence. "Elopements from St. Elizabeths Hospital in 1945." M.A. Dissertation. Washington, D.C.: Catholic University, June 1947.

Siebel, Julia Mynette. "Silent Partners/Active Leaders: The Association of Junior Leagues, the Office of Civilian Defense, and Community Welfare in World War II." Ph.D. Dissertation. Los Angeles: University of Southern California, 1999.

BOOKS

103 Rosie the Riveter Stories: As Told by Real Rosies Who Served in the Work Force or Who Helped through Volunteer Work During World War II. Warm Springs, Georgia: American Rosie the Riveter Association, 2001.

Abbott, Carl. *Political Terrain: Washington, D.C., from Tidewater Town to Global Metropolis.* Chapel Hill: University of North Carolina Press, 1999.

Abrahamson, James L. *The American Home Front.* Washington, D.C.: National Defense University Press, 1983.

Adler, Mortimer J., ed. *The Negro in American History I. Black Americans 1928-1971.* Encyclopedia Britannica Educational Corporation, 1971.

Alexander B. Callow, Jr., ed. *American Urban History.* New York and London: Oxford University Press, 1973.

Alsmeyer, Marie Bennett. *Old Waves Tales: Navy Women and Memories of World War II.* Conway, Arkansas: HAMBA Books, 1982.

Anderson, Karen. *Wartime Women: Sex Roles, Family Relations, and the Status of Women During World War II.* Westport, Connecticut: Greenwood Press, 1981.

Anderson, Madelyn Klein. *So Proudly They Served: American Military Women in World War II, A First Book.* New York: F. Watts, 1995.

Andrews, Maxene and Bill Gilbert. *Over Here, Over There: The Andrew Sisters and the USO Stars in World War II.* New York: Zebra Books, 1993.

Aron, Cindy Sondik. *Ladies and Gentlemen of the Civil Service: Middle-Class Workers in Victorian America.* New York: Oxford University Press, 1987.

Association of Retirees from the American Red Cross. *Our American Red Cross: Stories from Those Who Served.* Paducah, Kentucky: Turner Publishing Company, 2000.

Bailey, Beth. *From Front Porch to Back Seat: Courtship in Twentieth-Century America.* Baltimore: Johns Hopkins University Press, 1988.

_____ and David Farber. *The First Strange Place: The Alchemy of Race and Sex in World War II Hawaii.* New York: The Free Press, 1992.

Baldwin, Faith. *Washington, USA.* New York: Farrar & Rinehart, Inc., 1942.

Baxandall, Rosalyn, Linda Gordon, and Susan Reverby, eds., *America's Working Women.* New York: Vintage Books, 1976.

Bellafaire, Judith A. *The Women's Army Corps: A Commemoration of World War II Service.* Washington, D.C.: U.S. Army Center of Military History, 1993.

Bentham, Josephine and Herschel Williams, *Janie: A Comedy in Three Acts.* New York: Samuel French, 1943.

Bérubé, Allan. *Coming Out Under Fire: The History of Gay Men and Women in World War II.* New York: The Free Press, 1990.

Beuchner, Thomas S. *Norman Rockwell.* 2nd ed. New York: Harry N. Abrams, 1996.

Bloom, Vera. *There's No Place Like Washington.* New York: G.P. Putnam's Sons, 1944.

Boggs, Lindy. *Washington through a Purple Veil: Memoirs of a Southern Woman.* New York: Harcourt Brace & Company, 1994.

Borchet, James. *Alley Life in Washington: Family, Community, Religion, and Folklife in the City, 1850-1970.* Urbana, Illinois: University of Illinois Press, 1980.

Brinkley, David. *Washington Goes to War.* New York: Alfred A. Knopf, 1988.

Brokaw, Tom. *The Greatest Generation.* New York: Random House, 1998.

Bromley, Dorothy and Florence Britten. *Youth and Sex.* New York: Harper & Bros., 1938.

Brown, Carrie. *Rosie's Mom: Forgotten Women Workers of the First World War.* Boston: Northeastern University Press, 2002.

Brown, Gene. *Movie Time: A Chronology of Hollywood and the Movie Industry from Its Beginnings to the Present.* New York: Macmillan, 1995.

Brownlow, Louis. *A Passion for Anonymity: The Autobiography of Louis Brownlow.* Chicago: The University of Chicago Press, 1958.

Buchanan, Albert R. *Black Americans in World War II.* Santa Barbara, California: CLIO Books, 1977.

Cahn, Frances T. *Federal Employees in War and Peace: Selection, Placement, and Removal.* Washington, D.C.: The Brookings Institution, 1949.

Campbell, D'Ann. *Women at War with America: Private Lives in a Patriotic Era.* Cambridge and London: Harvard University Press, 1984.

Cantor, Milton and Bruce Laurie, eds. *Class, Sex, and the Woman Worker.* Westport, Connecticut: Greenwood Press, 1977.

Cary, Francine Curro, ed. *Urban Odyssey: A Multicultural History of Washington, D.C.* Washington, D.C.: Smithsonian Institution Press, 1996.

Chafe, William. *The American Woman: Her Changing Social, Economic, and Political Roles, 1920-1970.* New York: Oxford University Press, 1972.

_____. *The Paradox of Change: American Women in the 20th Century.* New York: Oxford University Press, 1992.

Chalou, George C., ed. *The Secrets War: The Office of Strategic Services in World War II.* Washington, D.C.: National Archives and Records Administration, 1992.

Chambers, John Whiteclay and David Holbrook Culbert. *World War II, Film, and History.* New York: Oxford University Press, 1996.

Clark-Lewis, Elizabeth. *Living In, Living Out: African American Domestics in Washington, D.C., 1910—1940.* Washington, D.C.: Smithsonian Institution Press, 1994.

Cobble, Dorothy Sue. *The Other Women's Movement: Workplace Justice and Social Rights in Modern America.* Princeton and Oxford: Princeton University Press, 2004.

Coffey, Frank. *Always Home: 50 Years of the USO.* New York: Brassey's, Inc., 1991.

Cole, Jean Hascall. *Women Pilots of World War II.* Salt Lake City: University of Utah Press, 1992.

Colman, Penny. *Rosie the Riveter: Women Working on the Home Front in World War II.* New York: Crown Publishers, 1995.

Conant, Jennet. *The Irregulars: Roald Dahl and The British Spy Ring in Wartime Washington.* New York: Simon & Schuster, 2088.

Connors, Jill, ed. *Growing Up in Washington: An Oral History.* Charleston, South Carolina: Arcadia Publishing, 2001.

Cooke, Alistair. *The American Home Front 1941-1942.* New York: Atlantic Monthly Press, 2006.

Coontz, Stephanie. *Marriage, A History: From Obedience to Intimacy or How Love Conquered Marriage.* New York: Viking, 2005.

_____. *The Way We Never Were: American Families and the Nostalgia Trap.* New York: Basic Books, 1992.

Costello, John. *Virtue under Fire: How World War II Changed Our Social and Sexual Attitudes.* Boston and Toronto: Little, Brown and Company, 1985.

_____. *Love, Sex & War: Changing Values 1939-45.* London: Collins, 1985.

Cott, Nancy F., ed. *No Small Courage: A History of Women in the United States.* New York: Oxford University Press, 2000.

Cox, Jim. *Historical Dictionary of American Soap Operas.* Lanham, Maryland: Scarecrow Press, 2005.

Cripps, Thomas. *Making Movies Black: The Hollywood Message Movie from World War II to the Civil Rights Era.* New York: Oxford University Press, 1993.

Culpepper, Marilyn Mayer. *Never Will We Forget: Oral Histories of World War II.* Westport, Connecticut and London: Praeger Security International, 2008.

Daniels, Les. *Wonder Woman: The Complete History, the Life and Times of the Amazon Princess.* San Francisco: Chronicle Books, 2000.

Decter, Midge. *An Old Wife's Tale: My Seven Decades in Love and War.* New York: ReganBooks, 2001.

Davies, Margery W. *Woman's Place Is at the Typewriter: Office Work and Office Workers 1870-1930.* Philadelphia: Temple University Press, 1982.

De Courcy, Anne. *Debs at War 1939-1945: How Wartime Changed Their Lives.* London: Phoenix, 2005.

D'Emilio, John and Estelle B. Freedman. *Intimate Matters: A History of Sexuality in America.* 2nd ed. Chicago: The University of Chicago Press, 1997.

Deutrich, Mabel E. and Virginia C. Purdy, eds. *Clio was a Woman: Studies in the History of American Women.* Washington, D.C.: Howard University Press, 1976.

Dick, Bernard F. *The Star-Spangled Screen: The American World War II Film.* Lexington: The University Press of Kentucky, 1985.

Ditzen, Eleanor Davies Tydings. *My Golden Spoon: Memoirs of a Capital Lady.* New York: Madison Books, 1997.

Doherty, Thomas. *Projections of War: Hollywood, American Culture and World War II.* New York: Columbia University Press, 1993.

Dos Passos, John. *State of the Nation.* Boston: Houghton Mifflin Company, 1943.

Douglas, Mary. *Natural Symbols: Explorations in Cosmology.* New York: Pantheon, 1970.

Dunnigan, Alice Allison. *Black Woman's Experience: From the School House to the White House.* Philadelphia: Dorrance & Co., 1974.

Early, Charity Adams. *One Woman's Army: A Black Officer Remembers the Wac.* College Station: Texas A&M University Press, 1989.

Ebbert, Jean and Marie-Beth Hall. *The First, The Few, The Forgotten: Navy and Marine Corps Women in World War I.* Annapolis: Naval Institute Press, 2002.

Ellwood, David, ed. *The Movies as History: Visions of the Twentieth Century.* Trowbridge, Wiltshire: Sutton Publishing, 2000.

Endres, Kathleen L. *Rosie the Rubber Worker: Women Workers in Akron's Rubber Factories During World War II.* Kent, Ohio: Kent State University Press, 2000.

Faderman, Lillian. *Odd Girls & Twilight Lovers: A History of Lesbian Life in Twentieth-Century America.* New York: Columbia University Press, 1991.

Fields, Joseph. *The Doughgirls.* New York: Random House, 1943.

Fitch, Noel Riley. *Appetite for Life: The Biography of Julia Child.* New York: Anchor Books, 1999.

Fitzpatrick, Sandra and Maria R. Goodwin. *The Guide to Black Washington*. New York: Hippocrene Books, 1990.

Fletcher, Commandant M.H. *The WRNS: A History of the Women's Royal Naval Service*. Annapolis: Naval Institute Press, 1989.

Flynn, George Q. *The Mess in Washington: Manpower Mobilization in World War II*. Westport, Connecticut: Greenwood Press, 1979.

Friedl, Vicki. *Women in the United States Military, 1901-1995: A Research Guide and Annotated Bibliography*. Westport, Connecticut: Greenwood Press, 1996.

Furman, Bess. *Washington by-Line: The Personal; History of a Newspaperwoman*. New York: Alfred A. Knopf, 1949.

Gavin, Lettie. *American Women In World War I: They Also Served*. Niwot, Colorado: University Press of Colorado, 1997.

George, Margaret Hewitt, ed. *We Knew We Were at War: Women Remember World War II*. Margaret Hewitt George, 2006.

Gilbert, James L. and John P. Finnegan, eds. *U.S. Army Signals Intelligence in World War II: A Documentary History*. Washington, D.C.: Center of Military History United States Army, 1993.

Gillette, Howard Jr. *Between Justice and Beauty: Race, Planning, and the Failure of Urban Policy in Washington, D.C.* Baltimore: The Johns Hopkins University Press, 1995.

Gluck, Sherna Berger. *Rosie the Riveter Revisited: Women, the War, and Social Change*. Boston: Twayne Publishers, 1987.

Godson, Susan H. *Serving Proudly: A History of Women in the U.S. Navy*. Annapolis: Naval Institute Press, 2001.

Goode, James E. *Best Addresses: A Century of Washington's Distinguished Apartment Houses*. Washington, D.C.: Smithsonian Books, 1988.

_____. *Capital Losses: A Cultural History of Washington's Destroyed Buildings*, 2nd ed. Washington, D.C.: Smithsonian Books, 2003.

Goodwin, Doris Kearns. *No Ordinary Time: Franklin and Eleanor Roosevelt: The Home Front in World War II*. New York: Simon & Schuster, 1994.

Goodwin, Sandra Fitzpatrick and Maria R. *The Guide to Black Washington: Places and Events of Historical and Cultural Significance in the Nation's Capital*. New York: Hippocrene Books, 1990.

Gordon, Ruth. *My Side: The Autobiography of Ruth Gordon*. New York: Harper & Row, 1976.

Graham, Katharine. *Katharine Graham's Washington*. New York: Alfred A. Knopf, 2002.

_____. *Personal History*. New York: Vintage Books, 1998.

Grahn, Elna Hilliard. *In the Company of Wacs*. Manhattan, Kansas: Sunflower University Press, 1993.

Green, Barbara. *Girls in Khaki: A History of the ATS in the Second World War*. Stroud, Gloucestershire: The History Press, 2012.

Green, Constance McLaughlin. *The Secret City: A History of Race Relations in the Nation's Capital.* Princeton, New Jersey: Princeton University Press, 1967.

————. *Washington: A History of the Capital.* Princeton, New Jersey: Princeton University Press, 1977.

Greenfield, Meg. *Washington.* New York: Public Affairs, 2001.

Gregory, Chester W. *Women in Defense Work During World War II: An Analysis of the Labor Problem and Women's Rights.* New York: Exposition Press, 1974.

Groneman, Carol and Mary Beth Norton, eds. *"To Toil the Livelong Day": America's Women at Work, 1780-1980.* Ithaca: Cornell University Press, 1987.

Gruhzit-Hoyt, Olga. *They Also Served: American Women in World War II.* Secaucus, New Jersey: Carol Publishing Group, 1995.

Gunter, Helen Clifford. *Navy Wave: Memories of World War II.* Fort Bragg, California: Cypress House Press, 1992.

Hanson, Joyce A. *Mary McLeod Bethune and Black Women's Political Activism.* Columbia: University of Missouri Press, 2003.

Harrigan, Robert E. *Pastimes in Washington: Leisure Activities in the Capital Area, 1800-1995.* Bowie, Maryland: Heritage Books, 2002.

Harris, Jonathon, Franklin D. Mitchell, and Steven J. Schechter, eds. *The Homefront: American during World War II.* New York: Putnam's, 1984.

Hart, Scott. *Washington at War: 1941-1945.* Englewood Cliffs, New Jersey: Prentice-Hall, Inc., 1970.

Hartmann, Susan M. *The Home Front and Beyond: American Women in the 1940s.* Boston: Twayne Publishers, 1982.

Haskel, Molly. *From Reverence to Rape: The Treatment of Women in the Movies.* 2nd ed. Chicago: The University of Chicago Press, 1987.

Heacock, Nan. *Battle Stations!: The Homefront World War II.* Ames: Iowa State University Press, 1992.

Hegarty, Marilyn E. *Victory Girls, Khaki-Wackies, and Patriotutes: The Regulation of Female Sexuality During World War II.* New York: New York University Press, 2008.

Heide, Robert and John Gilman. *Home Front America: Popular Culture of the World War II Era.* San Francisco: Chronicle Books, 1995.

Height, Dorothy. *Open Wide the Freedom Gates: A Memoir.* New York: PublicAffairs, 2003.

Herwig, David J. Bercuson and Holger H. *One Christmas in Washington: The Secret Meeting Between Roosevelt and Churchill That Changed the World.* New York: The Overlook Press, 2005.

Highsmith, Carol M. and Ted Landphair, *Union Station.* Washington, D.C.: Chelsea Publishing, Inc., 1988.

Higonet, Margaret Randolph, Jane Jenson, Sonya Michael, and Margaret Collins Weitz, eds. *Behind the Lines: Gender and the Two World Wars.* New Haven: Yale University Press, 1987.

Hine, Darlene Clark, ed. *Black Women in America: An Historical Encyclopedia.* Brooklyn, New York: Carlson Publishing, Inc., 1993.

Hirsch, Lewis A. Erenberg and Susan E., eds. *The War in American Culture: Society and Consciousness During World War II.* Chicago: University of Chicago Press, 1996.

Holm, Jeanne M., ed. *In Defense of a Nation: Servicewomen in World War II.* Washington, D.C.: Military Women's Press, 1998.

_____. *Women in the Military: An Unfinished Revolution.* Novato, California: Presidio Press, 1982.

Honey, Maureen, ed. *Bitter Fruit: African American Women in World War II.* Columbia, Missouri: University of Missouri Press, 1999.

_____. *Creating Rosie the Riveter: Class, Gender, and Propaganda During World War II.* Amherst, Massachusetts: University of Massachusetts Press, 1984.

Hoopes, Roy. *Americans Remember the Home Front: An Oral Narrative of the World War II Years in America.* New York: Berkley Books, 1977.

_____. *When the Stars Went to War.* New York: Random House, 1994.

Horten, Gerd. *Radio Goes to War: The Cultural Politics of Propaganda During World War II.* Berkley: University of California Press, 2002.

Humphrey, Mary Ann. *My Country, My Right to Serve: Experiences of Gay Men and Women in the Military, World War II to the Present.* New York: HaperCollins, 1988.

Israel, Betsy. *Bachelor Girl: The Secret History of Single Women in the Twentieth Century.* New York: William Morrow, 2002.

Jackson, Kathi. *They Called Them Angels: American Military Nurses of World War II.* Westport, Connecticut: Praeger, 2000.

Jackson, Robert. *Heroines of World War II.* London: A. Barker, 1976.

Jacob, Kathryn Allamong. *Capital Elites: High Society in Washington, D.C. After the Civil War.* Washington, D.C.: Smithsonian Institution Press, 1995.

Jeansonne, Glen. *Women of the Far Right: The Mothers' Movement and World War II.* Chicago: University of Chicago Press, 1996.

Jeffries, John W. *Wartime America: The World War II Home Front.* Chicago: Ivan R. Dee, 1996.

Jones, James. *WWII.* New York: Grosset & Dunlap, 1975.

Jones, Wilbur D., Jr. *The Journey Continues: The World War II Home Front.* Shippensburg, PA: White Mane Books, 2005.

Kanin, Garson. *Tracy and Hepburn: An Intimate Memoir.* New York: Viking Press, 1971.

Kendall, Elizabeth. *The Runaway Bride: Hollywood Romantic Comedy of the 1930s.* New York: Alfred A. Knopf, 1990.

Kessler-Harris, Alice. *Out to Work: A History of Wage-Earning Women in the United States.* New York: Oxford University Press, 1982.

Kiernan, Denise. *Girls of Atomic City and Good Girls: The Untold Story of the Women Who Helped Win World War II.* New York: Touchstone, 2013.

Klam, Julie. *The War at Home*. North Mankato, Minnesota: Smart Apple Media, 2002.

Koppes, Clayton R. and Gregory D. Black. *Hollywood Goes to War: How Politics, Profits, and Propaganda Shaped World War II Movies*. Berkeley and Los Angeles: University of California Press, 1990.

Langley, Wanda. *Flying Higher : The Women Airforce Service Pilots of World War II*. North Haven, Connecticut: Linnet Books, 2002.

Larson, C. Kay. *'Til I Come Marching Home: A Brief History of American Women in World War II*. Pasadena, Maryland: Minerva Center, 1995.

Laughlin, Kathleen A. *Women's Work and Public Policy: A History of the Women's Bureau, U.S. Department of Labor, 1945-1970*. Boston: Northeastern University Press, 2000.

Leder, Jane Mersky. *Thanks for the Memories: Love Sex, and World War II*. Washington, D.C.: Potomac Books, 2009.

Lepore, Jill. *The Secret History of Wonder Woman*. New York: Knopf, 2014.

Lesko, Kathleen M., Valerie Babb, and Carroll R. Gibbs, eds. *Black Georgetown Remembered: A History of Its Black Community From the Founding of 'The Town of George' in 1751 to the Present Day*. Washington, D.C.: Georgetown University Press, 1999.

Lewis, Brenda Ralph. *Women at War: The Women of World War II—at Home, at Work, on the Front Line*. Pleasantville, New York: Reader's Digest, 2002.

Lewis, David L. *A History of the District of Columbia, Unit IV*. Washington, D.C.: Associates for Renewal in Education, Inc., 1980.

Lingeman, Richard R. *Don't You Know There's a War On?: The American Home Front, 1941-1945*. New York: G.P. Putnam's Sons, 1970.

Litoff, Judy Barrett and David C. Smith, eds. *American Women in a World at War: Contemporary Accounts from World War II, Worlds of Women*. Wilmington, Delaware: Scholarly Resources, Inc., 1997.

_____. *Since You Went Away: World War II Letters from American Women on the Home Front*. New York: Oxford University Press, 1991.

_____. *We're in This War, Too: World War II Letters from American Women in Uniform*. New York: Oxford University Press, 1994.

Lombard, Helen. *Washington Waltz: Diplomatic People and Policies*. New York: A. Knopf, 1941.

Longworth, Alice Roosevelt. *Crowded Hours*. New York: Charles Scribner's Sons, 1933.

Lord, Alexandra M. *Condom Nation: The U.S. Government's Sex Education Campaign from World War I to the Internet*. Baltimore: Johns Hopkins University Press, 2010.

MacDonald, Elizabeth P. *Undercover Girl*. New York: The McMillan Company, 1947.

Man at the Microphone. *Washington Broadcast*. Garden City, New York: Doubleday, Doran & Company, Inc., 1944.

Martin, Ralph G. *Cissy*. New York: Simon and Schuster, 1979.

May, Elaine Tyler. *Homeward Bound: American Families in the Cold War Era*. New York: Basic Books, 1988.

McCluskey, Audrey Thomas and Elaine M. Smith, eds. *Mary McLeod Bethune: Building a Better World*. Bloomington: Indiana University Press, 1999.

McDermott, George L. *Women Recall the War Years: Memories of World War II*. Chapel Hill, North Carolina: Professional Press, 1998.

McIntosh, Elizabeth P. *Sisterhood of Spies: The Women of the OSS*. Annapolis: Naval Institute Press, 1998.

McLaughlin, Anne L. *The House on Q Street*. Santa Barbara, California: John Daniel & Company, 2002.

McQuirter, Marya Annette. *African American Heritage Trail, Washington, D.C.* Washington, D.C.: Cultural Tourism DC, 2003.

Melder, Keith. *City of Magnificent Intentions: A History of Washington, District of Columbia*. 2nd ed. Washington, D.C. and Silver Spring, Maryland: Intac, Inc., 1997.

Menefee, Selden. *Assignment U.S.A.* New York: Reynal & Hitchcock, Inc., 1943.

Mettler, Suzanne. *Soldiers to Citizens: The G.I. Bill and the Making of the Greatest Generation*. New York: Oxford University Press, 2005.

Meyer, Agnes Ernst. *Journey Through Chaos*. New York: Harcourt, Brace and Company, 1944.

Meyer, Leisa D. *Creating GI Jane: Sexuality and Power in the Women's Army Corps During World War II*. New York: Columbia University Press, 1996.

Meyerowitz, Joanne, ed. *Not June Cleaver: Women and Gender in Postwar America, 1945-1960*. Philadelphia: Temple University Press, 1994.

Milkman, Ruth. *Gender at Work: The Dynamics of Job Segregation by Sex During World War II*. Urbana: University of Illinois Press, 1987.

Monahan, Evelyn M. and Rosemary Neidel-Greenlee. *A Few Good Women: America's Military Women from World War I to the Wars in Iraq and Afghanistan*. New York: Alfred A. Knopf, 2010.

Moore, Brenda L. *To Serve My Country, to Serve My Race: The Story of the Only African American Wacs Stationed Overseas During World War II*. New York: New York University Press, 1996.

Morden, Bettie J. *The Women's Army Corps, 1945-1978*. Washington, D.C.: Center of Military History, U.S. Army, 1990.

Morehouse, Maggi M. *Fighting in the Jim Crow Army: Black Men and Women Remember World War II*. Lanham, Maryland: Rowman & Littlefield, 2000.

Mullener, Elizabeth. *War Stories: Remembering World War II*. Baton Rouge: Louisiana State University Press, 2002.

Murray, Florence, ed. *The Negro Handbook*. New York: Wendell Malliet and Company, 1942.

Murray, Pauli. *Song in a Weary Throat: An American Pilgrimage*. New York: Harper & Row, 1987.

Muzzy, Frank. *Gay and Lesbian Washington, D.C.* Charleston, South Carolina: Arcadia Publishing, 2005.

National Museum of African American History, ed. *The Scurlock Studio and Black Washington: Picturing the Promise.* Washington, D.C.: Smithsonian Books, 2009.

Norwalk, Rosemary. *Dearest Ones: A True World War II Love Story.* New York: J. Wiley, 1999.

O'Brien, Kenneth Paul and Lynn Hudson Parsons, eds. *The Home-Front War: World War II and American Society.* Westport, Connecticut: Greenwood Press, 1995.

Olmem, Martin A. *Rooming and Boarding House Manual: An Authentic Guide to Landlord and Tenant Conduct.* Washington, D.C.: Guest House Service, 1943.

Olson, Keith W. *The G.I. Bill, the Veterans, and the Colleges.* Lexington: University Press of Kentucky, 1974.

Olson, Lynne. *Freedom's Daughters: The Unsung Heroines of the Civil Rights Movement from 1830 to 1970.* New York: Scribner, 2001.

Parker, Pauline E., ed. *Women of the Homefront: World War II Recollections of 55 Americans.* Jefferson, North Carolina: McFarland & Company, Inc., 2002.

Parascandola, John. *Sex, Sin, and Science: A History of Syphilis in America.* Westport, Connecticut: Praeger, 2008.

Paton-Walsh, Margaret. *Our War Too: American Women Against the Axis.* Lawrence: University Press of Kansas, 2002.

Peiss, Kathy. *Hope in a Jar: The Making of America's Beauty Culture.* New York: Metropolitan Books, 1998.

Phillips, Cabell, ed. *Dateline: Washington, The Story of National Affairs Journalism in the Life and Times of the National Press Club.* Garden City, New York: Doubleday & Company, 1949.

Pitts, Lucia M. *One Negro Wac's Story.* Los Angeles: The Author, 1968.

Polenberg, Richard, ed. *America at War: The Home Front, 1941-1945.* Englewood Cliffs, New Jersey: Prentice-Hall, 1968.

Putney, Martha S. *When the Nation Was in Need: Blacks in the Women's Army Corps During World War II.* Metuchen, New Jersey: Scarecrow Press, 1992.

Rabinowitz, Harold. *A Sentimental Journey: America in the '40s.* Pleasantville, New York and Montreal: The Reader's Digest Association, Inc. 1998.

Reumann, Miriam G. *American Sexual Character: Sex, Gender, and National Identity in the Kinsey Reports.* Berkley: University of California Press, 2005.

Rexford, Oscar Whitelaw, ed. *Battlestars & Doughnuts: World War II Clubmobile Experiences of Mary Metcalfe Rexford—Her Journal.* St. Louis, Missouri, 1989.

Ritchie, Donald A. *Reporting from Washington: The History of the Washington Press Corps.* New York: Oxford University Press, 2005.

Rogers, Michael H. *Answering Their Country's Call: Marylanders in World War II.* Baltimore: Johns Hopkins University Press, 2002.

Rosenthal, Rose. *Not All Soldiers Wore Pants: A Witty World War II Wac Tells All.* Rochelle Park, New Jersey: Ryzell Books, 1993.

Ruble, Blair A. *Washington's U Street: A Biography.* Baltimore: Johns Hopkins University Press, 2010.

Rubin, Nancy. *American Empress: The Life and Times of Marjorie Merriweather Post.* New York: Villard Books, 1995.

Rupp, Leila J. *A Desired Past: A Short History of Same-Sex Love in America.* Chicago: University of Chicago Press, 1999.

_____. *Mobilizing Women for War: German and American Propaganda, 1939-1945.* Princeton, New Jersey: Princeton University Press, 1978.

Satterfield, Archie. *The Homefront: An Oral History of the War Years in America, 1941-45.* Chicago: Playboy Press, 1981.

Savage, Barbara D. *Broadcasting Freedom: Radio, War, and the Politics of Race, 1938-1948.* Chapel Hill: University of North Carolina Press, 1999.

Schrag, Zachary Moses. *The Great Society Subway: A History of the Washington Metro.* Baltimore: Johns Hopkins University Press, 2006.

Scott, Joan Wallach. *Gender and the Politics of History.* New York: Columbia University Press, 1988.

Seale, William. *The President's House, Volume II.* Washington, D.C.: The White House Historical Association, 1986.

Sinnott, Susan. *Doing Our Part: American Women on the Home Front During World War II.* New York, Franklin Watts, 1991.

Slayden, Ellen Maury. *Washington Wife: Journal of Ellen Maury Slayden from 1897-1919.* New York and Evanston: Harper & Row, 1963.

Sklar, Robert. *Movie-Made America: How the Movies Changed American Life.* New York: Random House, 1975.

Smith, Jesse Carney and Carrell Peterson Horton, eds. *Historical Statistics of Black America: Agriculture to Labor and Employment.* Detroit, Michigan: Gale Research, Inc.: 1995.

Soderbergh, Peter A. *Women Marines: The World War II Era.* Westport, Connecticut: Praeger, 1992.

Solomon, Burt. *The Washington Century: Three Families and the Shaping of the Nation's Capital.* New York: HarperCollins, 2004.

Sorel, Nancy Caldwell. *The Women Who Wrote the War.* New York: Arcade Publishing, 1999.

Spratley, Dolores R. *Women Go to War: Answering the First Call in World War II.* Columbus, Ohio: Hazelnut Publishing Co., 1992.

Stein, R. Conrad. *The Home Front During World War II in American History.* Berkeley Heights, New Jersey: Enslow Publishers, 2003.

Strom, Sharon Hartman. *Beyond the Typewriter: Gender, Class, and the Origins of Modern American Office Work, 1900-1930.* Urbana: University of Illinois Press, 1992.

Summerfield, Penny. *Women Workers in the Second World War: Production and Patriarchy in Conflict.* London: Croom Helm, 1984.

———— and Gail Braybon. *Out of the Cage: Women's Experiences in Two World Wars.* London and New York: Pandora, 1987.

Takaki, Ronald. *Double Victory: A Multicultural History of America in World War II.* Boston: Back Bay Books, 2000.

Terkel, Studs. *"The Good War": An Oral History of World War II.* New York: Pantheon, 1984.

Thierry, James E., ed. *Looking Back at War: Archives Volunteers Remember World War II.* Washington, D.C.: National Archives and Records Administration, 1993.

Thomas, Mary Martha. *Riveting and Rationing in Dixie: Alabama Women and the Second World War.* Tuscaloosa: The University of Alabama Press, 1987.

Treadwell, Mattie E. *The Women's Army Corps.* Washington, D.C.: United States Army, Center of Military History, 1954.

Troy, Thomas F., ed. *Wartime Washington: The Secret OSS Journal of James Grafton Rogers, 1942-1943.* Frederick, Maryland: University Publications of America, 1987.

Tucker, Sherrie. *Swing Shift: "All-Girl" Bands of the 1940s.* Durham, North Carolina: Duke University Press, 2000.

Verge, Arthur C. *Paradise Transformed: Los Angeles During the Second World War.* Iowa: Kendall/Hunt Publishing Company, 1993.

Vogel, Steve. *The Pentagon: A History.* New York: Random House, 2007.

Walker, Nancy A., ed. *Women's Magazines 1940-1960: Gender Roles and the Popular Press.* Boston: Bedford/St. Martin's, 1998.

Ware, Susan. *Holding Their Own: American Women in the 1930s.* Boston: Twayne Publishers, 1982.

Weatherford, Doris. *History of Women in America: American Women and Word War II.* New York and Oxford: Facts On File, Inc., 1990.

Weiner, Lynn Y. *From Working Girl to Working Mother: The Female Labor Force in the United States, 1820-1980.* Chapel Hill: University of North Carolina, 1985.

Wertheim, Albert. *Staging the War: American Drama and World War II.* Bloomington: Indiana University Press, 2004.

White, Leonard D., ed. *Civil Service in Wartime.* Chicago: University of Chicago Press, 1945.

Whitman, Sylvia. *Uncle Sam Wants You!: Military Men and Women of World War II.* Minneapolis: Lerner Publications Co., 1993.

Williams, Kathleen Broome. *Improbable Warriors: Women Scientists and the U.S. Navy in World War II.* Annapolis: Naval Institute Press, 2001.

Williams, Paul K. *Greater U Street.* Charleston, South Carolina: Arcadia Publishing, 2002.

————. *Washington, D.C.: The World War II Years.* Charleston, South Carolina: Arcadia Publishing, 2004.

Winchell, Meghan K. *Good Girls, Good Food, Good Fun: The Story of USO Hostesses during World War II.* Chapel Hill, North Carolina: University of North Carolina Press, 2008.

Wise, Nancy Baker and Christy Wise. *A Mouthful of Rivets: Women at Work in World War II.* San Francisco: Jossey-Bass, 1994.

Wright, David K. *A Multicultural Portrait of World War II.* New York: Marshall Cavendish, 1994.

Wright, Mary Herring. *Far from Home: Memories of World War II and Afterward.* Washington, D.C.: Gallaudet University Press, 2005.

Wright, William. *Heiress: The Rich Life of Marjorie Merriweather Post.* Washington, D.C.: New Republic Books, 1978.

Wynn, Neil. *The Afro-American and the Second World War.* New York: Holmes & Meier Publishers, 1976, 1994.

Yellin, Emily. *Our Mothers' War: American Women at Home and at the Front During World War II.* New York: Free Press, 2004.

Zeiger, Susan. *In Uncle Sam's Service: Women Workers with the American Expeditionary Force, 1917-1919.* Ithaca: Cornell University Press, 1999.

ARTICLES

Anderson, Karen Tucker. "Last Hired, First Fired: Black Women Workers During World War II." *The Journal of American History* 69 (June 1982): 82-97.

Buchholz, Margaret Thomas. "Josephine: The Washington Diary Of a War Worker, 1918-1919." *Washington History* 10, no. 2 (Fall/Winter 1998-99): 4-23.

Campbell, D'Ann. "Women in Uniform: The World War II Experiment." *Military Affairs* 51, no. 3 (July 1987): 137-39.

Davol, Leslie T. "Shifting Mores: Ester Bubley's World War II Boarding House Photos." *Washington History* 10 (Fall/Winter 1998-99): 44-62.

Gillette, Howard, Jr. "The Wartime Washington Of Henry Gichner." *Washington History* 7, no. 2 (Fall/Winter 1995-96): 36-53.

Horowitz, Roger. "Oral History and the Story of America and World War II." *Journal of American History* 82, no. 2 (September 1995): 617-24.

Johnson, David K. "'Homosexual Citizens': Washington's Gay Community Confronts the Civil Service." *Washington History* 6, no. 2 (Fall/Winter 1994-95): 45-63.

Johnson, Marilynn S. "Urban Arsenals: War Housing and Social Change in Richmond and Oakland, California, 1941-1945." *Pacific Historical Review* 60 (August 1991): 283-308.

Kammerer, Gladys M. "An Evaluation of Wartime Personnel Administration." *Journal of Politics* 10, no. 1 (February 1948): 49-72.

Kimble, James J. and Lester C. Olson. "Visual Rhetoric Representing Rosie the Riveter: Myth and Misconception in J. Howard Miller's 'We Can Do It!' Poster." *Rhetoric & Public Affairs* (Winter 2006): 533-570.

Koppes, Clayton R. and Gregory D. Black. "Blacks, Loyalty, and Motion-Picture Propaganda." *Journal of American History* 73, no. 2 (September 1986): 383-406.

————. "What to Show the World: The Office of War Information and Hollywood, 1942-1945." *Journal of American History* 64, no. 1 (June 1977): 87-105.

Leff, Mark H. "The Politics of Sacrifice on the American Home Front in World War II." *Journal of American History* 77, no. 4 (March 1991): 1296-1318.

Myerowitz, Joanne. "Beyond the Feminine Mystique: A Reassessment of Postwar Mass Culture, 1946-1958." *Journal of American History* 79, no. 4 (March 1993): 1455-1482.

Nichols, David A. "'The Showpiece of Our Nation': Dwight D. Eisenhower and the Desegregation of the District of Columbia." *Washington History* 16, no. 2 (Fall/Winter 2004-2005): 44-65.

Orbach, Barbara and Nicholas Natanson. "The Mirror Image: Black Washington in World War II Era Photography." *Washington History* 4, no. 1 (Spring/Summer 1992): 4-25.

Rung, Margaret C. "Paternalism and Pink Collars: Gender and Federal Employee Relations, 1941-50." *Business History Review* 71 (Autumn 1997): 381-416.

Silverman, Roselyn Dresbold. "World War II in Washington: Life at Dissin's." *The Record* 22 (1997): 42-44.

Schweitzer, Mary M. "World War II and Female Labor Force Participation Rates." *The Journal of Economic History* XL, no. 1 (March 1980): 89-95.

Tone, Andrea. "Contraceptive Consumers: Gender and the Political Economy of Birth Control in the 1930s." *Journal of Social History* 29, no. 3 (Spring 1996): 485-506.

Waller, William. "The Rating and Dating Complex." *American Sociological Review* 2, no. 3 (October 1937): 727-34.

Westbrook, Robert. "I Want a Girl Just Like the Girl That Married Harry James: American Women and the Problem of Political Obligation in World War II." *American Quarterly* 42 (December 1990): 587-614.

NEWSPAPERS CONSULTED

Baltimore Afro-American

Baltimore Sun

Chicago Daily Tribune

Des Moines Register

Los Angeles Times

New York Times

Washington Afro-American

Washington Post

Washington Evening Star

Washington Times-Herald

PERIODICALS CONSULTED

American Mercury

Atlantic

Architectural Forum

Business Week

Christian Science Monitor

Ebony

Good Housekeeping

Harper's

Independent Woman

Ladies Home Journal

Life

Monthly Labor Review

Nation

National Geographic

Newsweek

Reader's Digest

Saturday Evening Post

Time

Vogue

Woman's Home Companion

FEATURE FILMS AND DOCUMENTARIES CONSULTED

Best Years of Our Lives

Cry "Havoc!"

Glamour Girls of 1943

Government Girl

Government Girls of World War II

Homefront: WWII in Washington

Janie

Johnny Doesn't Live Here Anymore

Keep Your Powder Dry

Ladies of Washington

Never Wave at a Wac

Pin Up Girl

So Proudly We Hail

Since You Went Away

Stage Door Canteen

Standing Room Only

Swing Shift Maisie

Tender Comrade

The Doughgirls

The Life & Times of Rosie the Riveter

The More the Merrier

Washington Melodrama

Without Love

Why We Fight

Index

ABOUT THE AUTHOR

Cindy Gueli is an author and media professional who has worked as a consultant on Showtime's *The Untold History of The United States,* a reporter and producer for Associated Press Television News, VH1, and A&E, and host of the web series "Scandalous Washington."

Professor Gueli has written and lectured widely on American social, cultural, and pop culture history. She received a bachelor's degree from Georgetown University and a master's degree in Communications and master's and doctorate degrees in History from American University.

For more about Dr. Gueli and Washington's Lipstick Brigade go to www.cindygueli.com and @historybyte.

Made in the USA
Lexington, KY
20 September 2018